The Classic Car Book

First published in April 2006

A catalogue record for this book is available from the British Library

ISBN 1 84425 231 0

Library of Congress catalog card no 2005935257

Published by Haynes Publishing, Sparkford,
Yeovil, Somerset BA22 7JJ, UK.

Tel: 01963 442030 Fax: 01963 440001
Int.tel: +44 1963 442030 Int.fax: +44 1963 440001
E-mail: sales@haynes.co.uk
Website: www.haynes.co.uk

Haynes North America Inc.,
861 Lawrence Drive, Newbury Park,
California 91320, USA.

Designed by Richard Parsons

Printed and bound in Great Britain
by J. H. Haynes & Co. Ltd., Sparkford

Illustrations courtesy the author except where credited.

WARNING
While every attempt has been made throughout this book to emphasise the safety aspects of working on and restoring a car, the publishers, the author and the distributors accept no liability whatsoever for any damage, injury or loss resulting from the use of this book. If you have any doubts about your ability to safely work on or restore a car then it is recommended that you seek advice from a professional engineer.

Jurisdictions which have strict emission control laws may consider the running of certain vehicles or any modifications to a vehicle to be an infringement of those laws. You are advised to check with the appropriate body or authority whether your proposed purchase or modification complies fully with the law. The publishers accept no liability in this regard.

The Classic Car Book

The essential guide to
buying, owning, enjoying and
maintaining a classic car

Buying a
classic

Care and
maintenance

On the
road

When it
goes wrong

Restoration
& repair

Improving
your classic

Enjoy
your classic

50 classics
to consider

Introduction

Driving a classic car marks you out as an individual. Nobody drives a car that might be decades old because they have to – they do it simply because they want to. In a world of speed limits, congestion charges and excise duty, rare indeed are the motorists who can claim to derive pleasure from their time behind the wheel, but classic car enthusiasts enjoy their motoring. This book aims to make the experience even more enjoyable, and to bring that enjoyment to an ever wider audience.

That classic cars can deliver such pleasure – from their style, their character, and the nostalgia they engender – is a good enough argument for preserving and restoring them, but there are others reasons. The motor car, whether we like it or not, is part of our everyday lives and its development and its influence upon our culture and our environment is part of the social history of our times. Twentieth-century buildings are now being seen as important and worth saving, and industrial museums are fighting to save machinery which represents a way of life which is but a few decades removed from our modern world. Classic cars represent an equally important part of our history, and it is just as important that they be preserved.

Sometimes, classics appeal to enthusiasts because, despite their age, they are still very capable cars. But just as often these cars appeal precisely because they are outmoded and old-fashioned. Some people prefer to live in a Victorian house because it has more character than a modern property – just as classic cars often have more character than moderns.

This book will help you buy the right car, with the minimum of fuss and stress, and it will help you to understand it, to sensitively restore or modify it, and to fix it when it goes wrong.

What is a classic?

There are almost as many ways to define 'classic car' as there are classic car enthusiasts to argue over the definition. Like 'sports car', it is a term that can mean what you want it to mean.

Some definitions are simplistic. People will tell you that, to be a classic, a car must have wire wheels, or chrome bumpers, or carburettors. Or that it must be more than 10 years old, or 20 or even 30 years old. But then others say 'classic' defines a specific period in history, and is distinct from Veteran, Edwardian and Vintage, which define cars from the dawn of the technology up to the 1930s. Some enthusiasts contend that a classic is any car that is out of production, and others say classics must be designs with intrinsic merit – cars which moved vehicle design forward or achieved big sales and popular acclaim. An increasing number of car manufacturers think that 'classic' means any model that has just been superseded.

I subscribe to none of those viewpoints. For me, cars become classics when people begin to buy them or keep them because they offer something a newer car cannot. That might be

LEFT Few can afford the prices of rare, desirable machines like this Aston Martin DB4GT – but there are plenty of interesting classics with cheaper price tags

because their chosen car is one of the high achievers, the technically outstanding designs which have withstood the ageing process. But equally the car they call a classic might be one of the modest and sometimes mundane everyday cars of yesteryear, which are interesting precisely because they are out of date – because they are reminders of their age, and throwbacks to departed eras. Just as with people, character and achievement may be related but they are not the same thing.

It follows that a car of almost any age can be a classic, provided it is interesting and worthy enough – and that any car, however humdrum, can be a classic provided it is old enough. Outstanding cars become recognised as 'classic' before many other vehicles, but in the end every car becomes interesting simply because it becomes old.

OPPOSITE AND LEFT Classic sports cars line up at shows through the summer, but very often they will be joined by equally well-loved saloons. There are all sorts of classics, for every type of enthusiast

In the classic car heartland there are cars which are both old enough and interesting enough to merit the term; cars which practically all enthusiasts would readily admit to the classic car fold – the Jaguar E-type, for instance. The controversy begins with those machines which might be as old as an E-type, or perhaps even older, but which were everyday transport rather than objects of desire. They are often scathingly referred to as 'grey porridge'. Yet any major classic car event will see hordes of well-loved Hillman Minxes, Ford Populars and Austin Sevens lining up alongside the Ferraris, Jaguars and Aston Martins, and their owners are just as convinced of their machines' status. It is the character and the period charm of these once-everyday machines which make them classics, and those who deride their wheezy side-valve engines, flexible chassis frames and feeble performance are missing the point.

Even bigger arguments rage when you try to find the dividing line between those more modern cars which can be described as classics and those which are simply 'used'. One theory goes that your idea of a classic is governed by the cars that turned your head when you were a child: if you were born in the 1950s then that was probably XKs and E-types, DB Astons, maybe the Lamborghini Miura or the Mini Cooper S, and your heroes are the likes of Hawthorn, Moss and Hopkirk. But the impressionable 10-year-old of, say, 1985, will grow up with memories of Audi Quattros, Sierra Cosworths and Peugeot 205GTIs, of Toivonen, Kankkunen and Senna.

All these cars, and many more besides, can be claimed as classics, and I don't think it matters much whether or not we can arrive at a definition everyone agrees with – we never will, so there is little point trying. What is important is that enthusiasts of any age and type of vehicle co-

BELOW Middle-market saloons like this Ford Consul Classic might not have been world-beating designs, but today they have their place in the classic world (Ford)

676 VTW

LEFT Enjoying your motoring is what classic cars are all about – whatever the age or type of car you buy

exist with every other sort of classic car enthusiast, recognising that the same basic needs and desires are present no matter what the machine in question might be.

Owning a classic

Whatever the age or value of the classic that you currently own or long to buy, the hazards and hurdles you face in getting it on the road and keeping it there will be very similar. Buying the machine presents one set of problems, while maintaining it in the manner to which it is accustomed and fixing it when it inevitably goes wrong add another group of pitfalls and opportunities.

It is these, and plenty more, which are dealt with in this book, in an effort to bring light into some of the murkier areas of classic car ownership and to make the experience more fruitful for enthusiasts of all kinds.

Enthusiasts span a wide range of ages, abilities, interests and budgets, and I offer advice and assistance to all of them. So if, in the pages that follow, you find yourself reading something you consider to be obvious, spare a thought for the classic car owners with a different background from you. No doubt those sections of the book which you find most useful will strike others as 'obvious'. However, I hope that somewhere along the line there will be information and suggestions of value to everyone – for ultimately my aim is to offer more and more people the chance to enjoy owning their own classic car.

Acknowledgements

I have been learning about classic cars for about as long as the term 'classic car' has been in use, and over that time I've absorbed information, advice, hints, tips and tricks from numerous authorities, owners, enthusiasts, writers and specialists. I cannot possibly thank them all, but those who I mustn't fail to thank are:

Stuart Agar of Andrew Brodie Engineering, the late Graham Arnold, Charlotte Blight, Bill Blydenstein, Andrew Charman, Graham, Shaun and Danny at Classic Cars of Kent, Simon Coe, Julian Edgar, Clive Foskett, Ben Hardcastle, Kim Henson, Roland Hayes and Aaron Tucker of HT Racing, Joss Jocelyn, Trevor Kemish, Rod Ker, Peter Knivett, David Lazenby at Pace Products, Alastair Loxton, Chris Manning, Malcolm McKay, Melissa Moorhead, Tim Morgan, Danny Morris, Pete Nightingale, David Roberts, the late Roger Stowers of Aston Martin and the AMOC, Ian Strachan, David Vizard, Clive White and Tim Whittington.

I must also acknowledge the support of car makers who recognise and cherish their heritage, and who have supplied illustrations and information, including Aston Martin, Audi, BMW, Ford, Jaguar, Lotus, Mercedes-Benz, Volkswagen and Volvo.

The list of those, without whom ..., must also include my partner Paula Goddard who has put up with me working on a demanding classic car magazine and several demanding old cars, and has somehow remained cheerful throughout. And, of course, Lyn and Clive Noakes, my parents, who could have nipped all this in the bud when I was five.

Buying a
classic

Choose your **classic**

You know you want a classic car. You're not sure quite what sort of classic, what you ought to spend, who you should buy from or what you should be looking out for. So you pick up the first old-car magazine you see, scan the ads, make some calls, kick the tyres on some aged machinery and do a deal. What you've bought, more likely than not, is a pile of trouble.

Every classic car owner is an enthusiast to some degree, some more than others, but even the stoutest enthusiasm can evaporate away like coolant from a leaking radiator when the faults, problems and bills start to mount up. But it doesn't have to be like that.

Buying a classic car, like buying any car, needs a bit of prior thought, some research and, ideally, a degree of patience if it isn't to end up being more trouble than you expected and costing more than you bargained for. Follow a few simple rules, apply some common sense, contain the urge to allow your heart to rule your head, and you can pick up the right car for you, at the right price – and you'll enjoy it all the more as a result.

Given that the general heading of 'classic car' covers a wide range of machinery, your first step on the road to ownership ought to be to narrow down the field. For some people that's easy, because they've harboured a desire to own a particular car for years – perhaps since childhood. Others need to take a more analytical approach.

Get clear in your mind the uses to which you will put your classic car, and identify those aspects of the car's capability which are most important to you – not to friends, bar-room experts and classic car journalists, but to you. If you have a partner and a family, you will need to make early decisions about access and accommodation. Do you buy a car which can carry all the family? Or do you buy the two-door, two-seat sports car you really want and accept that the kids can't come along, with all the inconvenience and conflict that could cause? It's a decision only you can make.

The practicality, or otherwise, of your classic will probably be linked to the amount of use it is likely to get. If you plan to run a classic as an everyday car you need something that fulfils all the functions of a modern car, and in particular something that will cope reliably in all weathers and all situations. If, on the other hand, you already have a 'utility' car and your classic will only be for weekend use in summer, you are free to choose something a little less practical.

But even then, you may come to rue a decision in favour of a tiny, hard-riding sports car. Are you likely to go on a driving holiday – a thousand-mile tour of picturesque countryside in the summer, or a trip to the Nürburgring or Spa? Race-spec suspension might improve your circuit times, but it will rattle your fillings all the way there and back. And where do you intend to stow the luggage for you and your long-suffering partner, if the boot is full of a long-range works fuel tank?

The same principles apply when you make the choice between a convertible and a fixed-roof car. Convertibles have obvious attractions in fine weather, but there are inevitable compromises in safety and security. If your classic spends its winters tucked up in a garage, then this may not be an issue, or if a roadster really appeals you might choose to put up with the shortcomings. Perhaps a half-way house would be better, like a Porsche Targa or 'Surrey top' Triumph TR, or make sure your classic roadster has a removable hard-top.

If you'll be using the car regularly in traffic it would be worth considering an automatic transmission, as older manual gearboxes and clutches can be heavy to use. If it is to be a car for high days and holidays, you might be prepared to put up with fragility or fuel consumption that would rule out a car for everyday use.

You also need to consider the maintenance requirements of an older car, both from the financial and practical points of view. One of the biggest differences between classics and moderns is that older cars need far more frequent servicing, with all the cost and inconvenience that might entail. The cost, if not the inconvenience, can be cut by taking care of your own servicing. For many people, attending to simple spanner-work is one of the joys of owning a classic, in an age where it is almost impossible to work on a modern car without extensive training in electronic systems and masses of computerised analytical equipment.

But the more demanding maintenance schedule that is typical of an older car could be tiresome if you're planning to use the car extensively. Few classics have recommended service intervals of more than 6,000 miles, many demand workshop attention every 3,000, along with a touch of lubrication or adjustment every 1,000 miles or less. Clearly, if you intend to do a lot of miles it pays to look at the servicing requirements of the classic you are considering, and to consider modifications which can reduce the burden (see Chapter 4).

OPPOSITE Convertibles are great in summer, but can be drafty and leaky in the winter. The VW-Porsche 914 has a 'Targa' top with a lift-out roof panel which offers the best of both worlds

BELOW Think about how you will use your classic. If you'll be carrying the family, a saloon with some space might make sense

Where to
find them

The safest way to buy is through a specialist classic car dealership. The cars tend, at least, to be in reasonable condition, they are well prepared, and if you have a major problem with the car soon after purchase you will have some sort of warranty to fall back on; and the dealer will help to sort out the problem. That's partly because most dealers are keen to win, and then retain, a good reputation – and news travels fast around the classic car world. It's also because professional dealers are under a legal obligation to correctly describe the vehicles they sell, and if the car turns out to have hidden faults or a shady past the dealer, in law, is at fault and you, as the unlucky buyer, have a right of redress. If everything goes wrong, at least you have someone you can sue.

But you pay for the privileges: classics bought from dealers will be pricier than those from other sources. And dealers are professional salesmen, so you expose yourself to being manipulated into buying the wrong car, or paying the wrong price.

Buying privately can certainly net you a much better deal, but the attendant risks are much greater. Should a problem emerge after purchase you have almost no comeback against the seller, so it's essential to make sure that the car is in good condition, and to minimise the risk of being sold a car which is stolen or which has finance owing.

In the UK, that means it's sensible to pay for a vehicle data check, offered by several organisations, including HPI and the AA. This should tell you if there is outstanding finance, which could lead to the car being repossessed, and if there is any record of it being stolen. The checks often come with a guarantee, but read the small print: they guarantee to supply you with correct information, but they can't guarantee the information they supply is comprehensive. There

is no legal obligation for interested parties such as finance houses to register their details, though in practice most do.

It's also vital to look at the car's paperwork. The registration document should be the new form V5C introduced in 2004 – the old V5 ceased to be valid in July 2005, and all owners should have automatically been issued with a V5C when retaxing a vehicle. If all the owner has is the old V5 you should be suspicious. But even a properly completed V5C is only half the story, because it shows the name and address of the registered keeper – not necessarily the same as the legal owner. Ideally you want the history file that comes with the car to include an invoice from the previous owner, showing the current owner as purchaser. Without that, or equivalent evidence, it's difficult to prove that the seller actually owns the car you're trying to buy.

OPPOSITE Dealers are the safest source of classic cars, with the best back-up and legal safeguards for buyers – but, as a result, prices tend to be high

BELOW Wherever you buy, check the car's registration document and any other paperwork carefully – and get a receipt

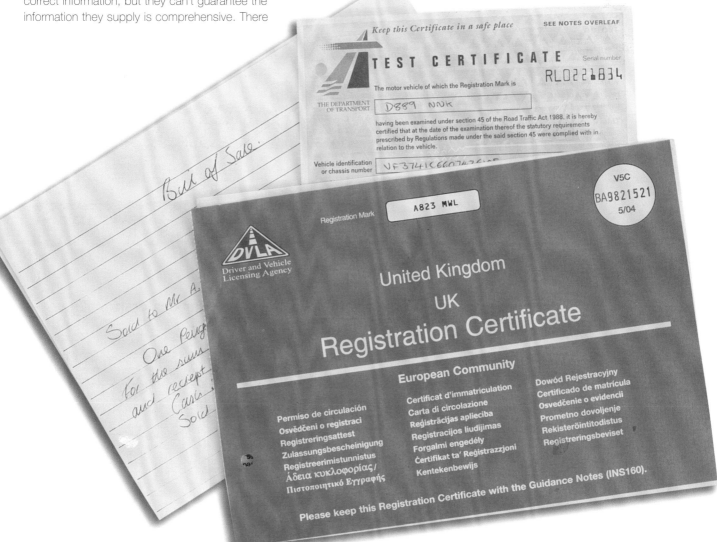

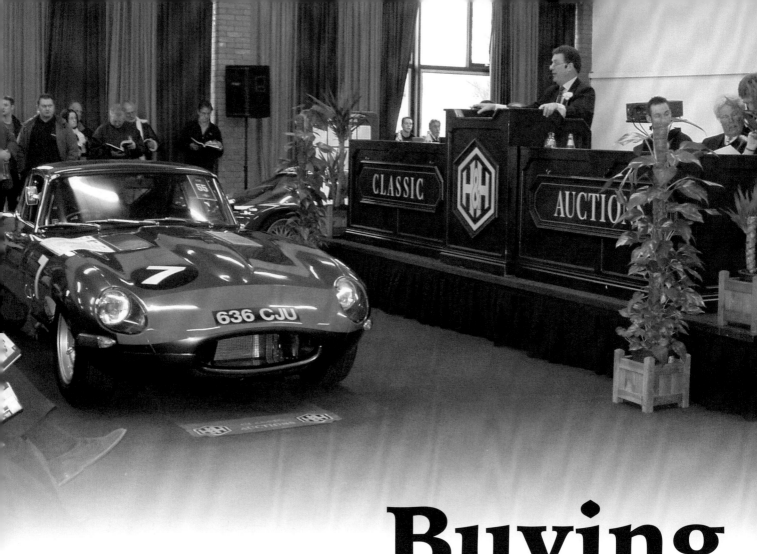

Buying
at auction

Auctions, another common route to classic car ownership, might seem to give you no chance to verify a car's previous history, but in practice auction houses tend to do everything they can to establish that the seller is genuine, and to sort out any problems which may occur post-sale. Some even perform data checks on all the cars they sell.

Auctions are useful because they can be quick and hassle-free, both for buyers and sellers. Buyers get to view potentially dozens of cars at once, and sellers get what can be a good price without having to deal with the inevitable time-wasters and joyriders.

To get a better idea of the atmosphere and the procedure of auctions, it's a good plan to visit a few purely as a spectator before you think seriously about buying. Don't fret about accidentally bidding for a rusty E-type because you innocently scratched your nose: a seasoned buyer might bid with no more than a nod to the auctioneer, but if the man with the gavel has never seen you before he'll expect your initial bid, at least, to be very obvious and unambiguous.

When you find a car you want, you will have the opportunity to examine it, though you probably won't be able to drive it. Go over the car carefully (see 'What to look for' below) and if you need assistance speak to the auction staff. You need to get a good idea of the car's condition, and then translate that into a current market price, from which you can work out how high you want to bid. Bear in mind that auctions charge premiums for buyers and sellers of around five per cent (sometimes more). Sellers receive the hammer price less that percentage, and the amount that you as a buyer will pay is the hammer price plus the commission.

Once you've arrived at the figure you are happy to bid up to, stick to it. This is the hardest part of buying at auction: it's so easy to get sucked into the drama and the excitement of the bidding process and to convince yourself that another £100 really doesn't make much difference and will win you the car. And then another £100, and another .... That's the point where sellers start to make real money, and auctioneers watch their commission mount up.

More and more auction houses now operate a 'bidding number' system, where you must register interest before the sale and obtain a bidding number, so if you're planning to bid, check the procedure. The professional buyers in the room will take advantage of your lack of experience if you let them, so your first step should be to find a place near the back of the room so it's harder for them to see you and recognise you as an amateur. Make sure you can still hear what's going on, that you can see the auctioneer, and that the auctioneer can clearly see you.

The auctioneer will take bids from two buyers until one drops out, then he will scan the room for another bidder. Assuming there is some interest in the car you've got your eye on, and that the early bids don't take the price over the ceiling you've set yourself, let those early bids go through until there's a lull and the auctioneer looks around for someone new. That's your moment to raise a hand, wave your catalogue, or whatever you need to do to attract his attention – shout 'over here' if you need to.

If another bid beats yours the auctioneer will keep coming back to you to bid again – perhaps with a comment like 'against you' – until you decline. Other comments from the auctioneer are worth listening for, too. You may find that early in the bidding the auctioneer is making remarks like 'long way to go', which is a hint that the reserve price agreed with the seller hasn't been reached and that the car will not be sold at this price. 'On the telephone' indicates a phone bid, obviously, while 'in the room' means the current bid is from someone present. Once bidding exceeds the reserve, you may find the auctioneer saying 'this will sell' or 'all your own money'.

If you're successful you will need to complete some paperwork and usually lodge a deposit – it's important to check the auction house's procedure before you bid.

The final word in this section concerns a very different type of auction – online auctions, which have their own set of pros and cons (discussed in more detail in Chapter 3). Buying a car from a private seller through an online auction site, such as eBay, is no different from any other private sale – in other words, the risks are predominantly the buyer's. It's important to view the car before you bid, and to satisfy yourself that the car and the buyer are all they claim to be.

OPPOSITE Classic auctions sell all sorts of cars, from classic family saloons to rare and famous machines worth millions *(H&H Classic Auctions)*

LEFT Work out how much to bid before the sale starts – then stick to your limit *(H&H Classic Auctions)*

What to
look for

A thorough examination of the car and the paperwork that goes with it can pay big dividends. But throughout this examination it's important to keep in mind what you're looking for – and it's not a simple case of assessing the car's current condition, important though that is.

Just as vital are clues about how the car has been treated, and evidence of its history. Comparing the clues the car gives you to the version of history the owner claims can identify any holes in the seller's story. So, with careful observation and a little simple detective work, you can establish how honest the seller is being about the car you are planning to buy.

Before viewing a car, do your homework on it. Find out where that model's weak spots are, and which components or repairs are expensive. You don't want to ignore some apparently trivial fault and find after you've bought the car that parts are difficult to get or the repair is long-winded and, therefore, expensive.

Get to know the original specifications, too. You need to be able to spot when the car you are looking at has the wrong trim or badges, or even the wrong engine for its year. Even if you're looking for an everyday classic and you don't care too much about every last nut and bolt being to original spec, you need to know – because the less original a classic is, in general, the less it's worth and the less you should pay for it.

That's particularly true of rare versions of common cars. A genuine Lotus Cortina or Mini Cooper S is worth far more than a base model Cortina or Mini with a few 'trick' extras. Find out if there are subtle differences in specification which would be unlikely to appear on a modified car, but which mark out the real thing. Learn about chassis and engine numbers so you can tell whether or not the car is from the right sequence.

It's also worth looking at other examples of the same model, to get a feel for their general condition. Cars which you know are original and unrestored are particularly useful: they will tell you, for instance, the consistency of panel gaps you could expect. Specialist companies, owners' clubs and even motor museums can be useful.

Start your assessment of a likely purchase by examining the bodywork. Stand at one end of the car and look along the side for dents and ripples in the panels. Then face one side from 10–12 feet (3–4m) away and look for colour variation between the panels, checking each side in turn. If you find a difference in colour, one or more panels has been repaired or replaced. Does that square with the owner's version of the car's history? Are there receipts in the file covering the work? Check also for variable panel gaps, indicating shoddy repairs or restoration – but be aware that not all cars had tight, even panel gaps

when new. Your homework should tell you how even the panel gaps ought to be.

Look carefully for paint 'overspray', particularly on the rubber seals around the windows – another indication that the car has been repainted (and badly, at that). You can also pull back the edge of the seal gently with a fingernail to see if there's a join in the paint underneath. Check if the colour inside

OPPOSITE Look along the side of the car from one end to show up ripples and repairs to the panels, then stand square on and check for colour variation between panels

FAR LEFT Check the mileage shown on the car's odometer against the service records and the MoT certificate

LEFT Does the condition of the interior back up the seller's claims about the car's history? If the gear knob, steering wheel and pedal rubbers are worn, a low mileage looks dubious

BELOW Several manufacturers can supply a certificate like this detailing a car's original specification. The certificate also hints at pride of ownership, which bodes well for the car's treatment over the years *(BMW)*

Inconsistent panel gaps might indicate poor accident repairs – but some cars were like that when they were new

Overspray on trim or window rubbers suggests a cheap respray: look for evidence of accident repairs, and check against the seller's version of the car's history

Original chrome is often preferable to modern reproduction parts, but check for serious pitting and flaking

Look for chips and cracks in the lights – they can be expensive to replace unless they are generic round lamps

the fuel filler flap and on the inner wings under the bonnet is different from the car's outer colour – these parts are often left untouched in a cheap respray.

Check all the exterior chrome for pitting and flaking. Look at the quality of the finish, too: original chrome is often preferable to modern reproduction parts, even if it is a little worn, because it tends to be of higher quality. The same goes for reproduction fittings, badges and mascots, which often don't have the attention to detail of original items.

Check the headlights and tail lamps for chips and cracks. The classic seven-inch and five-inch round headlamps are usually cheap to replace, though there are some unusual variations which are pricey. More modern lamps tend to be specifically made for a single model, which makes them much rarer and therefore more expensive. Try all the lights to see that they work correctly.

Examine the windscreen carefully for scratches, cracks and chips. Under UK MoT rules, any damage in the 'A zone' (essentially the area swept by the wiper on the driver's side) must be less than 10mm in diameter – about the width of the nail on your little finger. On laminated screens, check for fogging at the edges where water is forcing its way between the screen layers. Light scratches can be polished out, but if you find serious damage or discoloration, make sure the car's price reflects the expense of a new windscreen.

If there's a sunroof, check that it opens and closes smoothly. Stains in the headlining indicate sunroof leaks. If the car is a convertible, check the hood carefully and make sure all the latches and clips are in working order. Holes and tears in the material are bad news, obviously, but opaque or cracked windows in the hood can often be replaced without having to buy a new hood. Ask the vendor to raise and lower the roof for you to check that it is complete and operates correctly – and to get an idea of the care with which the vendor treats the car.

While we're on the subject of convertibles, it's worth noting they tend to suffer from rust problems, often caused by leaking hoods. Feel for damp carpets and check the floor underneath for rust damage, holes in the panels, and evidence of previous repairs. The floor should also be checked from under the car, at the same time taking the opportunity to examine the sills – a major structural element on many open-top cars. The fit of the doors often gives a good indication of the condition of the car: if they are difficult to open and shut, the body may be sagging because rust has destroyed much of the strength of the car.

On all cars, feel along the bottom of the sills and around the lip of the wheel arches for rust, but beware of sharp edges. A small magnet is a useful tool for finding filler in sills and arches. Wrap it in a tissue to avoid scratching the paint, then scan along the sill or round the arch: the magnet will be attracted towards a steel panel, but not to an area of filler hidden under the paint.

Check that all the door handles and locks work properly – often the passenger door lock seizes up through lack of use – and if the car has central locking, make sure it operates correctly. Usually the car will come with an ignition key, a door locks key and perhaps a fuel cap key, but if there are two door keys and they are different, that suggests a lock has been replaced. Check that the history file concurs.

Now you can move on to the engine bay. How clean is it? A concours-standard car should be spotless, but on an everyday classic a spotless engine bay might have been cleaned to hide evidence of fluid leaks. Check pipes and connections for any signs of seepage. You should be able to squeeze rubber water hoses with your hand: if cracks show up in the rubber when you squeeze, the pipes are on their last legs. The same applies to other flexible pipes in the engine bay, which often tend to crack on the outside of a bend where the rubber is in tension.

Is there overspray on any of the engine components, or evidence that bolt-on wings have been removed recently? Both suggest repairs to accident damage, which should be detailed in the history file. If the owner swears the car has never been bumped, be suspicious.

Check that the fluid levels in all the reservoirs are correct. When you remove the dipstick to check the oil, wipe a little of the oil onto your fingertips and feel its texture: it should feel smooth, not gritty. On some overhead-cam engines you can remove the oil filler cap and reach inside with a finger to rub one of the cam lobes, feeling for wear. Check that the cooling system has anti-freeze in it – normally the coolant will be a bright blue or green colour. Antifreeze should always be present, even in summer, because it helps cut down on internal corrosion.

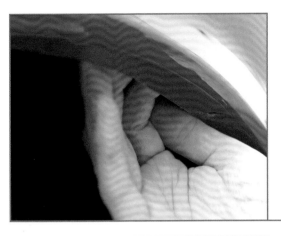

Feel around the lips of the wheel arches on a steel body – this is a common spot for rust to form

Exposed items like chassis outriggers, suspension mountings, jacking points and towing eyes are likely rust spots

Serious rust will be easy to spot. Be on the lookout for bubbles and ripples in paintwork which show the beginnings of rust, and for thick underseal applied to hide horrors

Uneven tyre wear points to problems with the suspension or steering: this tyre has worn on the shoulder nearest the camera. The problem might be wear or poor adjustment, but it could also be an indicator of crash damage

Raising and lowering the hood

On convertibles, ask the vendor to raise and lower the
hood so you can be sure it is complete and working

Remove the oil filler cap and check underneath for the gooey white substance which the trade calls 'mayonnaise'. If it's there it indicates either that the car has been used for lots of short journeys or that the head gasket is failing. Neither is good news.

Check the battery casing for cracks, and take a look at the connections – they should be secure, and preferably coated with petroleum jelly to fight corrosion. Frayed wires or corroded earth straps are bad news – they're probably not difficult to replace, but that being the case why hasn't the current owner attended to them? What else hasn't he bothered with?

Get underneath with a torch and examine the exhaust system, paying particular attention to joints and seams (which is where corrosion tends to strike). Many classic sports cars have very little ground clearance – Big Healeys are particularly notorious for it – so check the front of each silencer for impact damage. If one piece of the system looks cleaner and newer than the rest, it has probably been replaced, which suggests the rest of the system will need replacing before long. A shiny stainless steel exhaust is good news because it should last for years if not quite 'forever'.

While you're under there look for evidence of corrosion. The most important areas to check are those which provide the car's structural strength, which means the chassis members or the equivalent box-section structures built into a unitary body. Extremities such as outriggers, suspension mountings and jacking points often succumb to corrosion, so check these carefully. Don't assume that a layer of paint or underseal is protecting solid metal, because it might not be. Poke about to ensure that the structure is sound, but do remember that it is not your car yet, so don't go gouging huge holes in the bodywork with a screwdriver.

If the underside is painted with thick underseal, make sure that there are no gaps or cracks. Cracks allow water in (obviously), which defeats the object of the underseal. Even worse, once the underseal is cracked water tends to collect behind it which actually accelerates corrosion.

Look for evidence of rust or damage to the suspension and steering components. Grab each one in turn and try to shake it: you might be able to move them slightly, but you shouldn't find any suspension component which you can wiggle about easily by hand. Check rubber bushes for cracks.

It's a lot easier to inspect the brakes if you remove each wheel in turn, but on many disc-braked cars you can get by without doing this because you can see the pads through gaps in

BELOW If the car is fitted with locking wheel nuts, make sure the owner supplies you with the key

RVI 2430/01
SMITHS
MADE IN U.K.

IGNITION

ABOVE Check that the warning lights respond correctly – beware of an oil pressure light which does not light up with the ignition on but the engine not running

the wheel. Check how much material is left on the brake pads – if there's very little, the pads will of course soon need replacement. Look for scoring on the surface of the brake disc, and see if you can feel a lip forming at the outer edge: both indicate that the discs will need replacing.

Check for scrapes and dents in the wheel rims. Look for splits in the tyre sidewalls and check that all four tyres are wearing evenly across the treads – uneven wear suggests incorrect tyre pressures (a sign of bad maintenance) or suspension maladies. If you don't have a tread depth gauge, rest a 1p coin in one of the grooves. The tread blocks should at least reach the bottom of the '1' on the back of the coin if they're to exceed the minimum legal requirement of 1.6mm, but even this isn't really enough for safety on a wet road. A new tyre will have 5mm or more of tread depth.

If the wheels are fitted with locking nuts make sure a key is supplied so that you'll be able to get the wheels off for servicing or in an emergency.

Check the suspension dampers by pushing down each corner of the car in turn. When you let go, the car should spring back up, drop again, then settle at its normal height. If the car bounces several times before coming to rest, the dampers are worn out.

Inside the car, check for wear, damage, and cracks in leather, and for any missing items. Try all the electrical equipment to make sure it works – electric windows and seats, the heater fan, the radio, electric sunroof and so on. If you can lift the carpets, feel underneath for damp both in the passenger compartment and in the boot. At least feel under the floor mats.

While you're in the boot, check that the spare wheel is present and that its tyre is in good condition. Make sure the jack and tool kit are still there, as they can be difficult to replace.

Before you start the car, feel the cover on the top of the engine – is it warm? If so, the seller might be trying to hide the fact that the engine is difficult to start from cold. Check that the oil light comes on with the ignition and then goes out once the engine is running. If the car has a brake servo, hold down the brake pedal as you start the engine – the pedal should sink under your foot, indicating that the servo is working.

Check for smoke from the exhaust just after the car has started. Blue smoke suggests engine wear, black indicates excess fuel which could be a sign of poor maintenance. White 'smoke' is actually water vapour from inside the exhaust system, which will stop after a minute or two once the condensation in the exhaust is blown out. If it persists, suspect a failing head gasket. Let the engine run until it gets hot. If there's an electric fan, listen for it cutting in and out.

On your test drive, check that all the gears work, including reverse. Try driving along and suddenly pulling your foot off the accelerator, to show up any tendency for the gearbox to jump out of gear. Check that the clutch bites smoothly, with no juddering. Let the car labour in a high gear up a long hill – if the revs start to rise but the car goes no quicker, the clutch is slipping. To check that the handbrake works, try pulling away with it still engaged.

Check that all of the instruments work. If there's an oil pressure gauge, make sure the pressure reads in the middle or upper part of the gauge while you're driving – the pressure at idle will be lower.

LEFT To check the efficiency of the handbrake, try pulling away with it still engaged

Listen for engine noises during the drive: excessive, rhythmic tapping or heavy knocking signifies major wear. On a front-wheel-drive car, drive on full lock and listen for ticking noises indicating worn constant velocity joints.

Check that steering play is not excessive: exactly how much is 'not excessive' depends on the type of steering system, something you need to establish during your research. Hold the wheel gently, feeling for vibration which could be out-of-balance wheels or worn suspension.

Finally, on a quiet, empty road, hold the steering wheel gently and brake hard (check in your mirror first). The car should stop straight, not veer off to one side.

If all this sounds like too much to remember or you're not sure quite what you're looking for, consider getting a professional inspection. Motoring organisations offer them, and they're fine for relatively recent cars, but for older classics a specialist inspection company, marque specialist or club expert would be a better bet. Even a knowledgeable friend can provide a useful second opinion.

BELOW More modern classics have a wider selection of warning lights, but few more than this Alfa 164. Check that ABS, air bag and other lights operate correctly at startup

What **to pay**

Values of classic cars vary enormously. Nobody needs a classic, so their purchase is directed by enthusiasm and enjoyment, and some people are prepared to pay more to indulge their passions than others. Ultimately there is much truth in the old adage that a car is worth what someone is prepared to pay for it. One man's 'restoration project' is another man's pile of worthless scrap. At the other extreme it encouraged one wealthy investor to buy a Bugatti Type 41 'Royale' at a Christie's auction for no less than $5.5million. If you're considering a purchase in the latter category I would be pleased to assist personally – for a small commission, naturally – and can be contacted via the publishers.

Back in the real world, you will probably find a considerable variation in prices of outwardly similar cars. Some buyers are keen to spend more for low-mileage cars with one, or at least few, owners – though personally I don't see the point, unless you are buying the car to exhibit it in a museum. As soon as you use a low-mileage car you take away its greatest asset, so it becomes unusable. More relevant, in my view, is provenance: a bulging history file documenting the life of the vehicle is a great benefit, a subject we will come back to shortly. But the overwhelming consideration is the condition of the car: regardless of age or mileage, a classic in better condition is worth more. Buying the best you can afford is almost always going to be the most financially sensible route, because repair and restoration costs can quickly mount up.

Price guides in classic car magazines will give you some clues to a car's value, though you'll find the various guides rarely agree exactly – partly

Insurance for classic cars

In the UK and many other territories, car insurance is a legal requirement – and even if it weren't, effective insurance is vital for any classic. Though car insurance is always an unpleasant expense, there are ways of ensuring that the insurance on your classic provides good cover without costing a fortune in premiums.

Mainstream insurance companies will sometimes accept old cars, and these might be a reasonable option for 'modern classics' which are only ten years old or so. Indeed, many insurers give extra discounts for vehicles of this age, but for most classics there are significant benefits to be had by insuring with a classic car specialist.

One of the major benefits will be that premiums are likely to be much lower. A specialist will also be likely to cover your classic at an 'agreed value', which means that the car is valued at the start of the insurance period and should a 'total loss' claim be made, the company will pay that value rather than the market value, which is likely to be somewhat lower. For lower-value cars all you may need to do is fill in a form detailing your classic's condition, and supply recent photographs of the vehicle. More valuable classics will need a valuation from an expert, such as a marque specialist or club official.

But an essential point to note about classic insurance is that it sits outside the No Claims Discount (NCD) system. You can't use NCD to reduce your premiums, and even if you don't make a claim on your classic insurance, it won't earn you No Claims Discount.

With any insurance company, the premium you pay will be based on the insurance company's estimate of the risk you represent, and the more you can do to reduce that risk the lower your premiums will be. One of the best things about getting older is that you become, statistically, a safer driver and premiums reduce as a result. You can also reduce the risk by restricting cover to the minimum number of people, for example just yourself and your partner.

The location where you keep the car will also make a difference, and if you keep it in a garage when it's not in use, that will also alter your premium. Some insurers won't consider insuring a classic unless it's garaged overnight.

One potential difference between policies which is worth looking out for is the compulsory excess – an excess, in insurance-speak, is the amount of a claim paid by you rather than your insurer, so a '£100 excess' means you pay the first £100 of any claim. Some policies have a higher compulsory excess, but should offer a lower premium in return. It's up to you to decide whether the risk is worth the reward. If you wish, you can often opt to pay a 'voluntary excess' on top, reducing your premium still further.

OPPOSITE Classics are worth what someone will pay. For a rare and desirable machine like this Bentley Continental that means a price tag well into six figures

because of differences in the compilers' views about vehicle condition, and partly because price guides are sometimes compiled with less than the skill and care you might expect. A club official once confided to me that he had seen an entry for a certain rare classic in a magazine price guide, giving 'concours', 'average' and 'poor' values – yet only two were ever built!

More evidence comes from the ads in the same publications. Study ads for cars similar to the one you are considering, to see what sellers think they can get – bearing in mind that most cars sell for less than the asking price. Consider, too, that prices tend to be higher in summer when buyers are more active. Look at cars with higher and lower specification than the one you are thinking of buying, to see if that makes a difference, and look for the difference between good and bad condition examples of the same model. You may find the car you're looking at can be bought in better condition, or as a faster or more luxurious model, for very little more – in which case you either start looking at a different

car, or use that information to drive down the price on your current prospect.

Ads in club magazines, newspapers and online all provide further data to help you get a better idea of prices. Online auctions also provide useful information: most of the websites allow you to search for completed sales, and from this you can see the price the buyer paid rather than the price the seller hoped to get.

From all this data you will, hopefully, start to spot the patterns in the values of the cars you are considering – how much the values change depending on the car's condition, whether certain models are always worth more than others. You can then fit any likely prospects into this pattern and get a good idea of their value. But you might choose to pay a little more.

If you find the right car but it's a fraction expensive, bear in mind that if you walk away the next thing you'll do is start looking again – which will take more time, and cost more in magazines and travel. It might be worth spending the extra on the right car instead.

Doing the deal

Finance

The cheapest way to pay for a classic is to use your own money. However good the terms are on any sort of loan or finance deal, you are always paying for the privilege of borrowing money – so don't borrow unless you have to.

If you have to borrow, get the loan agreed in principle before you start looking for a classic. That way you can take time to investigate all the options and get the best possible deal, rather than arranging something at the last minute while the vendor waits impatiently to close the deal.

Secured loans tend to offer lower interest and longer repayment terms than unsecured loans, but remember that if the worst happens and you can't repay, the loan company can repossess whatever the loan is secured on – which might be the car, or even your house.

Payment

There are four common ways to pay: cash, personal cheque, building society cheque, and banker's draft.

Cash works for low-value transactions, but quite reasonably many people are wary of carrying large amounts of cash with them. So,

for most car purchases you will pay using some form of cheque.

Personal cheques are acceptable, but take a long time to clear. Building society cheques and banker's drafts used to be considered safer, but it's not unknown for them to be forged and building society cheques can still be stopped. So, however you pay, unless it's with cash, expect to wait for payment to clear before you can collect the car.

Paperwork

Rules about buying and selling vary in the UK, Europe and the US (and between states in the US) so make sure you understand your local regulations. In the UK the seller needs to fill in part of the V5C registration document and return it to the DVLA, giving you a tear-off slip with basic details about you and the car. You'll need this in case the V5C never makes it to the DVLA, and so the change of keeper is not recorded. That certainly can happen – it has happened to me, and only came to light when I tried to renew the road tax on the vehicle a year later. Provided you keep that slip showing the car's details, it's easy enough to sort out.

BELOW Make sure the new keeper's details are filled in on the registration document

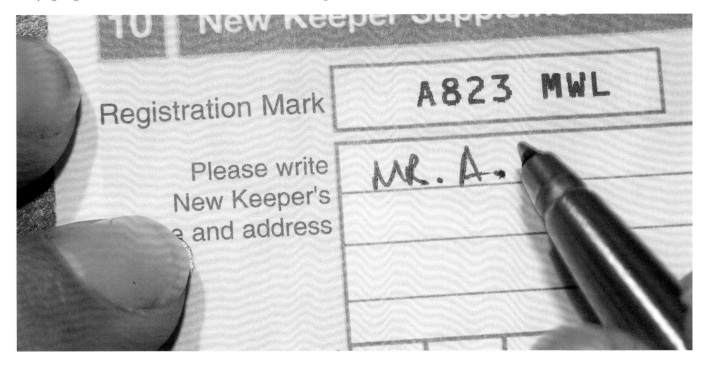

Selling a classic

If you thought buying a classic was a long-winded process full of pitfalls, problems, uncertainty and disappointment, wait till you try to sell one. Dealing with interested parties – ranging from timewasting tyre-kickers to serious buyers with pockets full of cash – can be a soul-destroying process. If it's one you can't face, there are other options you can consider: sell through auction, sell to a dealer or sell via a dealer on commission.

If you do choose to handle the sale yourself, you can save a lot of hassle by ensuring your advertising generates the right kind of enquiries. You want to make sure the ad is concise but informative, so you don't get dozens of phone calls asking for simple details, and at the same time encourages genuine buyers to call. The information you present is important, and so is the order in which you present it.

Usually you'll start with the make, model and year – though if you're advertising in a club magazine or other one-make publication and the make is obvious you might choose to omit it. Follow that with the most important and praiseworthy features of the car – for instance a new MoT, exceptional history or condition, or low mileage. If there's something unique about this car – it was once owned by a celebrity, or has had a £20,000 rebuild – then say so. If you include a sensible asking price, based on the same sort of valuation process we looked at earlier, you will filter out some of the timewasters and no-hopers.

Now you've made the car sound good in the ad, you need to make sure it lives up to that promise when prospective buyers come to see it. Before you even look at the car itself, spend some time going through the history file and making sure everything is in order and up to date.

A pampered garage queen might already be in a presentable condition, but if your cars (like mine) work for their living, a thorough clean will be the starting point – and that means outside, inside and under the bonnet.

So wash and dry the paintwork. If paint is dull, try using a cutting compound to bring back the shine. Tidy up the engine bay using an engine cleaner, and polish up any under-bonnet metal components like carburettor dashpots and rocker covers. Then turn your attention to the interior.

Vacuum the carpets, clean vinyl trim with a proprietary solution, feed the leather and empty the ashtrays. Clean the glass, too – visually it makes up a large proportion of the car body, so clean glass can make quite a difference.

Be very careful about test drives. Unless your car is covered on an 'any driver' insurance policy the buyer needs his own insurance covering him to drive your car – and you need to be aware that his insurance will probably not pay for damage to your car, only to others involved in any accident. If the car is not insured for your buyer to drive, don't let them drive it: both they and you will be committing a criminal offence.

If all goes well, your buyer will make you an offer for the car. It's unlikely to be as much as you asked in your advert, but you knew that and allowed for it when you wrote the ad. Don't be pressured into accepting less than you want for the car: if you've done your homework and valued your car correctly, there's no reason why you should. Be reasonable, but firm, in your negotiations.

As we've already seen, there are various ways of payment but one essential rule – do not release the car until the payment has cleared. Provide the new owner with the 'new keeper' slip from the registration document, together with a receipt detailing the car make and model, registration number, the amount paid and the date, and wave him on his way. Now you can start thinking about buying another classic.

BELOW Polish up any bright metal components under the bonnet to make a good impression

Care and maintenance

Servicing
your classic

Careful maintenance is, or should be, a major part of running a classic.
You cannot escape the fact that classic cars need more maintenance
than moderns. You can choose to ignore that and simply run your car
until it breaks, then fix it, but a cheaper and better approach is to plan
for maintenance that ensures your classic never lets you down. Even if
you are not the most mechanically adept, there are jobs you can do
which can help your classic maintain its condition, and you will enjoy it
all the more as a result. Tackle these simple items yourself, and when
you are faced with a more involved task which is beyond your skill or
confidence, take the car to a specialist.

Classic service schedule

Wherever possible, follow the manufacturer's recommended service procedures, as detailed in the owner's handbook or workshop manual. Requirements vary from classic to classic, so your car may not need every operation listed below, or it may need attention more frequently or in areas not mentioned here. But this checklist is reasonably comprehensive, and should provide a good starting point if you are unsure.

Daily or weekly

Check levels of engine oil, brake fluid, clutch fluid, other hydraulic fluids (e.g. power-steering), battery electrolyte and windscreen-washer fluid. Replenish as necessary.

Intermediate service

- Clean or replace engine air filter (depending on type).
- Change engine oil and filter.
- Check levels of brake fluid, clutch fluid, other hydraulic fluids (e.g. power-steering), battery electrolyte and windscreen-washer fluid.
- Check gearbox and rear axle oil levels. Replenish as necessary.
- Lubricate suspension/steering points, distributor, dynamo and throttle linkage.
- Check condition of brake pipes, fuel pipes, steering joints and gaiters, cooling system hoses and radiator, lights and windscreen wipers. Replace as necessary.
- Check spark plug condition, replace if electrodes are worn or the insulator is cracked. Adjust plug gaps as necessary.
- Check condition of contact-breaker points and replace if necessary. Adjust points gap as necessary.
- Check condition of fan belt and other drive belts. Replace if necessary. Check and adjust belt tensions.

Main service

- All intermediate service items.
- Change spark plugs and HT leads.
- Check valve clearances and adjust as required.
- Check brake pads/linings for wear. Replace/adjust as necessary.
- Check wheel bearings for wear. Replace/adjust and lubricate as necessary.
- Check clutch operation. Replace/adjust as necessary.

How often your classic needs simple checks on tyres and fluids and the like will depend on how much you use it. Daily checks would not be excessive if you use the car every day and rack up a considerable mileage, but for most classics a check each week, after each period of inactivity, and before a long trip will suffice.

Whenever you top up a fluid, ask yourself where it went – most classics will slowly consume oil and water, but a sudden drop could be a sign of trouble in store. Tyre pressures and condition should also come in for frequent scrutiny. Many classics need regular suspension lubrication, which can be as simple a matter as pumping a plunger sited under the dashboard, or it might involve you crawling under the car with a grease gun. Rapid wear is the likely result if lubrication is neglected.

Traditionally, service work has been split into 'intermediate' and 'main' services, which will be described in the owner's handbook or workshop manual, to be carried out at mileage or time intervals – perhaps every 6,000 miles or six months. Because most classics cover low annual mileages the original schedule may no longer be appropriate, but all cars will benefit from at least one thorough service each year. There is little point servicing a car which is in storage, but it ought to be thoroughly checked over before it is put back into use, and for many people this translates into a major service and preparation for the MoT test when the car is brought out of storage in the spring.

Convenience dictates that if your car is serviced by a specialist, all the work will be carried out in one go, but if you are doing the majority of the work yourself there is no reason why everything must be done in one great frenzy of activity. It is often easier to carry out a few jobs at a time, perhaps split into areas of the car – engine one weekend, brakes the next, suspension and steering the weekend after that. Splitting the work into chunks can make it more manageable, and causes no problems as long as you keep careful records of which jobs have been done and which remain.

Keeping
records

A classic with a well-recorded maintenance history is worth more and is easier to sell, so taking the time to organise the paperwork and keep up-to-date notes on the work done to your car will pay dividends in the end. Your classic's history file should include every 'official' bit of paper relating to the vehicle. You might inherit a pile of papers when you buy the car, but even if the car is accompanied by only skeletal paperwork you will soon begin to generate your own, beginning with the purchase invoice, road tax discs and registration documents. The maintenance records might include MoT test certificates and failure sheets, emissions analysis printouts, rolling road tuning printouts and – most important – bills for work done on the car and for parts you have bought.

Usually invoices from specialists detail the work done and the parts used, and if you keep these invoices in order they provide a comprehensive record of the service and repair work on your car. Record-keeping is more complicated if you work on your classic yourself, because the invoices you have relate only to parts and consumables – there will be no record of the work done, though the parts you bought are a good clue. What I do is to keep notes of all the work I do myself, each one including the date and mileage, which a prospective buyer will be able to relate to the parts invoices to build up a picture of my classic's history. How you store all this paperwork is up to you, and I have seen

everything from grubby manilla envelopes to slip-cased, leather-bound albums with gilt-embossed titles. A ring-binder works well, because it keeps everything in order and is easy to add to.

Your own notes can also help you to fine-tune your maintenance schedule, and to plan ahead for the service work your classic needs in the future. Over time you might be able to work out, for instance, how long a set of brake linings will last, and you will be able to predict roughly when to expect that expense to arise again. And it helps if you fit a new component which fails soon after: if you have the invoice to hand you may be able to claim under the guarantee.

OPPOSITE Keep records of all the work done on your classic, and all the parts bought – they can be useful if something goes wrong in future, and help a prospective purchaser to verify the car's history when the time comes for you to sell

Choosing a specialist

Word of mouth recommendation is the best way to choose a specialist, so talk to friends and club members. Some of the bigger clubs run their own approval schemes, which can also give you a clue. But there are other ways to assess a specialist before you start spending too much money.

Permanence is one key factor. A company that has managed to stay in business for several years without going bust or acquiring notoriety is likely to be doing good work. Try looking through copies of classic car magazines or owner's club newsletters that are three or four years old – if you can find mentions in the news and features columns, or adverts from the company in question, then at least you know that they have been around a while.

Another useful clue is to look at the work they do: you want to see evidence of cars going in and out, of jobs being finished. Be wary of a company which seems to have lots of cars around, but nothing much happening. Yours could end up being the next long-term project to sit around waiting for attention.

You can also tell a lot from the type of car you see. Whatever the value of the make or model the company specialises in, there are always cheaper ones and more expensive ones; ideally you want to see a mixture. Tattier cars in for MoT repairs, say, suggest that the more impecunious owners use the company, so their prices cannot be too daunting. Shiny concours winners, on the other hand, suggest that the company must

be capable of a good standard of work, otherwise those who can afford to pay more and demand the best quality would take their custom elsewhere. The ideal is a healthy blend from the two extremes and everywhere in between.

Find out whether the company prepares racing cars, and if so whether they are successful. Nobody can be consistently successful in a well-populated racing category without knowing what they are doing, and provided day-to-day work on customers' cars is never neglected in favour of the racing machines, that expertise should filter down to the bread-and-butter work. Just don't expect such a company to have all the staff on site every Saturday morning, particularly in the summer, because there is a good chance they will be at a racing circuit at the other end of the country.

Choosing and
using tools

Received wisdom is that you should always buy the finest tools you can afford, but I am not convinced it is always the best idea. Quality tools certainly make tasks easier, they last longer, they often do the job better and (which can be just as important) they are far more enjoyable to handle. But much of that only applies once you have some experience of the tool and the job in question.

There's not much point buying the best quality tool when you have little knowledge of how to use it, and none of the skill that experience brings. It's like a would-be racing driver beginning his career in a Formula 1 car rather than in karts or Formula Ford – a waste of good machinery on an unproven talent.

Some tools, particularly power tools, vary enormously in price and durability, and somewhat in performance. If you are aiming to buy a tool which you have no previous experience of using, consider buying something relatively cheap (which, in the case of a power tool, might mean it lacks the power or the build quality of something more expensive). The advantage is that you get to acquire experience and find out what you like and dislike about the tool, without committing yourself to an expensive purchase. If it turns out you rarely use the tool, it will matter less that it is not of the highest quality. If you use it constantly, you can cheerfully accept that your cheap tool will one day wear out or break, and by that time you will know enough about the job, and the tool you need to do it, to enable you to replace it with something more robust. So, use a cheap tool until you know what you're doing. Once you do, apply the old adage: buy the best you can afford, and look after it.

Spanners & sockets

Spanners divide into two main categories, ring and open-ended (plus a hybrid – the combination spanner, with a ring at one end and open jaws at the other). Open-ended spanners can be applied to the head of a nut or bolt from the top or from the side, making them useful in confined spaces. Their jaws are generally angled, and wherever possible the spanner should be used in such a way that the angled jaws point in the same direction that your hand is moving – if you are tightening the fastener, the jaws should point towards you as you are pulling the spanner handle towards you. This gives the spanner the best purchase on the nut or bolt head, making it less likely to slip.

Ring spanners can only be applied from above, but redress the balance by offering a far more secure grip on the fastener, making them less likely to slip. Also, they usually have 16 teeth, which means they can be used in a small arc – useful in a crowded engine bay. Sockets share the pros and cons of ring spanners, but with added versatility. Ratchet handles are serious time-savers, and this is where quality really is worth paying for. Quality socket sets work better and last longer than cheaper ones. The points of the teeth on cheap sockets tend to wear quickly with use, reducing their grip and making them very prone to slippage.

An innovation of recent years is the 'wall-drive' system, where the socket or spanner is shaped so that it bears on the flats of the fastener rather than the corners. Wall-drive sockets and spanners are less likely to round-off a nut or bolt head, and can undo fasteners previously rounded-off by conventional tools. Some types fit several different spanner sizes, reducing the number of tools you need to cover a range of sizes and doubling up for metric and imperial. But some wall-drive systems wedge the nut or bolt into the jaws, and it can be difficult to separate the fastener from the tool. Test before you buy.

ABOVE A wall-drive socket (right) can be useful, but fasteners tend to wedge inside as with wall-drive spanners

OPPOSITE Spanners come in all shapes, sizes and conditions. Second-hand spanners are usually fine, though the jaws on cheaper open-ended types can splay over time

LEFT Open-ended spanners (top) are useful if there is only access to the fastener from the side, not the end. Ring spanners (bottom) are less likely to slip and can operate through a smaller arc in a confined space. A 'combination' spanner has a ring at one end and open-ended jaws at the other

CAUTION:
Bend this tab after
inserting ratchet bar

⚠ WARNING   SWL
3000KG

Clarke INTERNATIONAL Epping, Essex, CM16 4LG, England

3 TONNE HEAVY DUTY
AXLE STAND
MODEL:CAX-3TBC

CAUTION

• USE STAND IN PAIR

Tightening & torque wrenches

With a bit of practice you will be able to get a
'feel' for the right tightness on most fasteners –
tight enough not to undo by itself, but not so tight
that threads are stripped. What you are actually
feeling is the stretching of the bolt shank, and that
feeling varies with the size and material of the
bolt. It helps to use a tool 'in scale' with the
fastener, because then the leverage you have at
your disposal will be appropriate to the size of the
bolt. That is why quarter-inch ratchets, designed
for small fasteners, have short handles.

Where the exact tightness is critical, use a
torque wrench. It is best to think of a torque
wrench as a measuring instrument rather than a
fancy spanner, and treat it as such. Use a
conventional ratchet to 'nip up' the nut or bolt,
then switch to the torque wrench for final
tightening. Always grip the torque wrench by its
handle, to avoid inaccurate results.

Jacks, stands & ramps

A trolley jack is almost essential. Buy one with a
weight rating which comfortably exceeds that of
your vehicle – a two-tonne rating is usually
sufficient. Heavier-duty jacks are bulkier and
heavier, which makes them more difficult to use.
Carrying handles and detachable jacking handles
make transport and storage easier. Sports car
owners should look for a jack with a low 'saddle
height' to ensure that it will fit under a car with
limited ground clearance.

It is often wise not to trust jacking points built
into bodywork or chassis outriggers, because
they are exposed to the elements and are often
prone to rust. Consult your workshop manual for
alternatives: a strong chassis member is a good
bet. Chock the wheel diagonally opposite the one
you are raising, and never work under a car which
is supported only by a jack: support it properly
using axle stands or ramps.

Workshop practice

Good 'workshop practice' might sound like a set of rules designed by management to make a job harder, but in fact the whole idea is to make every job simpler, quicker and less liable to error. Simple things can make a big difference, like organising your tools and then putting them back in the same place each time – that way you always know where to find a tool and never waste time searching.

There is no substitute for prior planning if you want to make sure a job goes smoothly and takes as little time as possible. Before you get going, read the relevant section in the workshop manual and get the procedure straight in your mind – you don't want to be reading it for the first time while you're in the midst of the job. Then work out which tools you are going to need, and collect them together. Decide what spares, if any, you are going to want and make sure you have them. Consider, too, whether you might need replacements for torn gaskets or disintegrating seals which are not likely to become apparent before you start the job.

If you are doing a job where you have to carry out the same procedure more than once – like rebuilding a pair of carburettors, or overhauling the brakes – fight the temptation to strip everything down at once. Work on one carburettor, or one brake, so that if you have trouble putting it back together you still have an untouched example to use as a reference.

Whenever you remove a component from the car, note the orientation in which it was fitted if that is relevant. Write notes, take photographs or draw diagrams to remind yourself. As you remove things, put them down in order, so they are easy to find when refitting – and for tiny components like nuts, get a container like a biscuit tin or an old hubcap to keep them in. If you don't lose anything, the job will be that much quicker.

OPPOSITE A trolley jack is more versatile and more secure than the jack supplied with the car, but you should also support a car with axle stands before working underneath

OPPOSITE RIGHT Use a torque wrench if it is vital to get the tightening torque correct. Always hold a torque wrench by the end of the handle, or it will produce inaccurate results

BELOW A test lamp makes tracing electrical faults easier

Other useful tools

There are all sorts of tools you can buy, but few you actually need. A test lamp is very useful for tracking electrical faults, and a multimeter can do the same job and much more – particularly a purpose-designed automotive meter, which will be able to measure engine rpm and dwell angle.

Pliers are invaluable, and it is useful to have two pairs – one with strong jaws for general use, and a needle-nosed pair for confined spaces. Self-locking pliers can be a useful 'third hand'. You will no doubt have an army of screwdrivers of different sizes, but one useful addition is a medium-sized 'chubby' screwdriver with a short blade and handle – ideal for setting the points on inaccessible distributors.

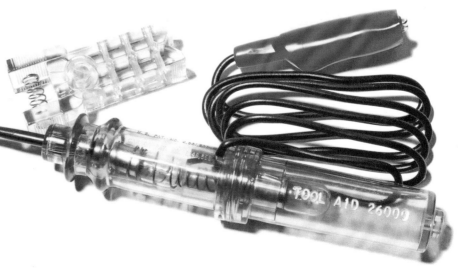

Routine
maintenance

Classics need regular servicing, but most of the jobs involved are easy to do once you've had a bit of practice and learned a few tricks of the trade. Do your own servicing and you save the cost of regular visits to a mechanic. But even if you choose to leave maintenance in the hands of the professionals, it's useful to know a little about the care your classic needs.

Engine oil and oil filter

Checking the engine oil level should be second nature, but remember not to do it immediately after the engine has run, as it takes a while for the oil to drain back into the sump and you would get an incorrect reading. Pull out the dipstick, wipe it clean with a rag, reinsert as far as it will go and remove it again – the level of oil on the dipstick should be between the maximum and minimum marks. After an oil change the clean oil can be quite tricky to see, but even new oil will turn black very quickly because additives in the oil clean the engine and hold the contaminates in suspension.

Warm up the engine before you drain the oil, because warm oil is thinner and will drain faster

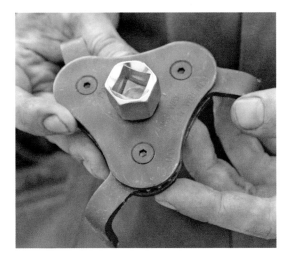

FAR LEFT Spin-on oil filters can be difficult to get at. A filter wrench like this, with geared legs which grip the sides of the filter, can help

LEFT Before discarding any old component, it is good practice to check that the new one matches it – sometimes specifications change, or the wrong part gets packed in the box. Here the new and old oil filters match perfectly

OPPOSITE Check the oil level frequently, but if the engine has just been run, leave it for a minute or two to allow the oil to drain back to the sump

and more completely. But take care when you remove the drain plug and, inevitably, the oil spills onto your fingers – it will be boiling hot. Drainer cans are ideal for catching the old oil but too deep to fit under some ground-hugging sports cars, so you will have to find a shallower receptacle or raise the car.

Cartridge-type oil filters are contained in a filter bowl secured by a bolt, and these are easy to undo, but disposable canister-type filters can be trickier. Band-type filter wrenches are effective if you have enough space to wield them, or you can try the claw-type wrench if you have access to the end of the filter rather than the sides. If all else fails, punch a long screwdriver straight through the canister to act as a lever.

Refit the sump plug, with a new sealing washer. Fill a new canister-type filter with oil before fitting it, and smear some oil on the rubber sealing ring so that it seals more effectively, then

screw on the filter hand tight. The bolt on a cartridge filter bowl should be tightened to the torque recommended in the workshop manual. Fill the engine with fresh oil, taking care not to overfill: it takes a minute or so for oil to work its way down into the sump, so fill in stages and keep checking the level on the dipstick. Wipe up any spills and check for leaks. Then start the engine, making sure the oil pressure warning light goes out, and check again for leaks. Stop the engine and, after a few minutes, recheck the oil level.

Choosing oil can be tricky for classic engines, and recommendations differ depending on the type of engine, its age, what it gets used for and your personal preference. Take advice from marque experts. As a general rule, run the engine on the grade of oil it was originally designed for – which for most post-war classics means a standard 20W/50 oil is fine. Many modern motor oils are thinner and crammed full of additives, both of which work well in modern cars but can be inappropriate for an older engine. 'Classic' oils generally have fewer additives for that reason.

Ignition and electrical system

Most breakdowns are caused by electrical faults, and the lion's share of those are ignition problems. Good maintenance here will make a real difference to your classic's reliability.

Clean, correctly-gapped plugs are essential, so periodically pull the plugs out and check them. Clean the area around each one before you remove it to avoid foreign material dropping into the combustion chamber – either sweep around the plug with an old paint brush, or use an air-line. Ideally, you want the plugs to have a grey/brown appearance, with only light deposits. Heavy

LEFT Details count: replace the sump plug washer (where fitted) when you change the oil to help prevent leaks

RIGHT Some alternators and dynamos have a lubrication hole at the back

FAR RIGHT The ignition timing may need to be checked with the distributor's vacuum connection removed – check your workshop manual

BELOW Check the plug gaps using a feeler gauge. The earth electrode on the plug can be bent carefully in or out to adjust the gap. These days plug manufacturers advise against cleaning plugs – if they are heavily soiled they should be replaced

deposits suggest fuelling or ignition faults, while an oily appearance indicates engine wear. Cleaning is not recommended for modern plugs – going at them with a wire brush is not a good idea. Measure the gaps using feeler gauges, adjusting the earth electrode if necessary.

With the engine switched off, look along each of the HT leads for any signs of cracks or deterioration in the insulating material – if any lead is suspect, replace the whole set. Wipe off any oil or grease from the leads, as this can result in 'arcing' from one to another. Check that all the connectors are pushed firmly onto the plugs and the connections at the distributor and coil. A loose connector can usually be tightened up by squeezing it gently with pliers, but be careful not to damage the insulation. Finish off by spraying a water dispersant over the leads and the connectors at both ends, to keep damp out of the ignition system.

Regular checking and setting of the points gap will also pay

dividends in keeping your classic running sweetly. Look out for pitting on the face of one of the contacts, often accompanied by a 'pip' of deposited metal on the other, which will prevent you being able to measure the gap correctly. You can clean up the faces using a file and then readjust the gap, but eventually the points will need to be replaced. Use feeler gauges to measure the gap, then adjust by slackening the securing screw and moving the fixed contact. Recheck the gap after you tighten the screw, in case anything moved. While you are in there, apply a little grease to the operating cam and the heel of the points onto which the cam bears. The distributor will benefit from a few drops of light oil at the top of the shaft to lubricate the bearings, and if there are gaps in the baseplate you should be able to drop a little oil into the advance mechanism. When you refit the rotor arm try to rock it from side to side – there should be a tiny amount of movement, but if the motion is considerable the distributor's bearings are worn, and consequently the ignition timing will be all over the place.

LEFT Setting the tappets, using a feeler gauge to measure the gap and the screwdriver to adjust it. The adjusting screw will have a locknut which must be tightened once adjustment is complete

Once set, the ignition timing is unlikely to change much over time, so it will not need to be rechecked frequently. Ideally, check the timing with a stroboscopic timing light with a xenon lamp (much brighter than neon, making it easier to see the timing marks in a dark engine bay). It is also helpful to have a timing light on which you can set the required timing advance. Most strobe lights are built for a 12-volt, negative earth supply, so if your classic is positive earth or has 6-volt electrics, power the timing light from an auxiliary 12-volt battery. Make sure you check the timing at the engine speed quoted in your workshop manual, and with any vacuum advance connected or disconnected according to what the manual says.

The heart of the electrical system is the battery, and you can get a simple estimate of the state of the battery by checking its voltage – like taking its pulse. On a 12-volt system the voltage across the battery should be 12V or slightly more when the engine is not running. It will drop to 10–12V during cranking and then recover to 13–14V with the engine running. Unless you have a 'maintenance free' battery, keep an eye on the electrolyte levels, topping up as necessary with distilled water. If the same cell always needs topping up, look for cracks in the casing. If all the cells lose electrolyte at about the same rate, the battery is probably being overcharged, suggesting faults with the alternator or regulator. Check regularly that the connections are sound and secure, and smear a little petroleum jelly on the terminals to deter corrosion.

Alternators and more modern types of dynamo have 'sealed for life' bearings, but older dynamos will have an oil hole at the back, opposite the drive pulley.

Valve clearances

'Setting the tappets' is a ritual which has long since died out for modern car owners, even those rare few who still do their own maintenance. For a classic it is likely to be an essential job, and rarely a particularly difficult one.

What you are adjusting is the free play in the valve gear, usually measured between rocker and valve stem (or cam lobe and tappet in an overhead-cam engine). Adjustment methods vary, but the most common is a screw at the end of the rocker, secured by a locknut. To adjust, you undo the locknut, turn the screw, and retighten the nut.

Each clearance is checked with the valve fully closed. It is actually easier to see when a valve is at full lift, because its motion is more pronounced, and you can work out from the engine layout which corresponding valve is fully closed. Sounds complex, but for in-line four-cylinder engines there is a rule, the 'rule of nine', which works it out for you. Number all the valves from one end of the engine: take away the number of the open valve from nine and you get the number of the closed one. So when valve one is fully open, valve eight is closed. When valve two is open, seven is closed – and so on. For in-line six-cylinder engines, you can use the 'rule of 13' in the same way, but in both cases be warned that the rules only work if the valves are in the conventional order, where they swap sides in adjacent cylinders (inlet/exhaust, exhaust/inlet and so on).

The clearance is measured by inserting a feeler gauge into the gap – if it is correct you should feel a gentle dragging as you pull the feeler gauge out. Keep your screwdriver pressed onto the adjustment screw while you measure, or you will get a false reading. When you have adjusted and tightened the locknut, check again with the feeler gauge to make sure nothing moved.

ABOVE Give each water hose a squeeze, and look for cracks appearing in the rubber

Fuel system

The air filter should be cleaned or changed regularly, depending on the design. Gauze filters are cleaned in petrol and fresh engine oil added to the filter bowl. Paper elements are disposable. K&N filters should not need attention for 50,000 miles or more, unless driven in adverse conditions. They can be brushed to remove the worst of the debris, or properly cleaned by spraying on a special cleaning fluid and rinsing with water. In both cases the filter should be re-oiled before being refitted.

Make sure throttle and choke cables are free to move – if not, you can try introducing a little light oil to the cable inner. Lubricate joints in rod-operated throttles and linkages on the carburettors to avoid sticking throttles, and check flexible fuel hoses for signs of cracks or chafing.

Once correctly set, carburettor settings should not drift far over time, so there should be no need to spend time tweaking the idle mixture and balancing twin-carb set-ups at every service. But if you dismantle the carburettors – for instance, to clean the piston in an SU carb which controls the position of the needle in the jet – you will need to re-check the settings. The correct procedure varies between engines, so consult your workshop manual.

Cooling system

Most classics are water-cooled. The coolant water level will be measured either at the radiator or in a separate header tank, and generally needs to be filled to an inch or so below the filler neck. If in doubt, overfill because the system will expel excess coolant through its overflow. Anti-freeze should always be used, even in summer, because it cuts down on internal corrosion – particularly important if the engine has any aluminium alloy components, like the cylinder head or water pump. Brightly-coloured anti-freeze makes it easier to see the coolant level.

Give each water hose a good squeeze and look for any cracks starting to form: these cracks will take a while to go through the hose completely, but if they are visible when you squeeze the hose it means it is time to think about replacement. Pay particular attention to any hose which has to turn a corner, as these often crack on the outside of the bend where the rubber is under greatest stress. Also prone to failure are hoses which are subjected to high temperatures because of proximity to the exhaust manifold. Check, too, that the clips retaining all the hoses are tight.

Every year or so it is worthwhile draining the coolant, flushing out the system and refilling with fresh anti-freeze mixture. Back-flush the radiator, with water flowing in the opposite direction to normal: wrapping the end of a hose in rags helps provide a good enough seal when you insert it into the stub on the radiator. The radiator matrix will also accumulate debris, so this is a good time to wash out the dirt and dead flies to make sure air can get through.

FAR RIGHT Lubricate carburettor linkages to avoid sticking throttles

Steering and suspension

Many classics have stringent greasing requirements, and it is wise not to put off attention with the grease gun. You may not be able to get round all of your classic's grease points in a short session, particularly if you need to jack up the car and remove wheels for access to suspension or chassis grease nipples, but you can divide the job into several smaller ones, taking one end or one corner at a time.

Clean off any road dirt or hardened grease from around a grease nipple before you apply the gun. A quick squirt is not enough – keep on going until clean grease exudes from the nipple or the joint. That way you can be sure that fresh grease is getting to the joint, and you are also cleaning out any debris. Wipe away any excess grease.

Regularly check the rubber boots on the ends of the steering rack. If they split the rack will lose oil and may wear rapidly as a result.

Braking system

Mechanically-operated brakes were used into the 1950s, and are still adequate provided they are well maintained. Make sure rods and cables are in good condition and that all the joints and pins in the system are well lubricated. The same applies to the handbrake linkage. With hydraulic systems, inspect the pipework to check for leaks, and regularly check the fluid level. Investigate any sudden level changes. To ensure that no debris enters the system, always clean around the neck of the reservoir before removing the cap. Replace the fluid at least every two years or so, as brake fluid is usually hygroscopic – it absorbs water.

Disc brakes adjust themselves as the pads wear, marked by a slight drop in the level of fluid in the system. Check the pads regularly, particularly on cars where the brakes work hard, and replace when the friction material is worn down to about 3mm thick. To get the thicker new pads into place you will need to force the caliper pistons back into their bores using a special tool, or a piece of wood, as a lever. Be aware that when you do this the fluid level in the reservoir will rise, and that spilt brake fluid will attack paintwork! Apply copper grease to the backs of the new pads before fitting them.

Drum brakes usually require periodic adjustment, and an adjusting screw, or peg, is provided on the brake backplate. Some thoughtful manufacturers provide an access hole for a screwdriver in each wheel, so that the brakes can be adjusted without removing the wheels – provided whoever last fitted the wheels put them on in the correct orientation. The brakes should be adjusted up so that the wheel locks, and then backed off until it can rotate freely.

Air in the fluid will prevent a hydraulic system from operating correctly. To remove trapped air the system must be 'bled' one brake at a time, starting at the brake furthest from the master cylinder. A small length of rubber or plastic tubing is connected to the bleed nipple (on the side of the disc brake caliper, or on a drum brake backplate) and the free end of the pipe immersed in brake fluid in a small container – a jam jar is ideal. The bleed nipple is opened and the brake pedal pumped until only clean fluid, with no air bubbles, emerges from the pipe. The bleed nipple must then be tightened while the brake pedal is held down, to avoid air being drawn back into the system. Brake bleeding takes two people, unless you use a pressure-bleeding system like Gunson's Eezibleed.

Safety: tyres, windows, wipers and lights

Check tyre pressures regularly, using a good pressure gauge, and correct any deficiencies at once. If one tyre always needs air – suspect a

ABOVE Disc brakes automatically adjust themselves, but drums will need period manual adjustment

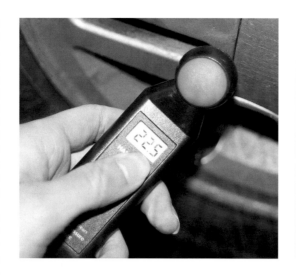

slow puncture. Look carefully for any cracks or abrasions to the tyre sidewalls, as these can cause sudden tyre failures at high speed. Inspect the tyre tread regularly, ensuring you have a good thickness of tread across the whole tyre – the legal minimum in the UK is just 1.6mm, but for safety you really want double that. Feel around the tread of the tyre for stones and foreign bodies in the tread – remove them before they cause a puncture.

The wiper mechanism will have been part of your lubrication routine, but take a look at the rest of the system, too. Run your thumb down each wiper blade in turn – if the edge of the blade feels rough then the wiper rubbers are worn and should be replaced. If the wipers judder, twist the wiper arms slightly so the blades lie flatter to the screen. Look for water leaks in the washer pipework, and check the aim of the washer jets – the jets of water should hit the windscreen about in the centre or slightly higher. On many cars the jets are affected by the airflow over the bonnet, so check them out on the road and then make further adjustments if necessary.

Keeping the windows and lights clean is an obvious must for visibility, though the lights in particular are often neglected. Glass cleaners work well on both, but even a good rub with a damp rag is better than nothing as it will remove most of the road dirt and give you a fighting chance of seeing where you are going.

Bodywork

Cleaning is maintenance. Keeping your classic clean cuts down the chances of rust forming, and washing by hand also gives you the chance to thoroughly inspect the bodywork on a regular basis. Wash the car with a proprietary car shampoo – never use washing-up liquid, which

dulls and scratches paintwork. Remove mud (and salt, in the winter) using a hose pipe or pressure washer inside the wheel arches and underneath the car. Finish by applying a good wax polish to protect the paint. To fight corrosion, regularly apply rustproofing materials inside box sections and cavities.

Hinges will squeak and start to wear if lubrication is neglected, so go round them with an oil can on a regular basis, moving the hinge back and forth to work the oil into the mechanism. Remember to oil bonnet and boot hinges as well as door hinges, and to grease lock pins and latches. Another worthwhile way to spend a few minutes is to go round every nut, bolt and screw on your classic, making sure they are tight. Old cars seem to have an infinite capacity for vibrating things loose. Get to know if anything on your car is always coming undone, and pay particular attention to it – you might even consider replacing an always-loose nut with a Nylock, or adding a lock nut if there's enough exposed thread on the bolt. Or you can apply a thread lock to ensure things don't shake loose. Where possible, tighten nuts and bolts to a specified torque using a torque wrench – it's not necessary to try to tighten any further, and it can often cause damage to the fixings if you do.

Other maintenance jobs

The fan belt usually drives the dynamo, or the alternator, and the water pump; and, depending on what is fitted to your classic, there could be other drive belts for power-steering, air-conditioning and other systems. Each belt needs to be correctly tensioned – too tight is almost as bad as too slack because it will eventually wreck the bearings in the device it is driving. Check your manual for specific advice on belt tensions, but a good rule of thumb is that you should just be able to twist a belt through 90 degrees with your fingers in the middle of its longest run.

The more recent your classic is, or the more expensive it was when new, the more likely you are to have extra pumps and compressors and hydraulic systems running a variety of ancillaries – air-conditioning, power-steering and self-levelling suspension being the common ones. Check any hydraulic fluid reservoirs, and top up using the recommended fluid and the appropriate procedure (which may mean with the engine running). Examine drive belts for signs of wear, replacing any which look past their best, and adjust the belt tensions.

As you look over the hoses in the engine bay, you might well find that clips intended to keep the hoses in place have disappeared or detached themselves. Replace any that have gone completely, and refit those that have worked loose. Do the same thing with wiring runs, and operating cables for throttle, choke, bonnet catch and perhaps even radiator blinds. Keeping hoses, wiring and operating cables neatly clipped in place improves the engine bay appearance, improves reliability because things cannot flap about and break, and makes working on the engine quicker and easier.

Unless you have a garage with a lift or a pit, there isn't much maintenance you can do under

your classic without spending a fair amount of time jacking up, securing and lying on the floor. But you can perform a visual check on the underbody, and in particular on the exhaust, looking for corrosion and impact damage to the system. A powerful torch helps and, strangely, it's often easier to see under the car at night – because your eyes are adjusted to gloom instead of sunlight. If you can reach the exhaust and its hangers you can try waggling the exhaust pipe – it should be flexibly mounted, but still retained in position – and squeezing any rubber 'doughnuts' just as you would a heater hose, to look for cracks.

ABOVE The fan belt tension will usually be set by swinging the alternator or dynamo on its off-centre bracket. If there is more than one bolt fixing the position, loosen them all before trying to adjust

LEFT Keeping your classic clean is about more than just appearances – regular cleaning helps keep corrosion at bay, and gives you the opportunity to inspect the bodywork as you go

Preparing for the MoT test

Most countries have a vehicle roadworthiness check. In Britain all passenger cars over the age of three years are required to undergo the annual 'MoT test' which concentrates on safety-related items. Because some areas of the test require the examiner to use his or her judgement it is wise to get your classic MoT'd at a testing station which is used to dealing with old cars. Many items covered by the test are easy to check at home.

The vehicle structure must be sound and, in particular, rust may not encroach within 30cm of a load-bearing structure, such as a suspension or seat-belt mounting point. Sharp edges or projections caused by damage or corrosion, which may be dangerous to pedestrians or other road users, are not allowed. Doors must be openable from inside and out, and doors, bonnets, tailgates and boot lids must latch securely.

The steering system must be in good condition, securely fixed to the vehicle and without excessive wear or play. The efficiency and balance of the brakes will be checked on a rolling-road brake tester. The hydraulic system must not show evidence of fluid leaks or corrosion. Mechanical linkages must operate correctly and must be in good condition. Suspension joints must not be worn to excess, and dampers must not be leaking or ineffective. Tyres must be of an appropriate type and size with no serious damage, and have at least 1.6mm of tread depth across three-quarters of the tyre all the way round. Wheels must be in good condition and securely attached. The spare wheel, however, is not tested.

All the lights must be intact and must work correctly – check stop lamps and indicators function with and without other lights on. Indicators must flash between 60 and 120 times a minute, which old flasher units sometimes struggle to achieve. Hazard warning lights, if fitted, must work.

Chips or cracks in the windscreen must be less than 10mm in diameter if they occur in the 'A zone', an area 290mm either side of the centre of the steering wheel, swept by the windscreen wiper.

Elsewhere they may be up to 40mm in size, but they must not compromise the integrity of the screen glass. The wiper blades and washers (where fitted) must be effective. Requirements for mirrors vary with the age of the car, and additional mirrors are not part of the test.

Seat belts must be securely fitted and in good condition, and must lock and release correctly. The seats themselves must be securely fitted and generally must lock in the upright position – but seats in two-door cars which tip forward for access to the rear, and were never designed to have a locking mechanism, should be accepted.

Any fuel leak will result in an MoT failure, so check the fuel hoses and connections. The exhaust system must be effective, securely fitted, and have no major leaks. Vehicles first used from the mid-1970s onwards must pass emissions tests which vary depending on the vehicle's age.

OPPOSITE Classics need more maintenance than moderns, but servicing and repairs need not be daunting

MOT requirements – major changes with vehicle age

1906
- Audible warning horn (on cars built prior to 1906 a gong, siren or bell is acceptable).
- Parking brake.

1 January 1915
- Service brake must have minimum efficiency 40 per cent.
- Parking brake must have minimum efficiency 25 per cent (16 per cent for dual systems).

1 January 1931
- Headlamps.

2 January 1933
- Minimum tyre tread depth 1.6mm (1.0mm on cars first used prior to this date).

1 January 1936
- Stop lamp, on vehicle centre-line or to the offside.
- Direction indicators, which may be incorporated into stop lamps, side lamps or rear lamps; may show white to front and red to rear.

Approx pre-1960
- Diesel vehicles which emit 'unavoidable' smoke due to their design should not be failed; after this date vehicles must not emit dense smoke.

1 September 1965
- Direction indicator must be separate from stop lamp and amber in colour.
- Front seat belts restraining the torso (lap belts optional).

1 January 1968
- Service brake must have minimum efficiency 50 per cent.
- Parking brake must have minimum efficiency 25 per cent (16 per cent for dual systems); parking brake must be mechanically locked and released.

1 January 1971
- Two stop lamps.

1 August 1973
- Horn must be a continuous, non-varying note (i.e. musical horns no longer acceptable).

1 August 1975
- Petrol cars must pass basic emissions test (CO limit 4.5 per cent, HC limit 1,200ppm).

1 August 1978
- Cars must have an offside exterior mirror, and either a nearside exterior mirror or an interior mirror; additional mirrors are not subject to the test (vehicles used prior to this date must have at least one rear view mirror, of any type).

1 August 1979
- Diesels must pass a smoke emission test.

1 August 1980
- Must display a Vehicle Identification Number (VIN).

31 March 1981
- Front seat three-point (lap and diagonal belts) or other three-point belt with British Standard markings.

1 April 1986
- Hazard warning flashers.
- Side-repeater indicators or wrap-around indicators.
- Emissions: CO limit reduced to 3.5 per cent.

31 March 1987
- Rear seat belts (where rear seats are fitted).

1 August 1992
- Exhaust catalyst; emissions must conform to manufacturer's specifications.

Winter preparation

Many classics are 'laid up' during the winter months to avoid the worst of the weather, but there are thousands of classics which are on the road all the year round. Whether you choose to use your classic or garage it for the duration, prior preparation is essential.

Cold weather makes the battery less efficient, so if you plan to run your classic through the winter, make sure the electrolyte is topped up and check the battery voltage as described earlier. Check the fan belt tension. Make sure there is sufficient anti-freeze in the cooling system to prevent freezing at the temperatures you are likely to encounter – a one third anti-freeze, two-thirds water mix is common. You will be using the lights, wipers and washers much more frequently, so make sure everything is in good order. Finally, check that the tyres have sufficient tread to deal with wet roads.

The optimum environment for storing your classic during the winter is clean, dry and secure.

The ideal way of achieving this is to use a dehumidifier 'bubble', of which there are several types. These filter and dry the air inside the 'bubble' to avoid corrosion and keep out dust. Failing that, at least use a dust cover to keep your classic clean. If you have to store your classic outside, use a proper 'breathable' car cover – a thick plastic tarpaulin probably does more harm than good, because it traps moisture underneath.

Before you store the car, change the oil to remove any contaminants, and lubricate each cylinder through the spark plug hole to prevent corrosion – either use engine oil or an upper-cylinder lubricant. The cooling system can be drained, but it is probably better to flush it and refill with a water/anti-freeze solution to prevent corrosion. Disconnect the battery, which will need charging occasionally. Protect the electrical system with a water-repellent spray, lubricate the door locks and hinges, and apply a thick coat of wax polish to exterior chrome. Leave the handbrake off and wedge the clutch pedal down to avoid them sticking. If possible raise the car on axle stands or fit 'slave' wheels, because tyres will tend to form flat spots through prolonged standing.

OPPOSITE If you have to store your classic outside, use a 'breathable' car cover. A plastic tarpaulin does more harm than good

LEFT Kits are available to convert your classic from tungsten-filament headlamps to halogen units

BELOW Your classic's cooling system should contain a water/anti-freeze mixture, whether or not you intend to run the car in the winter

Restoration
& repair

Buying a project car

Twenty years ago speculators gave up betting on the prices of Van Goghs and started buying classic cars instead. Values rocketed, resulting in hundreds of unsuspecting classics being unearthed and treated to nut and bolt restorations, and being rebuilt with far more time and care than would ever have been expended on them when they were new. Such was the state of the market that even after a multi-thousand-pound rebuild these cars could still be sold at a considerable profit.

Eventually the bubble burst, of course, and values dropped back to more sensible levels. Today there are few classics which you can buy as a wreck or a box of bits, restore to its former glory and sell on at a profit: most cars will cost more to rebuild than they will be worth when the job is finished, and in many cases the rebuild costs will far outweigh the eventual value. Restoring a classic will not make you rich. So, some might ask, why do it at all?

There are a variety of answers. Some people just enjoy working on cars, and restoring an old vehicle to its former glory is more interesting than just servicing and general maintenance. Other people do it because they want to save a dejected classic from terminal decline, or because they can rebuild the car to the specification they want. Sometimes a rebuild can be the only way to get a rare classic.

But a full restoration is not easy. You need a wide variety of skills, an array of tools, somewhere to work, money for parts and specialist services and, perhaps most important of all, the time and patience to do the job.

Buying a car to restore can be even trickier than buying one which is in good condition. You can never really be sure just how much work is going to be involved, not until you start pulling things apart – and by then it's too late. Though many of the tests you can apply to a running car are useless with a project car which may well be immobile (and even if it runs is almost certainly not road legal), I suggest you take the same approach. Check as much as you can, so you know as clearly as is possible what you are letting yourself in for.

Try to get an idea of which parts of the car are salvageable, which can be replaced by new parts and which will need to be built up from scratch. Ideally you want the car to be complete, with no major parts missing or beyond saving. It's also worth checking more minor items, if they are rare and sought-after parts which could easily go missing – like Colin Chapman signature steering wheels on Elans, for instance.

Modifications can also be a headache if you're planning to restore the car to its original condition. Find out how much work it will take to put the car back to its standard specification: not all modifications are easily reversible.

Enthusiasm is usually abundant at the beginning of a project – it is other qualities which can be in short supply. Consider the limits of your own expertise as a restorer: it would be wise to start with a relatively simple project, rather than jump in at the deep end with a restoration project which needed money, skill and luck in huge amounts. Many projects founder once the initial wave of enthusiasm dies down and the would-be restorer realises the harsh reality of the task, so abandoned projects are often found for sale. These have their pros and cons: you might be able to get a better idea of the work required if the car is already partially stripped down, but the bad news is that you cannot be sure everything is there and it may not be obvious how everything goes together. It is much easier to put something back together if you saw it come apart in the first place.

Into the class of 'restoration projects' come a very wide range of vehicles, from slightly shabby runners to cars that were parked in a field in the mid-1950s and have trees growing through them. No car is unrestorable, provided you have enough time, money and enthusiasm. But there comes a point where, arguably, what you've done is build a new car rather than 'restore' an old one. Unless you're looking at something incredibly rare, it won't be worth taking on a really derelict car, certainly not in financial terms – as already stated, it's very easy for a restoration bill to far exceed what the car will ever be worth.

OPPOSITE Is this a viable project, or just a pile of scrap? Project cars are often difficult to assess properly until you start pulling them to bits – and by then you are committed

LEFT Dirty, damp, full of rubbish and attacked by mildew – but at least this TR7 interior looks complete. A thorough clean will work wonders

How cars deteriorate

Rust is the obvious enemy, but not the only one. Rust is iron oxide, caused by the reaction of iron in the steel components of the car with the oxygen in the atmosphere. Water, particularly salt water, accelerates the formation of rust because it provides an effective pathway for electrons to be swapped around as the chemical reaction takes place – effectively it acts like the acid in a battery. Rust will only occur if bare iron or steel is in contact with air, which is why good preparation and careful painting makes such a difference.

Aluminium alloys do not rust, but they can still corrode to form a powdery white deposit of aluminium oxide. Where there is a mixture of aluminium and iron/steel components (aluminium heater taps on iron block engines, aluminium panels on steel chassis) and water is present, the aluminium will corrode preferentially through what is called 'galvanic corrosion'. It is the same process which makes the zinc coating on galvanised steel protect the steel underneath – the zinc corrodes preferentially. Aluminium panels are separated from the steel chassis or body frame to which they are mounted by either a paint film or a cloth tape along the join, the latter working well as long as it never gets wet.

Light also causes problems. Over time the dyes in trim materials are bleached by exposure to sunlight, and sometimes trim fabrics degrade because of the action of the ultra-violet part of the spectrum – so you will find holes and wear on the tops of seats where they catch the sun.

Obviously, mechanical components eventually fail because of wear, but lack of use can be just as bad. Most lubricating oils and greases break down over time, allowing corrosion and seizure.

Planning
the rebuild

If your project car is complete, running and roadworthy rather than a complete wreck, you will have to decide whether to take it off the road to tackle the restoration, or to keep it in use. Many classics are sound enough to use but not nearly as good as they could be, and for these cars a 'rolling restoration' is perfectly possible. The advantage is that you get to use your classic while you are rebuilding it, instead of having to put in plenty of effort before it ever turns a wheel. But the rebuild can be more complex and involve more work if you want to tackle the job in bite-size pieces which never leave the car immobilised for long. To minimise the time the car spends off the road, make sure you have all the parts and tools you need for each job before you begin.

A rolling restoration should begin with all the work necessary to ensure the car is safe and, hopefully, reliable. A thorough service is a good

idea, paying particular attention to tyres, brakes, steering, suspension and the structural integrity of the chassis or bodyshell. Submitting the car for an MoT test (or the equivalent in other countries) can be useful, even if the test is not yet due – it will give you a good idea of any areas on the car which render it unroadworthy. Once those are attended to, you will be able to use your classic while you are bringing other areas up to scratch.

If you plan to take the car off the road during the restoration – or it is in such poor condition that you have no option – you do have the advantage that you can tackle the work in any order you wish. If, like the majority of restorers, you are happy to tackle some areas of work but not so keen on others, you can plan the restoration so that sub-assemblies can be sent away for refurbishment while you concentrate on another area of the car.

ABOVE A rolling restoration allows you to enjoy driving your classic while you work on improving it

Stripping

Removing components for refurbishment or for access to other items can be difficult and long-winded. Many of the nuts, bolts, screws and other fasteners which hold your classic together will have been there for decades, and may well have been affected by corrosion. Clean around the head of the nut or bolt, using a wire brush to remove any surface corrosion so that your spanner or socket can get a good purchase. Soak overnight with a releasing agent to aid removal. You can try extra leverage by slipping a piece of tubing over your spanner or socket T-bar handle, but be wary of shearing the head of a bolt. You can also try applying heat to a nut, if access is good enough to allow the use of a blowtorch without causing damage to adjacent componentry. If all that fails, more drastic measures will be called for.

Often a nut can be removed by cutting down through it next to the bolt threads using a hacksaw or angle grinder – be careful not to cut too close,

to avoid damaging the bolt. The remains of the nut can usually then be unscrewed or broken away using a cold chisel. Another option is a hydraulic nut splitter, which will slowly bite through a stubborn nut. Immovable screws can often be loosened using an impact driver, which has a screwdriver bit which turns when the tool is struck with a mallet.

Take notes and photographs as you go, so that you will be able to figure out how everything goes back together later on – do not rely on memory, because your memory can play tricks on you, and if things do not quite go to plan it may be much longer than you expect before you start putting things back together. Label everything you remove, either by applying a sticky label or tying on a tag, and if there are any fixings, brackets or mounting screws keep them with the component to which they belong. It is tedious, but you will thank yourself later.

BELOW Take notes and photographs as you strip things down so you will know how to put it all back together

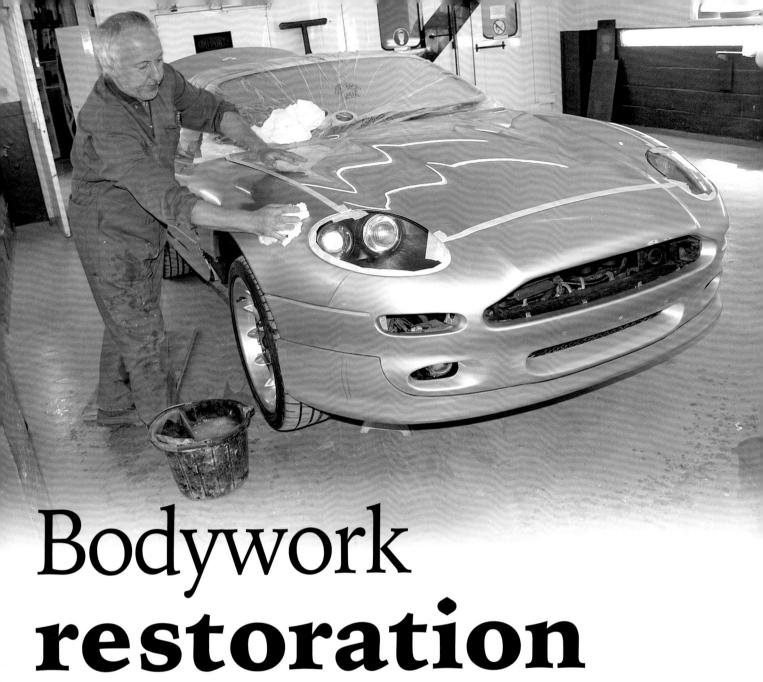

Bodywork restoration

Rust is a big enemy of most classics, so much of the time spent on a restoration will go into the bodywork. Probably more time than you expect, in fact, because the true extent of the corrosion in your classic's body will only become fully apparent when you start to strip off the outer panels. Repairs require a combination of four skills: making up of repair sections, welding, filling and painting.

Panels in very poor condition, and those which are reasonably easy to remove – such as lids, doors and bolt-on wings – can be replaced with new or better-condition second-hand items. If rot is less severe, or corrosion is localised, it might be a better idea to tackle the problem by cutting out the affected area and welding in new metal. To

prevent rust coming through again it is vital that all the affected metal is cut away, which might mean cutting out far more than you originally bargained for. In situations where significant lumps of the body are being cut away, it may be necessary to use props to keep the body square while repairs are made. It is often a good idea to fit a hard top on convertibles, and to leave the body on the chassis at least until it is structurally sound. Repair panels will be available from specialists for popular classics, but for some repairs and particularly for rarer machinery you might have to make your own. Simple repair sections can be made up using nothing more complicated than tin snips, a vice, a pair of pliers and a hammer, but it does need

ABOVE Preparation is the key to a high-quality paint finish. Professional body shops spend a great deal of time and effort ensuring that the surface is right before the paint is applied

some skill. Restoration courses spend a lot of time teaching these techniques, and are a good place to start for a beginner.

Modern techniques make welding much easier than it used to be. In the old days, amateur welders had a choice of two systems: electric arc welding and gas welding. Arc welding is tricky to get right because you have to wear a dark welding mask to protect you from the bright light of the arc, and the arc is only 'struck' when the tip of the welding rod is close enough to the workpiece. So you can't see what you're doing until it's too late. It is also difficult to get the speed of movement right when arc welding, and if you move too slowly there is a good chance you will melt a hole in your panel. Gas welding is a bit less frightening, but it needs considerable skill to get a neat, clean result, and the heat generated can easily cause distortion to the surrounding metalwork. So neither is the ideal technique for the tyro welder.

Metal inert gas (MIG) welding is easier. It works on the same principle as arc welding, melting the welding rod and the metal of the panel using an electric current, but instead of welding using a stiff filler rod you use a 'gun' with a trigger. When you press the trigger, narrow-gauge welding wire is fed from a drum inside the welder into the gun, emerging from the centre of its tip. At the same time the gun supplies an inert gas (usually argon) which shields the weld from air to prevent oxidisation. The power and feed rate can be varied to suit the thickness of the material.

Whatever welding technique you use, consider the effect of the heat generated on any trim, wiring or fuel lines running nearby. Protect or remove anything likely to be affected. Clean up surrounding metal before you attempt to weld in a repair section, and begin by 'tack welding' the new metal in just a few places. Check that it is correctly positioned and aligned before completing the welding. Finish by applying a seam sealer to prevent ingress of moisture.

Traditionally, seams and dents were 'lead loaded', by applying solder to the surface and then carefully shaping the cooled lead to match the profile of the panel. Lead is the 'authentic' method, but modern plastic fillers are far more convenient and easier to work with, so it all depends on the kind of standards you are applying to your restoration. Whichever you use, the filler must be shaped to suit and then rubbed down using progressively finer grades of wet and dry abrasive paper.

Spray painting is another skill to learn, and one that requires considerable practice to achieve a good result. Cellulose paint is the only type which a home restorer could consider using, and it is the 'authentic' finish for most classics. But modern two-pack paints – which must be applied in professional spray booths using specialist equipment – are tougher and more durable. So, if your main concern is for your restored classic to keep its condition for some years to come, it is worth thinking about a professional paint job using two-pack materials.

RIGHT Welding a chassis frame is a skilled job, but professional results can be achieved with practice and the correct equipment *(Lionel Baxter)*

Interior **trim**

Classic interiors come in a multitude of materials and styles, from austere efforts with painted tin dashboards and rubber mats, to leather, wool, Wilton and wood veneer. Whatever the level of luxury in your classic, you will appreciate the time and effort you spent on the interior every time you use the car. Improvements inside are good value for the time and money they cost.

Thorough cleaning should be your first job, to give you a better idea of which parts of the interior can be rescued and which will have to be replaced. Use a vacuum cleaner to remove dust, loose dirt and cobwebs. Specialist cleaning agents for various interior surfaces often do a good job, but so too do common household cleaning solutions, so see what you have in the kitchen cupboards first. If in doubt, test the cleaning solution on a hidden piece of trim – under a seat, for instance – to make sure it causes no damage to the surface.

Small tears are common on vinyl and leather upholstery. Repairs will always be visible, but might

be preferable to replacement of the whole panel, which is the only other solution. The best repair is a patch on the underside of the material, to which the torn piece can be stuck using trim adhesive. Leather tends to show signs of age quite quickly unless cared for, but can be rejuvenated by recolouring – and, unless the rest of your restoration is to 'showroom' concours standards, restored leather with a bit of honest ageing will almost always look more convincing than brand new replacements.

Door panels often warp and crinkle with age, but can often be restored by removing the vinyl

ABOVE Painted dashboards, vinyl trim and even rubber mats are found in the simplest classic interiors

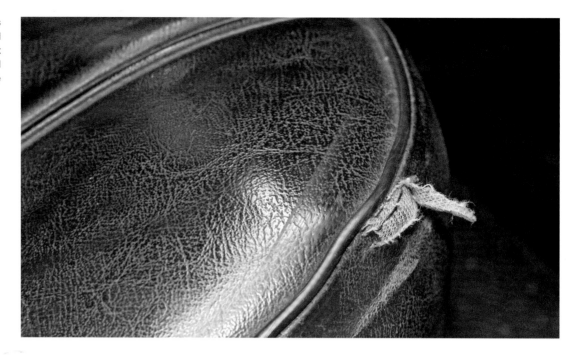

RIGHT Small tears can be patched from behind, but the damage will always be visible

covering from the fibreboard, hardboard or plywood backing, and cutting a new backing panel to suit. If the fixings are not obvious, try levering the edges of the panel gently using a broad-bladed screwdriver or a tyre lever – many are held in place by spring clips. Thin marine plywood is a good choice for the new backing, because it is resistant to moisture.

The simplest dashboards will be painted metal, either painted in the body colour or in black 'wrinkle finish' paint. If the paint is cracked and

flaking, the best bet is to remove the panel, take out all the controls and instruments, strip it to the bare metal and apply new paint. Wrinkle finish paints are available from specialists, but be careful about how and when you use them because the wrinkle effect depends upon the right ambient temperature.

'Wood' dashboards can be problematic, because they generally aren't wood. If they are the 'real thing' the surface is likely to be paper-thin veneer, applied to a humble timber base. Many

RIGHT Even leather apparently damaged beyond repair can respond well to remedial treatment. The driver's seat of this Alfa Romeo looked in a bad way …

FAR RIGHT … but careful application of a specialist leather treatment made a huge difference

mass-market cars with upmarket aspirations did not even use veneer, instead relying on a wood-grain pattern which set into a plastic film or was screen-printed onto a metal or Bakelite panel. You need to be absolutely sure that you are dealing with real wood before you set about stripping the varnish away, or you might find that you strip away all the 'wood' at the same time. Wood-grain finishes can only be restored by skilful hand painting: if you decide to have a go, practice on a scrap panel first.

Real wood trim can be stripped of its varnish using a paint stripper, but be careful to choose one which will not affect the colour of the wood underneath. Repairs can be made to veneer by cutting a patch of new veneer, then using it as a pattern to cut away the old veneer. The patch can then be stuck in place using water-resistant woodworking glue. Matching the grain and colour of the old wood is likely to be tricky, but slight variations can be hidden by applying a stain across the whole piece. Staining may be necessary to correct colour variations anyway – the wood in some cars was covered with coloured varnish to hide imperfections. Once any repairs are complete, rub down the surface using fine glasspaper (carefully, because veneer is very thin) before applying several coats of new varnish. Modern polyurethane varnish is easy to apply and will give the most durable finish.

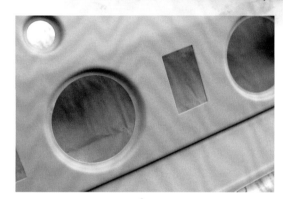

ABOVE Painted dashboards can be stripped to bare metal using a chemical stripper

LEFT Refinishing this painted dashboard began with a zinc-rich primer to fight corrosion in the future

LEFT Resplendent in new wrinkle-finish paint, this MG dash is returned to the car

Engine and transmission

It is much easier to deal with engine ancillaries on a workshop bench than in the engine bay, so start by removing all the bolt-on bits – the carburettor(s), distributor, dynamo or alternator, starter motor, water pump and so on. In each case you can then decide whether the item simply needs cleaning, or rebuilding (with new seals, bearings or brushes as appropriate) or whether it is best replaced with a reconditioned or new component.

Removing the ancillaries will also give you more space to work around the engine itself. The cylinder head can be removed and stripped down on the bench, keeping the valves, springs and rockers in order. Look for cracks and pitting on the seating faces of the valves, and signs of wear on their stems. Check that the springs are all the right length. Check the combustion chambers for damage and cracks, particularly between the valve seats, and run a straight edge over the head to check for warping. Slight warping can be corrected by machining.

With the head off, you can check for damage to the piston crowns, and feel for bore wear. If the engine is well worn you will probably be able to feel a small lip near the top of the cylinder. If wear is minor, new piston rings may be all that is needed, but if bore wear is significant, a rebore and the fitment of oversize pistons will be necessary. The crankshaft, main bearings and big-end bearings should also be checked and, if necessary, the crank can usually be reground to eliminate uneven wear. If the engine is removed for overhaul, then it makes sense to fit a new clutch plate and release bearing, saving work later.

Many restorers are wary of delving into gearboxes because of their complexity, and there is no adequate way of testing the 'box except by driving the car. If you expect the worst, you can remove the 'box for a full rebuild, either by yourself or by a specialist, or replace it with a reconditioned item. If you are an optimist, you might choose simply to renew the gearbox oil, re-grease the shift mechanism, and hope for the best – but there is always the chance that when the car is back together and running, you might find a gearbox problem you hadn't bargained for.

RIGHT It is much easier to work on ancillary components once they have been removed from the car

Brakes, suspension and steering

Any car which has sat around unused for some time is likely to have surface rust on the brake discs and drums, but if the rust has been there for some time there might be significant pitting of the surfaces. The only cure is to skim the friction surfaces in a lathe, and that can only be done if there is sufficient thickness of metal. Skimming can also be the answer if the discs or drums are scored or warped. Drums can often be difficult to take off, but once the retaining screws are removed and the adjusters slackened, if possible, a good thump with a mallet (not a hammer, unless you protect the drum with a block of wood) should free them.

Caliper pistons and the sliding sleeves on more modern calipers often seize in their bores, and if they cannot be removed or the caliper is damaged they must be replaced. If you can

remove them without damaging the caliper, new sleeves and seals can be fitted. Drum brakes can be overhauled in the same way, either by fitting new cylinder seals if the piston and bore are undamaged, or by fitting complete new cylinder assemblies. In both cases it makes sense to fit new brake linings, which should be replaced as axle sets (in other words, do both sides of the car at the same time). New seals can also rejuvenate the master cylinder, provided there is no sign of internal corrosion or damage.

Cable-operated brakes, including handbrakes, will often show signs of wear because of neglect. Fit new cables if you have any doubts about the existing ones, and check that compensators and equalising mechanisms are free to operate – if not they should be freed up and lubricated, or replaced.

ABOVE Brake calipers can be rejuvenated with an overhaul kit

Repair, recondition
or replace

Deciding how to deal with failed components is a key part of the restoration process. Essentially there are three possible options: overhaul the component you already have and make such repairs as are necessary, replace the component with a reconditioned item, or replace it with a brand new one. But your choice might be limited to two (or even just one) of those options, depending on the age and rarity of the components you are dealing with. How you make the choice between the available options depends on the relative importance of cost, convenience and originality.

Originality demands that you retain as much as possible of the original vehicle. In practice this applies most if the car you are restoring has a unique history (such as an important competition record) and to large sub-assemblies such as the engine block. Worn blocks can be bored out and re-sleeved, and even quite major damage can be rescued by specialist welding and 'stitching', but the costs involved need to be weighed against the consequences of losing the car's originality: unless there is an important, unique story to tell it might be better to admit defeat and fit a replacement. For more popular classics an exchange engine will be an option, but be sure to check what is supplied with an exchange reconditioned unit because ancillaries such as oil filters, and even timing chains, may be extra.

Cylinder heads can usually be restored to health by stripping and rebuilding, ideally with new valves, guides and seat inserts. Fitting guides and seats, and cutting the seats to the correct profile, requires specialist machining, but there's no reason why a competent mechanic cannot strip down the valve gear and refit it afterwards. As with blocks, even quite severely damaged heads can often be rescued, but the costs involved will only be justified if originality is vital or if a replacement cylinder head is impossible to find.

Unusual period modifications such as aftermarket tuning parts might also be so rare that they are worth saving, even the standard parts can be substituted at lower cost – but only you can decide what is restorable and what is beyond saving.

Dynamos, alternators and starter motors can be treated to new brushes and a clean-up, but burnt internals and complex faults are best dealt with by swapping to a new or reconditioned unit. Carburettors are expensive to buy, and even if the same type of carb is still available it will often be a slightly different specification – which might work fine, but will irritate the perfectionist in search of a truly 'showroom' standard rebuild. Overhauling the existing carburettors might be a better move, and for most types rebuild kits are available to replace aged seals and worn valves. The spindles on which the throttles rotate can usually be rebushed to eliminate wear, though this is not always a simple job. Fuel pumps can also be rebuilt, though for common types a reconditioned unit might prove to be economically more viable.

Gearboxes and differentials are complex beasts, so problems here are best dealt with either by despatching the unit from your car to a specialist for a rebuild or by fitting an exchange unit – the latter usually being cheaper, but not always an option for rarer classics.

OPPOSITE This engine sucked water into the intake and 'hydraulicked' – a conrod broke and punched this hole in the side of the block. Rare blocks can be repaired, but often it is easier to rebuild the engine in a new block

LEFT Wheels are usually easy to refurbish, but you might be able to find secondhand replacements in better condition – and new wheels will still be available for some classics

Finding parts

Inevitably it is more difficult to find parts for classic cars which may have been obsolete for years. Just how difficult will depend on how popular the car is and how many owners are spending money on them. If there is a healthy market for spares, then specialist companies will secure supplies of new parts and recondition old units. If the commercial case for supplying parts is less clear, owners' clubs often step in to make sure parts are available. But even then, some parts will apparently be made of that rarest of metals, 'unobtainium'.

Commonality of parts between cars of the same make, and from one make to another, boosts the supply of second-hand spares and the market for new ones. You might find parts for your car were used on something else, and that applies just as much to rare classics as common ones. Many classics use standard parts from an army of specialist suppliers, like electrical components from Lucas, Smiths or Bosch; running-gear components from Armstrong, Alford & Alder, Girling, Lockheed, Dunlop; fuel system parts from SU, Weber, Lucas and Bosch. Porsche often used Volkswagen parts, and specialist British manufacturers like Reliant, TVR and Lotus regularly rifled the parts bins of bigger manufacturers such as Ford and British Leyland. It is bespoke parts such as body panels, glass and unique engines or suspension components which can be hard to find.

Cars and parts do still turn up in scrapyards, but the older and rarer the classic the less likely you will be to find one. Nevertheless it's worth looking, and in drier climates like those of the warmer US states, where corrosion is less of an issue, a scrapyard could yield many useful parts. It is a good idea to buy rare parts when you see them, instead of waiting until you actually need them. One problem is that the parts you are most likely to need are those which fail or wear on that particular model, and examples in scrapyards may be suffering from the same wear or failure.

Sometimes the biggest problem is making sure you and the vendor are talking about the same type of car, particularly where there are several very different models with the same name – a Sunbeam Alpine, say. One good idea is to carry a wallet-sized photo of your classic. If there is ever any doubt over which model you are talking about, you can pull out the photo as an example.

New, old and reconditioned

Specialist suppliers deal in three main types of parts: new, second-hand and reconditioned. New parts are recently manufactured to original specification, or something approximating it. A sub-category is 'new, old stock', parts manufactured some time ago (perhaps when these cars were still in production) but never used. These are sometimes better quality, but problems can arise from deterioration over their many years of storage.

Reconditioned parts are second-hand components which have been completely overhauled. Often they will be supplied on an exchange basis, which means the supplier expects you to return the non-working component you are replacing so that it can be rebuilt – if not you will be subject to a surcharge. Quality varies, but a good 'recon' item can be almost indistinguishable from new and yet significantly cheaper. But check exactly what is required of your exchange item – certain types of wear or failure might render it unacceptable – and check what is supplied with your recon unit. Recon engines, for instance, are supplied as basic units without ancillaries, so make sure you remove everything you might need from your existing motor.

Online auctions

For classic car enthusiasts one benefit of the internet has been the emergence of online auctions, the best known of which is eBay (www.ebay.co.uk), although there are several others. The eBay auctions provide an interesting and effective way to buy and sell classic car parts, so it's worth understanding how the auctions work and how to get the best out of them.

Anyone can buy or sell using online auctions once they've registered with the auction website. Sellers choose when to start and end their auctions, provide information and, optionally, photographs of the item they are selling, and bidders choose how much and when to bid. The winning bidder enters into a binding contract with the seller to pay for the item. The auction website usually charges the seller a fixed fee plus a small percentage of the final selling price.

For sellers, eBay and its rivals have several advantages over conventional advertising methods. For one thing, it's cheap: the costs of auctioning a relatively inexpensive item on eBay are far less than the equivalent cost of advertising, particularly if you choose to include pictures. Provided you have a digital camera, the cost of illustrating your item for sale is so small that it's hardly worth setting up an eBay auction without photographs.

Another advantage of the auction sites is their vast coverage. Buyers come from, literally, all over the world. I've sold parts to Australia, the US, the Philippines and, a little closer to home, all over Britain and Northern Ireland.

Buyers benefit in a similar way. When you're looking for that rare item, you're not limited to local sellers – you can buy from anywhere in the world. The only drawback can be shipping charges, which will often be more than the final auction price of the item itself, so make sure you understand the seller's shipping fees before you bid. These should be explained in the auction details, but if they are not or you are in any way unclear, contact the seller before you place the bid, leaving plenty of time before the auction ends for them to reply to you.

The best news of all with sites like eBay is that the computer does all the searching for you: you search the auctions by entering keywords, and though this often brings up plenty of unrelated items alongside the ones you are interested in, it certainly weeds out the bulk of the uninteresting stuff. If you're trying to find that elusive part, you can even set up a 'favourite' search and then wait for the system to e-mail you when it has found what you are looking for, which has to be better than searching through the classified columns.

Driver : John Dando
Co-Driver: Alexis Dando

MOTORSPORT CHALLENGE

Improving your classic

Original
or modified?

Modifying classic cars causes all kinds of controversy. Old cars are lasting reminders of bygone times, and some people seem to think that means they should all be preserved in every original detail. Those who choose to do otherwise are regarded in some circles as 'boy racers' with no respect for heritage and tradition. Generally the people holding these views don't actually drive the old cars they so vigorously defend.

As is often the case, such extreme views have an element of sense buried deep within them. Of course classic car enthusiasts, as a community, should seek to preserve excellent, original examples of all sorts of classic cars, and in particular those which are rare or significant. If your classic is a rare, original, museum piece it would be a shame to modify it, even if those modifications would make it a more capable car. But most classics are not rare or original or displayed in museums, and I don't see why their owners shouldn't modify them, if that's what they want.

Engine tuning

The 'horses for courses' principle is clearly demonstrated when it comes to engine tuning. Engine modifications which will produce a lively road car might be very different from those which make a race car competitive. There are all sorts of options, ranging from simple bolt-on jobs to complex conversions and transplants, and if you want to get the best out of your classic you need to choose carefully.

Most people start with two modifications to engine breathing – a free-flow air filter and a performance exhaust. Both can bring useful performance gains on some engines and both are relatively inexpensive and easy to fit.

Air filters

Performance air filters either fit into the original air filter housing or replace it entirely, in which case they might create a little more intake noise. There are two main categories: cotton gauze filters like the well-known K&N, and foam filters from the likes of Pipercross and Ramair. Arguments rage over which is the 'best'.

Years ago I organised a test at MIRA which showed that gauze filters offered the maximum filtration, trapping even the tiniest dust particles and providing cleaner air to the engine than any other type of filter. But it is quite likely that very tiny particles don't actually do any harm to an engine, in which case a foam filter – which lets

RIGHT A good race engine and a good tuned road engine may look similar, but some details will be very different

through some of these minuscule particles, but generates less of a pressure drop at the engine intake – might be a better bet. On road-going classics, gauze filters are more popular, largely because they look the part with shiny chrome or cast-aluminium endplates. Both gauze and foam filters reduce maintenance, needing attention less frequently than conventional paper filters.

Ignition system

Fitting electronic ignition brings a string of potential benefits: more power, smoother idling, better fuel consumption, better reliability and less maintenance. Electronic ignition systems have been around since the 1960s and have gradually increased in popularity, and are universal on new cars today. There are several different types, but all replace the mechanical contact breakers with an electronic 'black box' which switches the low-tension current to the coil. This removes the need for periodic cleaning and re-gapping of the contact breaker, eliminates 'points bounce' at high engine speeds and can provide more consistent ignition timing. The timing of the spark is usually achieved using a magnetic or optical sensor fitted into the

BELOW K&N filters reduce resistance to intake airflow and reduce maintenance

distributor. Some systems are so small that all the electronics sit under the distributor cap, which is useful if you want to retain an 'original' appearance in the engine bay.

Because the speed at which fuel burns is constant, regardless of the speed of the engine, ignition has to start earlier in the cycle the faster the engine is rotating in order for combustion to be completed in time. This is commonly achieved using a centrifugal advance mechanism inside the distributor – rotating weights fly out against spring pressure, and the further the weights move the greater the spark advance. The size of the weights, the strength of the springs and the design of the linkage all have an effect, and changing them can retune the advance curve to suit a modified engine.

Most classic cars also have a second advance mechanism operated by manifold vacuum, which reduces the amount of ignition advance when it is not needed, at idle and at full throttle. Many competition engine builders remove vacuum advance systems.

'Sports' coils are an easy fitment and can provide more reliable starting and better combustion, though I suspect that on most engines you would be hard pressed to spot the difference. Spark plugs are commonly upgraded in the quest for power, again because they are easy and cheap to fit, but whatever the claims may be by some manufacturers, the power gains are minimal.

Exhaust systems

Standard exhaust systems were usually designed with low manufacturing costs in mind, and often do a poor job of extracting exhaust gases efficiently. Cast-iron manifolds, standard ware on most cars, can be 'gas flowed' by smoothing out any internal corners, but better results are available at moderate cost by replacing a cast-iron manifold with a tubular steel item. The manifold 'primaries' (the pipes directly connected to the exhaust ports) can be connected together in different ways for different results. For example, on a normal four-cylinder engine, a four-into-one manifold tends to favour top-end power, while a four-into-two-into-one sacrifices outright power for a boost in mid-range torque, and is often a better bet for a road car.

Free-flow exhaust systems are often noisier than standard, partly because it is difficult to combine easy gas flow and good silencing, and partly because enthusiasts often want their modified cars to be a bit louder than standard. Very loud exhausts, as well as being anti-social, can also cause you problems if you run your car on a track day, because noise limits tend to be lower than they are during race events. If you're not keen on a rise in the noise level, speak to other owners to find out which exhausts are the subtlest.

Most exhausts are mild steel and will rust, usually from the inside outwards. Stainless steel exhausts are much more resistant to corrosion, and the best ones carry a 'lifetime guarantee'. If off-the-shelf stainless systems are not available for your classic, specialist companies such as Double S in Devon can build a bespoke system to fit.

Fuel system

The carburettors supply the air/fuel mixture the engine burns, and a bigger and more efficient engine can burn more fuel, which means it needs bigger carburettors. But at low engine speeds the air flow rate through a big carb is much less than a small one, which can create some odd flow effects inside the carbs and destroy the uniformity of the mixture. The result is rough running at low engine speeds, which is of no consequence on a race car but is a pain on a road car. Ideally, then, you use the smallest carburettor(s) which can deliver the air the engine needs at its maximum power.

Those carburettors will need to be set up correctly. Changing jets, needles and springs can have a big effect on the way the engine runs and the power it can produce. Getting it right is a painstaking job best left to professionals, unless your engine is built to an established specification and suitable carburettor settings are well known.

Other parts of the fuel system can also benefit from attention. Older electric fuel pumps incorporate contact breakers which eventually wear and fail like those in the ignition system, but they can now be replaced with 'breakerless' electronic pumps – which still tick authentically! More extreme modifications are required for some cars: petrol-injection Triumphs are well known for overheating fuel pumps, but well-designed pump systems are available to replace them.

Cylinder head

Often the greatest potential for power increases is locked inside the cylinder head, which affects the way the engine breathes and the efficiency with which it burns fuel. Improvements can usually be made in both areas.

Breathing can be improved by 'gas flowing', carefully shaping the inlet and exhaust ports and the valve seats to reduce resistance to the flow of gas through them. The ports are usually opened out using a grinder to match the apertures in the

manifold gaskets (and the manifolds are also modified to suit). This eliminates any step in the port caused by a mismatch of the manifold and the head which might impede the gas flow. Bigger valves can be fitted and the ports enlarged to match, though its wise not to go too large on a road car because bigger ports mean lower gas flow speed, which can hurt low-rev flexibility.

The combustion chambers, which are usually recessed into the cylinder head, can also be smoothed out with the grinder and their volumes precisely matched – often a mass produced head will show slight variations from one chamber to another. The area around the valves can be opened out to avoid 'shrouding' of the ports. On some engines, experienced tuners add metal to the walls of the combustion chamber with a welder to change its shape, or to reduce the chamber volume to increase the compression ratio.

A more usual way of increasing compression is to skim the cylinder head, taking a horizontal slice out of the combustion chamber. This works on engines with their combustion chambers in the head: engines with flat-faced heads, like the 'cooking' Ford Crossflows, have their combustion chambers recessed into the piston crowns, and on these engines the compression ratio is raised by fitting different pistons with taller crowns or smaller chambers.

ABOVE Over-sized carburettors can cause lumpy low-rev response, but liberate extra top-end power. For road engines it is generally best to fit the smallest carbs you can get away with

Too high a compression ratio leads to pinking and ultimately engine damage, and usable compression ratios are limited by the octane rating of the fuel you use. Many classics were produced in an era when 100 octane 'five star' fuel was commonly available, but today fuels with an octane rating greater than 98 RON are rare. Octane-booster additives can help, but for most road cars it is safest to stick to compression ratios no greater than about 10:1 (though it varies from engine to engine). You should then be able to use pump fuel without problems.

Camshaft and valve gear

Because the camshaft controls the operation of the valves, the cam profile dictates the power output of the engine and the shape of the torque curve. The three design factors to look for are lift, duration and overlap.

Lift is the height of the 'peak' of the cam profile, which will control the amount that the valves are lifted off their seats. Duration measures the period the valves are open. For optimum breathing the intake and exhaust valves will both be open for a period at the top of the exhaust and intake strokes, and this is known as overlap.

Higher lift, longer duration and greater overlap all tend to improve power, but you never get something for nothing and the payback comes in driveability. Though they work well at high engine speeds, these high lift, long-duration cam profiles tend not to be so good at mid-range speeds and part throttle. A race cam is fine for racing, where low-rev response is unimportant, but is a disaster on the road because it cannot work properly at the engine speeds you use most often. For a

road car a 'fast road' cam with a less aggressive profile is a better bet.

Where the camshaft operates the valves directly, the cam lift and valve lift will be the same, but where the valves are operated by rockers, the rocker ratio will increase valve lift. Fitting different ratio rockers is an alternative to fitting a higher-lift cam – an attractive one on engines where removal of the camshaft is a long-winded job.

With any sort of performance camshaft it is essential that the camshaft position in relation to the crankshaft is absolutely correct. The timing of the cam can be set up exactly using a vernier timing gear, which allows a few degrees of adjustment either way.

Bottom end

Improvements to the bottom end of the engine aim at greater strength, sharper throttle response and reduced stress at high engine speeds.

The crankshaft itself can usually be lightened by grinding away excess metal around the webs, an operation best left to an expert. When the crankshaft turns at high speed its own weight tries to pull it apart, so if the crankshaft is lightened without compromising its strength by careful reshaping, the engine will have better throttle response and will be more reliable at high revs.

The flywheel can also be lightened to reduce rotational inertia, allowing the engine to spin up faster. The crank and flywheel should be rebalanced after lightening, and balancing to tighter tolerances will allow the engine to spin smoothly at higher speeds. A similar process can be applied to the conrods, which can be smoothed out and their weights matched to each other as closely as possible. They can also be shot peened to discourage the formation of surface cracks.

Boring and stroking

There's some truth to the oft-quoted American expression that 'there ain't no substitute for cubic inches'. Bigger engines, all things being equal, produce more power, so one tuning option often worth exploring is to increase either the bore or the stroke – or both.

Boring is generally easier and often cheaper, requiring only some simple machining and bigger pistons. An increase in stroke, by contrast, means a new or modified crankshaft, and possibly modifications to the crankcase, new pistons and conrods, and changes to the valve timing. The crankshaft can either be a new cast or forged item with greater throw, or sometimes the big end bearings on the original crankshaft can be

BELOW A Kent Cams high-performance camshaft kit for a BL A-Series engine *(Tim Mundy)*

'stroke ground' on new centres to give an increase in stroke.

The basic geometry of the engine often gives clues to the best approach. An engine which is already heavily oversquare, in other words with a bore much greater than its stroke, will probably respond better to stroking. Boring might be a better idea on an engine which already has a long stroke. Broadly speaking, a big bore engine will rev smoothly to high speeds and can produce a high power output, while a long-stroke engine will be rougher and less inclined to rev and is better suited to mid-range punch.

Sometimes the decision will be made for you. The engine can only be bored out if there's enough extra 'meat' in the block to allow the increase in bore. Similarly, an increase in stroke is only possible if there is physically enough space in the crankcase to allow for the greater throw of the crankshaft. You need to take advice from an engine builder with experience of your engine before you make plans.

Cooling

Modified engines may generate more excess heat than standard ones, and are likely to be used harder than standard engines, so efficient cooling is a must. A bigger radiator can sometimes be fitted, either from another model in the range or from a specialist such as Pace Products. Remember that it's the air passing through the matrix which takes the heat away, so a clear

passage of air into and away from the radiator is just as important.

The oil system has a vital cooling role which should not be overlooked. A hard-worked engine – used for competition or motorway cruising – might benefit from an oil cooler to keep oil temperatures down and pressure up. Various kits are available, and specialists like Think Automotive can supply oil cooler radiators and pipes individually so you can make up a bespoke system of your own. But overcooling the oil is to be avoided: either cover up the oil cooler radiator in cold weather or fit the system with an oilstat.

ABOVE An alloy radiator can save weight and improve cooling, but only if sufficient cooling air can flow through the matrix

BELOW Few classics were designed with motorway cruising in mind. An oil cooler can help keep your classic reliable if you plan to use it for long journeys

Transmission

An increase in engine power puts more stress on the driveline components, which can be uprated to cope. A competition clutch, for instance, will provide greater resistance to wear and slip, though potentially at the cost of a heavier action and sharper engagement which can be irritating in stop-start traffic. Stronger driveshafts are another common upgrade to avoid breakages.

Engine tuning can increase power while reducing the effective rev range, and the more extreme the power increase the more restricted the range is likely to be. A standard gearbox is unlikely to get the best out of this sort of engine, because the ratios will be too widely spread and at each gear change the engine will drop out of its useful rev range. The answer is a close-ratio box which can keep the engine on the boil.

The rear axle ratio can also be changed depending on the way the car is used. A numerically lower ratio axle offers higher gearing, giving relaxed cruising at lower engine speeds and perhaps a higher maximum speed. A numerically higher axle gives lower gearing

which tends to improve acceleration, but at the cost of fussier high-speed cruising.

With more gear ratios, you can get the best of all worlds – low ratios for acceleration and higher ratios for cruising, but without wide gaps between ratios. Five- and six-speed gearboxes are the norm these days and for some classics a five-speed box might have been available as a period tuning part, but a more likely option would have been overdrive.

An overdrive unit is an auxiliary gearbox which sits behind the main gearbox and offers either 1:1 gearing or an 'overdriven' ratio where the output to the propshaft turns faster than the input from the gearbox. Normally this is engaged by a solenoid, operated by a switch on the dashboard or gearknob. Usually the overdrive is locked out in first gear but can be engaged in second, third or top to provide three extra ratios – two of which plug the gaps between the existing ratios, and another which is higher than top gear in the normal gearbox. If an overdrive was available as an option on your classic when it was new, retro-fitting one should be a fairly simple job.

RIGHT A typical four-speed synchromesh gearbox *(Austin)*

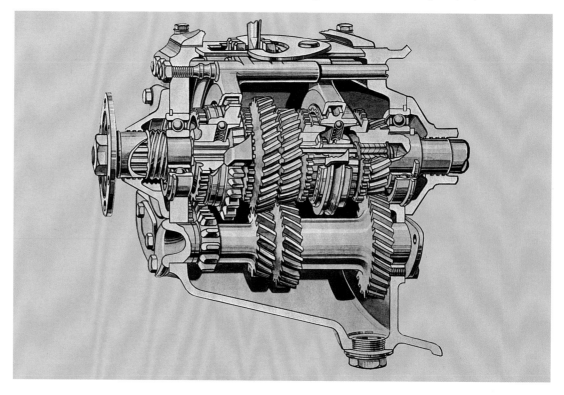

Engine and gearbox
transplants

Tuning is one way to improve performance. Replacing the existing engine with a bigger or more modern unit is another. Simplest of all is the swap to a bigger, more powerful variant of the same engine – like a 1275 A-series into a Minor 1000, or a 3.8-litre XK into a Jaguar 2.4.

Next on the scale of complication comes the fitting of a different engine, but one which was used in that type of car – Rover V8s into MGBs and TR7s, for example, or Lotus twin-cams into Cortinas and Escorts. These tend to be reasonably easy, too: the list of parts required might be a little longer, but at least the swap itself is a known quantity.

The most challenging transplants are those which use an entirely different engine. Some of these transplants are now well documented, so they shouldn't pose too many problems – there are plenty of Spridgets with modern Rover K-series power, for instance. Gearbox swaps are also common, and many specialists can supply kits to convert to modern five-speed gearboxes. Stick to a well-known swap and at worst you will be able to get advice from someone who has already done it – at best you will find a specialist with a comprehensive kit of parts to do the job. More esoteric transplants leave you on your own, solving all the problems yourself. But if you're feeling brave, why not?

ABOVE An extreme engine transplant – an Audi 20V engine fitted to a VW Golf GTI Mk1

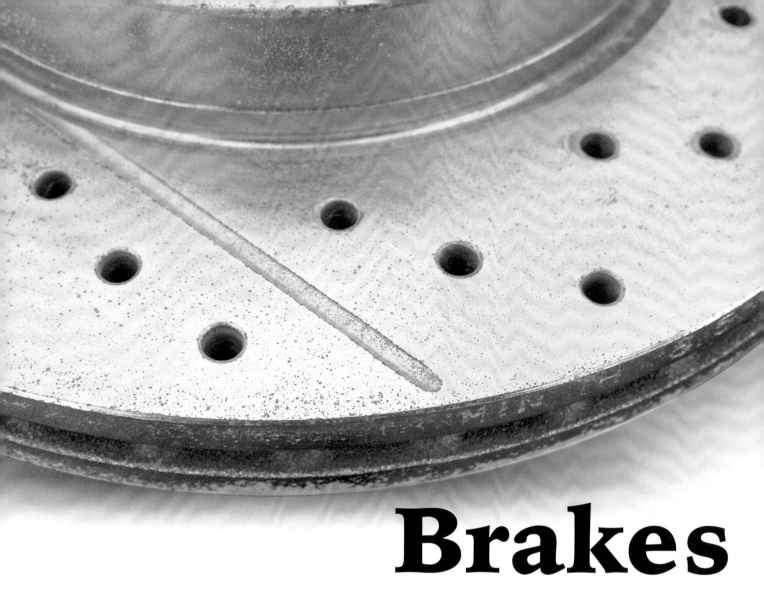

Brakes

Brake upgrades can provide greater stopping power, more resistance to fade, more adjustability to suit conditions or greater capacity to cope with wear. The simplest upgrade is to change the lining material to a high-performance specification, which can be effective against fade and, sometimes, wear but is unlikely to give you considerably better stopping power. 'Fast road' linings should work reasonably well even when cold, which is most of the time on a road car, while materials intended for racing will only be effective when hot – so choosing the right material is important.

Drum brakes can sometimes be swapped for finned alloy drums (which have iron friction surfaces inside) to improve cooling. Discs can be cross-drilled or grooved, or both, to promote cooling air flow and to help remove water or vaporised lining material from the face of the pad.

Conversions from drums to discs are another option, which is well worth considering on a hard-driven classic with front drum brakes. Swapping from drums to discs does not necessarily stop the car any faster, but it will help with fade – the main advantage of discs is that the air flow has easy access to the friction surfaces so discs cool quicker than drums. If discs were available on a later model or a sporting version they should be easy enough to retro fit to your classic. If not, talk to specialists who have prepared racing versions of your car to find out the best options: they may be able to supply a kit based on proprietary brake parts from the likes of AP Racing, together with the bespoke brackets and pipework needed to make it all fit.

Many classics will be fitted with single-circuit hydraulic pipework instead of a dual-circuit system, the latter being safer in the event of a leak because at least one circuit will remain operational. For road cars it is common to connect one front brake and the opposite rear brake into each circuit, but for competition cars the front and rear brakes can be given individual circuits and master cylinders with a 'balance bar' between the cylinders. The ratio front to rear can be altered by adjusting the balance bar to suit the driver's preferences or the road conditions.

Improving the ultimate stopping power of the car is more difficult. Bigger pads or wider shoes do not increase stopping power to any great degree, though they do provide more lining material so they need to be changed less often,

and they may reduce fade. To brake harder the brake system needs to generate more torque at the wheels, and your choices are to clamp the lining material to the disc or drum with greater force, or to increase the leverage with which the pad or shoe operates.

Applying greater force to the lining material is done most simply by pressing the pedal harder, but there are mechanical options, too. Greater piston area at the wheels is one way, and competition cars often use four- or six-piston brake calipers to increase piston area. Or you can increase the line pressure generated in the brake system for a given pedal pressure by adding a servo or fitting a smaller master cylinder (though the latter will increase brake pedal travel). Increasing leverage means making the brakes bigger, which might mean using bigger wheels, perhaps with low-profile tyres – which can in turn affect the way the suspension is set up.

OPPOSITE Grooving and cross-drilling help to delay the onset of brake fade by improving air flow and keeping the pads clean

BELOW High-performance brake pads, like these from Mintex, offer improved resistance to fading in heavy use

Suspension

Modifications to the suspension are usually aimed at improving grip and handling. Shorter, stiffer springs are often adopted to drop the centre of gravity of the car, which reduces lateral weight transfer in cornering and gives the outer tyres a chance to retain their grip on the road. Shorter springs also limit suspension travel, reducing the camber change that the tyres experience – and, provided the static suspension settings are correct, that too can help generate the best possible grip from the tyres. Control of suspension movement in this way is also vital if the car will be fitted with lower-profile tyres, which are much less tolerant of camber changes.

But it is very easy to go too low and too stiff – and that won't just hurt the ride quality, it will also have a detrimental effect on grip. A race car will only ever run on smooth race tracks, so it can run close to the ground with short, stiff springs, wide wheels and fat tyres. A road car has to deal with much bigger, more aggressive deviations in the road surface, so it needs softer springs and more suspension travel to keep the wheels on the ground. Run race-car springs on a road car and not only will the ride be excruciatingly uncomfortable, grip levels will be unpredictable and the car will be difficult to drive fast.

Damping must be matched to the springs, so shorter, stiffer springs need uprated dampers. Lever-arm dampers can be refilled with thicker fluid, revalved, or replaced with stiffer telescopic dampers. Telescopics can be replaced with uprated items, many owners opting for adjustable units which can be set softer for day-to-day use and then stiffened up for competition or track days.

OPPOSITE Careful choice of springs, dampers and anti-roll bars can make a big difference to the way a car handles

LEFT Shorter, stiffer springs lower the car's centre of gravity and reduce camber changes, which generally means more grip – but handling on rough roads will suffer

Anti-roll bars can be added to many classics, or existing bars can be replaced by thicker items. The choice of anti-roll bar needs to be carefully matched to the springs to ensure the two work in harmony, so this is another area where it is sensible to take advice from an expert. Go too stiff and the anti-roll bar will start to have an adverse effect on the ride quality.

Many classics have live rear axles with leaf springs, and these can be fitted with additional links to control axle movement. A Panhard rod eliminates sideways movement during cornering, and 'anti-tramp' bars control axle hop during acceleration.

On road cars, the moving suspension components are usually mounted in rubber bushes, which provide a small amount of compliance and a damping effect, reducing road noise, vibration and harshness (what vehicle engineers call 'NVH'). Stiffer bushes can be fitted to improve wheel location, which makes for better grip and handling precision – but noise and vibration may increase, so careful specification of the material is essential to get the best compromise. On road cars, polyurethane bushes like the SuperPro range are a good bet, while a competition car might benefit from stiffer nylatron bushes and the replacement of some rubber-insulated joints with metal Rose joints.

LEFT Suspension settings ideal for circuit use will be too stiff on the road. The result will be unpredictable handling and a harsh ride

Wheels and **tyres**

Alloy wheels carrying bigger tyres are popular because they are easy to fit and can make a significant difference to a car's appearance, and possibly to its handling. If grip and handling are the priorities, though, you should first choose the size and type of tyre, and then the appropriate wheel to carry that tyre – but more often than not the appearance of the wheel is the deciding factor.

Steel, wire and alloy wheels

Steel wheels are seen as the least sophisticated option, but it has to be said that the supposed advantages of other types are difficult to discern on a road car. Steel wheels are strong and cheap, and some of the motor sport wheels from the likes of Weller can look attractive on the right car.

Wire wheels are the classic 'sports car' option, and on some cars nothing else looks quite right. Sadly, wires come with a host of potential drawbacks, starting with their considerable cost. It is also very difficult to keep them clean, so they are prone to rapid corrosion, and they are flexible, which does nothing for the car's handling. Bolt-on wire wheels look like the travesty they are: wires should be mounted on splined, centre-lock hubs with knock-off wheel nuts which are 'handed' to ensure that the nuts self-tighten. It's essential to get the hubs and the matching nuts on the right sides of the car otherwise they become self-loosening, with obvious results.

Alloy wheels are a more modern option. The most 'classic' style is the Minilite, originally a magnesium-alloy wheel but also now available in a cheaper aluminium-alloy version which is suitable for all but the most ardent race competitor. There are also numerous lookalikes which are generally cheaper – but they're not the real thing. Modern alloys are styled to suit modern cars, so they can easily look totally out of place on a classic car even if an appropriate size is available. But sometimes the old and new combination works well, so keep an open mind.

Wheel and tyre sizes

Modern trends in tyre technology have led to the use of wider and lower profile tyres: road-going supercars now routinely wear fat 35-series rear tyres. The wider a tyre and the lower its profile the less tolerant it is of wheel camber changes as the suspension moves, so the suspension must be carefully designed to keep the wheels upright in all conditions, which is not nearly as easy as it sounds. The suspension system on your classic is unlikely to control camber changes to the degree necessary, because it was designed for narrower tyres which are much less demanding. Shorter, stiffer springs limit wheel movement and reduce the camber changes, but at the expense of poor ride and, if you go too stiff, unpredictable handling.

Because there is a limit to the effectiveness of stiff springs on a road car, there is a limit to the width and profile of tyre a road car can sensibly use. There is also a limit to the size of tyre which will physically fit without fouling on the bodywork, suspension or steering. Often the 'return' around the inside of the wheel arch can easily be modified to allow slightly bigger tyres to fit, or you might be prepared to add wheel arch extensions.

Another consideration is the rolling radius of the tyre, which should be kept as close as possible to the original to avoid changing the gearing or ruining the speedometer calibration. If you want wider rubber, you can at the same time move to a lower profile and retain roughly the same rolling radius.

Wheel width and diameter should be chosen to suit the tyres you are using. Generally a given

tyre will fit a range of rim widths, narrower rims giving a slightly softer ride and wider rims giving optimum steering response.

Another important wheel dimension is offset, often denoted by the German abbreviation ET. This is the distance between the centre line of the wheel and its mounting face; if the mounting face is outboard of the centre, offset is positive, and if it is inboard of the centre, offset is negative. Positive offset pushes the wheel inside the arch, while greater negative offset makes it project further out. Offset affects steering geometry and wheel bearing load, and determines whether the tyres foul on the body or suspension, so take expert advice before fitting wheels with an offset which is considerably different from standard.

PCD or 'pitch circle diameter' is the size of a circle passing through the centres of the wheel mounting holes. With an even number of bolts or studs, PCD is the distance between any bolt and the one directly opposite. With a three-stud wheel, PCD is the distance between any two adjacent bolt centres multiplied by 1.16. On a five-stud wheel it is the distance between two adjacent bolt centres multiplied by 1.7. PCD is surprisingly easy to get wrong, because both imperial and metric measurements are in use – a 100mm PCD is very close to, but not the same as, a 4in (101.6mm) PCD.

Centre bore is the final important wheel dimension, and is simply the diameter of the hole in the centre of the wheel. This acts to locate the wheel on the centre of the hub. A wheel with too small a centre bore will not fit, while too large a centre bore allows the wheel to move on the hub and applies extra loads to the wheel studs. Many aftermarket alloy wheels are machined with large centre bores and supplied with adaptor rings to match the wheel to the hub.

BELOW Alloy wheels usually have their size and offset (or 'ET') marked on the wheel rim or under the nave plate in the centre

Second-hand wheels

There are two problems with second-hand wheels. The first is how to work out whether they will fit your car, which is not always obvious, and the second is how to establish that they are in a usable condition.

Take measurements yourself, if possible, rather than relying on the vendor. Remember that the diameter is measured to the base of the rim flanges, not right to the edges, and similarly the width is measured between the inner and outer flanges. PCD is easy enough to measure, but measuring offset is tricky. The easiest way is to measure the 'backspace' of the wheel, which is from the mounting face to the rearmost edge of the rim, and the overall width from flange to flange. Offset is the backspace measurement less half the overall width.

Condition is obviously crucial, because your wheels and tyres are the only connection you have with the road. Look for cracks around the bolt holes and cracks or dents around the rim. If possible, rest each wheel on a flat surface to check that the rim is true. An even better test is to mount the wheel on a hub and spin it while holding a pointer (a pencil is ideal) near to the wheel rim – this makes it easy to see any wobble or 'run out' in the rim.

Tyre pressures

Useful changes in a car's handling can be effected by tweaking the tyre pressures from the basic settings recommended by the manufacturer. Increase the tyre pressures on your classic and, very broadly, you will improve grip at the expense of ride comfort. Increase the pressures in the front tyres only and you will reduce understeer, increase the rear tyre pressures only and you cut oversteer. In all cases, avoid exceeding the tyre manufacturer's recommended maximum pressure, and make changes in small increments. Also, be aware of any local laws which might require you to stick to the standard pressures.

Clearly, non-standard pressures might be appropriate if your classic is fitted with larger-than-standard wheels and tyres. Generally, bigger tyres run at slightly lower pressures, but beyond that it is hard to generalise. Your best bet, short of a trial-and-error approach starting with the standard pressures, is to seek advice from other owners or specialists for your car.

Crossply or radial?

Crossply tyres were standard wear on most cars until the 1960s, when radials started to take over. The main difference between them is the angle of

the threads in the fabric layers making up the tyre carcase: in a crossply the threads run diagonally under the tread, in a radial they run straight across. Radials have stiff treads and flexible sidewalls, while crossplies have much more uniform stiffness throughout the tyre. As a result, a crossply's tread distorts under cornering loads, limiting grip. A radial's tread stays flat against the road, so grip is maintained. The downside is that at low speeds the stiff tread can result in a harsher ride and stodgy steering. Early radials also gave little warning when they finally did reach their limit, but modern tyres are much more forgiving. Generally, the benefits of radials outweigh their disadvantages, and unless originality is of the utmost importance to you, radials are the best option.

Tyre markings

Size markings are moulded into the sidewalls of most tyres. Crossplies have markings in the form '5.60-13' which indicates the section (tread) width is 5.6 inches and the wheel rim diameter is 13 inches. A radial might be marked '165/70SR13', which indicates a 165mm wide tyre with a 70 per cent profile, speed rating S, on a 13-inch rim. The speed rating letters denote the maximum speed at which the tyre can carry its designed load:

Speed Rating	Maximum Speed
Q	100mph (160kph)
R	106mph (170kph)
S	113mph (180kph)
T	118mph (190kph)
H	130mph (210kph)
V	150mph (240kph)
Z	over 150mph (240kph)

A more modern version of the same tyre would be marked '165/70 R 13 79S', in which the '79' is a load rating. Radials without a profile number (marked, for instance, '165R13') have an 82 per cent profile.

In recent years, US regulations have demanded that tyres be rated for tread wear rate, traction and running temperature. The tread wear rating is a number, usually between 60 and 500 – the higher the number the longer the tyre should last. The traction rating is actually a measurement of straight-line wet braking ability, not resistance to wheelspin or side slip in corners, and is rated from A to C (where A is the best). The temperature rating, also a letter from A to C where A is the best, denotes the tyre's ability to dissipate heat. But before you go searching for new tyres based on the ratings,

LEFT Good tyres are an essential safety requirement on any car. Michelin offer one of the biggest ranges of tyres for classic and vintage vehicles

bear in mind that they apply only to a specific test load, road surface and ambient conditions. Your local road surface and weather might be quite different, so the ratings can only ever be a very general guide.

Tyres sold in the US must carry a DOT (Department of Transportation) mark. All tyres manufactured for sale in Europe since October 1977 have been required to carry the EU 'E mark'.

TRX and TD tyres

The vast majority of tyres are designed to fit rims sized in inches, even though the width of a modern radial is measured in millimetres. The exception is the Michelin/Dunlop TRX and TD tyre range, which was designed to fit a special rim design. To ensure that these tyres were never accidentally fitted to conventional rims, the rims were 'half a size' bigger (11.5 inches, 12.5 inches and so on, up to 16.5 inches) and were measured in millimetres.

TD tyres have an extra bead-retaining lip around the inside (giving it a limited run-flat capability) which requires a specially-shaped rim, so they can only be fitted to TD rims. TRX tyres can be fitted to either TR or TD rims. Both TRX and TD tyres are still made by Michelin and Dunlop, and are available through specialist suppliers, such as Longstone Tyres, for those owners who wish to keep metric-rimmed wheels on their classics for the sake of originality. But they are produced in small numbers, so they are expensive, and a set of accessory alloy wheels in a conventional size, plus a set of normal tyres, might well work out cheaper.

Interior

Useful modifications can often be in your classic's cabin, whether you're looking to improve comfort, convenience or safety. Fitting accessory steering wheels or seats is usually no more than a bolt-on job, which makes them easy to accomplish. But if you want your new seats or steering wheel to work well and complement your car's interior, you'll need to choose with care.

Steering wheel

Even some cars with fairly serious sporting intent were provided with vast, flexible steering wheels which do little to improve the driver's precision of control. It's easy to see why replacement wheels have always been among the most popular accessories.

You can improve control and sharpen up the feel of the car by fitting a steering wheel of smaller diameter, but be wary of going too small. With a smaller wheel, the reduction in leverage at the wheel rim makes the steering heavier, which can be a pain when parking and can mask feedback when pressing on. So don't bin your 16-inch standard wheel and bolt on a 9-inch single-seater item: even a reduction of two inches in diameter will have a significant effect on the way the car feels to drive. Try talking to other owners to get opinions on the optimum size for your car.

Wood is the most traditional rim material, and was popular in the 1950s and 1960s. A good wood-rim steering wheel can look fantastic in the right car, though I find they only work well if you wear driving gloves – with bare hands they can be a bit slippery and they provide none of the cushioning of a leather rim. Vinyl is no more than a cheap leather substitute. Suede, as used on modern racing wheels, is grippy and looks great in the right setting when new, but soon becomes dirty and worn.

Modern wheels often look out of place in a classic interior (though some of the simple racing wheels can look the part in the right car), but classic-styled wheels are still available from the likes of Moto-Lita and Mountney, the former being much nicer but priced accordingly. Look for 'spats' covering the ends of the spokes where they meet the rim, making the wheel more comfortable to use, and check the quality of the stitching on a leather wheel.

Accessory steering wheels were sold in their thousands in the 1960s and 1970s, but where they've all got to is anyone's guess: they seem rare on the second-hand market and those you do see are invariably in appalling condition. Look for cracks and wear, particularly on the top half of the rim (which has the greatest exposure to sunlight). On a leather wheel feel all the way round the rim for soft spots.

As an alternative to an accessory wheel you might be able to find a better item from a more sporting model, if there is one, in the same range as your car, or from another car in the same manufacturer's range. That can often be a good option where a wheel boss (the adaptor which mates an accessory wheel to a given steering column) is not available for your classic.

Fitting is usually a reasonably simple process, though the wheel will probably be splined onto the top of the column and you may need a puller to get it loose. It's a good idea to mark the 'straight ahead' position on the top of the column so you have a datum for the position of the new wheel.

Seats

This is another area where you have to make a decision, not just about what will do the job but also about what is going to look right. Do you opt for a classic-style seat or a modern one? In an out-and-out competition car a modern seat makes sense from a safety and efficiency point of view; in a road car you might choose something more 'in keeping' with the style of the rest of the machine.

'Classic' seats are built on steel tube frames, upholstered in cloth, vinyl or leather. The two

OPPOSITE A replacement wheel like this Moto-Lita is a popular option, but don't pick one that's too small

BELOW Race-style seats like this offer more support for competition or spirited road driving, but many look out of place in a classic – so choose carefully

best known UK seat manufacturers, Corbeau and Cobra, both have classic style seats in their range, and Ridgard now concentrates on seats for classic cars. Modern seats are usually constructed in a very different way, using composite shells. Good ones are strong and comfortable, and they tend to be lighter than steel-framed seats.

Seat mounting is very important, particularly in a car which is going to be used for competition. More than once in recent years, drivers have been hurt, not because their seat belts failed but because the seat became detached. Seats or seat runners need to be firmly fixed to strong areas of the body, using spreader plates if necessary to distribute the load.

Seat harnesses

Many sports car owners add racing-type harnesses either in place of or in addition to the standard seat belts. As with seat mountings, the eyebolts to which the harnesses attach need to be securely mounted with spreader plates where appropriate to ensure that they can cope with the loads imparted in a collision. Ideally, the lap straps should be mounted close to your hips by the sides of the seat, and the shoulder strap mountings should be arranged so the straps are at or slightly below the horizontal.

The harnesses themselves differ in the number and size of straps and the way they buckle up. In the cheapest harnesses the two shoulder straps join together behind the seat to mount at a single point, and are sewn into the lap straps at their bottom ends. These harnesses usually have a buckle similar to a normal seat belt, with a push-button release. The problem with these is you have to insert your arms into them between the straps, which is difficult unless the straps are loose, and loose straps will not do their job properly. Proper race-style harnesses have four individual straps, one of them permanently attached to a buckle which is released by a knob or lever. These are easier to get into because you can fix each strap individually. In the UK, theoretically, all harnesses used on the road should be E-marked.

Two-inch straps have been the norm for some time, but three-inch straps are now available which spread load better. Wider straps, as well as being theoretically safer, may also be more comfortable provided they are mounted sensibly – it is easy to put the shoulder strap mountings too close together, which makes wider straps rub on your neck.

Security

Modern ideas about security are far more extensive than they were when classic cars were new. Few classics have locks which are difficult to defeat, or electrical systems which are complex enough to baffle a would-be thief. So, if you are concerned that your classic might be a target, you need to think about some form of extra protection.

Defence is needed against three potential forms of attacker, the first of them being the thief who gains entry to the car to remove any valuables. Convertibles are particularly at risk (even with the roof up – most folding roofs are easy to cut through). The obvious advice is not to leave valuable items on display inside the car. Alarms can also help by providing a warning that the vehicle is being tampered with. Period alarm and immobiliser kits still turn up occasionally and, in working order, they are no less effective today than they were then, and would certainly look the part if you were aiming to preserve your classic's period style. But modern systems offer greater protection and greater convenience, with remote arm/disarm using a key fob radio transmitter.

Simple mechanical immobilisers such as steering wheel or handbrake locks can be very effective against thieves who are trying to steal the vehicle, though they are designed for modern interiors so they will not fit every classic. A cunningly hidden 'kill' switch to interrupt the ignition feed (the low-tension side, of course!) is an alternative which will slow down an opportunist, but it will not defeat a serious thief. Electronic immobilisers can also be fitted to classics, and can be hidden away so they will not spoil your classic's appearance. The system's radio receiver can be hidden behind the dashboard or under the carpet, and simply holding the key fob transmitter nearby triggers the immobiliser – some give a gentle electronic bleep to confirm.

The final form of attack is more problematic. Classics are often stolen not by opening them, but by craning the whole vehicle onto a truck. The car can then be taken away and opened at the thieves' leisure. Often this method is used for cars which are to be broken up and sold as spares, often overseas – something which affects classic Mercedes saloons of modest value (because they are still in front-line service in Africa) as much as it affects Ferraris and Bugattis. A good investment here is a tracking device, which is hidden on the car and can be used to locate it should it be stolen. Many stolen vehicles, using tracker systems, have been recovered from shipping containers at docksides, where they were about to sail away forever.

OPPOSITE Three- or four-point harnesses hold you into the seat more effectively, and are essential for racing

LEFT Old-style alarms like this Selmar still turn up at autojumbles and in car-boot sales, but a modern system will protect your classic more effectively

Electrical accessories

In a steel-bodied car one terminal of the battery will be connected to the body, so that the steel body panels act as an extension of that battery terminal. Any component can be earthed simply by giving it an electrical connection to the bodywork. As a general (but not infallible) rule, older cars with dynamos are 'positive earth', with the positive terminal of the battery connected to the body, and more recent cars with alternators are 'negative earth'.

For many electrical accessories it makes no difference which way the car is wired, but if you intend to fit modern electronic devices, such as in-car entertainment systems and alarms, the car will need to be negative earth. Changing polarity involves swapping the battery terminal connections (usually its easier to turn the battery around, or fit a new one with the terminals in the reverse positions). If a dynamo is retained it will have to be re-polarised, connections to motors might have to be reversed, and some equipment like radios and clocks may no longer work at all. Consult an auto electrician with experience of working on classic cars to get the full story, or see

Haynes's *Classic Car Electrical Systems Repair Manual* by Dave Pollard.

Upgrading to an alternator is a good move if extra electrical accessories are to be added, because an alternator generates useful power even when the engine is idling. With more accessories to power it makes sense to go for an alternator with greater capacity. If you do plan to add many electrical accessories it would be sensible to begin by adding an auxiliary fusebox with a heavy-duty power supply lead direct from the battery, from which the new electrical items can be powered.

Lighting

Tungsten-filament bulbs are the standard wear for many classics, either in the form of conventional bulbs or 'sealed beam' lamps where the whole headlamp is one big bulb. Kits to convert to more efficient quartz halogen bulbs are available, and will make a significant difference. The next step is to fit auxiliary lamps, which will need to be wired through a relay using the correct grade of wire for their power consumption.

Make sure any lamps you fit meet local rules on type and position. In the UK, driving lamps must be positioned symmetrically and can only operate with main-beam headlamps. Fog lamps must also be positioned symmetrically, no more than 400mm from the sides of the car and no more than 1,200mm from the ground, and should be operable with the sidelights, dipped beam or main beam.

Air horns

Another classic accessory. Standard horns are usually one of two types, high frequency or wind tone, both of which use a vibrating diaphragm to produce sound. An air horn, by contrast, has a small compressor which sends high-pressure air to metal or plastic trumpets, which make the sound.

The compressor will pull several amps of current, so it should have a fused power feed taken from the battery, fuse box or starter solenoid, switched by a relay. If the air horn replaces the car's original horn, the old wiring can operate the new relay. Alternatively, the old horn can be retained and a switch provided to alternate between it and the air horn. Proponents of this approach suggest the original horn can then be used 'in town', but I've never quite understood why. I doubt I'd remember to flick the switch every time I entered or left a town, and certainly wouldn't have time to select the right horn in an emergency. It seems to me a better idea just to have the strident air horn available for any eventuality.

In-car entertainment

Modern in-car entertainment equipment causes several problems in classic cars – polarity we have already dealt with, but there are more pitfalls in store. One is simply that it looks wrong: multi-coloured vacuum fluorescent displays rarely sit happily in a classic interior. Another is that modern DIN-sized units are too big to fit into the old-style 7in x 2in radio aperture which your classic will have – if it makes any provision for a radio at all.

One solution for both problems is to hide your modern equipment. Amplifiers and CD-changers are usually designed for this, but the same principle can be applied to a head-unit, which can be fitted in the glovebox. Another solution is to fit modern radio electronics inside a 'classic' radio casing, a service which several vintage radio repairers can provide. This should give you reliable FM radio reception, but do not expect to get all the features of a modern RDS-equipped, Bluetooth-enabled head unit. If the looks of a modern unit are acceptable to you, there is usually space to hang it under the dash, in which case any in-dash aperture can be blanked off or, with a bit of ingenuity, turned into a handy cubbyhole.

A final option is to rely on portable equipment – from now old-fashioned 'personal stereos' to modern MP3 players – and provide a hidden amplifier and speaker system in the car with nothing showing but a power switch and a line-input jack socket. That way you can have music on the move and, if you take your iPod with you when you leave the car, there's nothing left to steal.

OPPOSITE Modern DIN-sized radios are bigger than the old 7in x 2in units

BELOW Air horns provide strident audible warning. Because the compressor draws a lot of current, it should be powered via a relay

On the
road

Driving position

Driving a classic car takes you back in time to an era when technology was less advanced, safety was less of a priority and when drivers were expected to think for themselves. It is because of this that classic cars offer a driving experience all their own – but it also means that they demand care, concentration and commitment from their drivers.

To drive a classic safely and well you need to appreciate that the bad habits displayed by many drivers, which rarely get them into trouble, can have more serious consequences in an older car. Some of the driving techniques that were commonplace in the 1960s have now all but disappeared, but learning them can be essential if you want to drive your classic smoothly and safely, and particularly if you want to extract the best performance from it – either for fun or for competition.

But even if you only ever use your classic for gentle touring, optimum control should be

paramount – and that begins with the way you sit in the car.

Your position at the wheel needs to take into account several factors: operation of the controls, visibility, safety and comfort. Different authorities give different advice about how to set up the correct driving position, many of them apparently ignoring the fact that the ideal position is sometimes impossible to achieve, and what is needed is the best compromise.

Usually the pedal positions will be fixed and the seat will be adjustable at least fore-and-aft, and probably (but not always) the seat backrest angle will be adjustable. The steering may be fixed or provided with adjustment for either reach, or rake, or both. The range of adjustments available will dictate both your approach to setting up your driving position and the amount you will need to compromise.

The basic principle I work on is that too far away from a control is hopeless, because you can't work it properly, whereas too close is usually uncomfortable but operable. So I start by getting close enough to all the controls to ensure I can operate them, and then if necessary use whatever adjustments are available to give myself more room and therefore a more comfortable position.

So, start by adjusting the fore/aft position of the seat to give you good control over the pedals – a good starting point is a position where you can just about press the clutch pedal to the floor without fully extending your leg and ankle. With luck this will sit you a reasonable distance from the steering wheel.

The ideal position is with your elbows bent at about 120 degrees as you grip the wheel at the usual 'ten-to-two' or 'quarter-to-three' position – a more relevant measure is that you should be able to grip the top of the wheel with either hand with your arm almost fully extended but without leaning forward from your seat. This gives you optimum control over the wheel, and should also enable you to reach dashboard switches and the gearlever in its furthest position.

Adjusting the seat backrest or steering column extension might help you achieve this position. If the seat and column are fixed or do not provide enough adjustment to do the job, you will have to compromise.

Further compromises might come to light when you drive the car. If the steering is heavy you might find it easier to sit a little closer to the wheel, likewise if the wheel is particularly big. Unassisted brakes or a heavy clutch might prompt you to sit closer to the pedals.

Safety belts

Seat belts did not become a regular fitment until the 1960s, though many classics which did not have belts fitted when they were new will have been retro-fitted with them. Seat belts are a very effective safety aid, but they must be adjusted correctly.

Seat belts in classics might be of the modern lap-and-diagonal inertia-reel type, but cars from the 1970s or earlier are likely to be fitted with 'static' belts and you will find some classics fitted

only with lap straps or diagonals, but not both – or perhaps with no belts at all.

An inertia-reel belt will adjust itself, though if you are very lucky you may have an extra adjustment for the top mounting of the diagonal strap. This should be set so that the belt crosses your shoulder, not so low that it slips off or so high that it cuts into your neck.

Static belts should be adjusted to suit your size. The lap belt should sit snugly across your hip bones, so that in an accident the loads are carried by the pelvis and not the unsupported abdomen area. The length of the belt should be adjusted so the diagonal strap (if there is one) allows you a small amount of movement, but only a small amount – you may have to sit closer to the dashboard to reach the switches, because a static belt will not allow you to lean forward for them as an inertia-reel belt does.

Competition-type three- and four-point harnesses are adjusted in the same way as a static lap-and-diagonal belt. Tightening the shoulder straps can cause the lap strap to ride up, so make sure the lap strap is very tight first, and that it fits across your pelvis.

OPPOSITE Often classics have steering wheels which are large by modern standards, and your steering technique has to take account of that. This is the 1959 Le Mans-winning Aston Martin DBR1

LEFT Adjust the seat to give you good control over the steering wheel. Ideally you should be able to turn the wheel 90 degrees in either direction without having to stretch forwards

LEFT Static seat belts must be adjusted to the user. Make sure the lap strap bears on the pelvis

Starting

Starting cars has become progressively simpler for drivers as more and more systems have been automated. Today, starting a cold engine requires no more than a turn of the ignition key, but an older car might need a little more technique and can certainly benefit from a little more care.

Some classics have manual control of the ignition timing, in which case the ignition should be set to the 'retard' position. A manual choke or starting enrichment control is almost universal, and is usually operated by a pull knob on the dash. Usually the best ploy is to pull the choke knob out fully if the engine is cold, even in reasonably warm weather, but different engines prefer different treatment – often engines with big twin-choke Weber carbs start more easily if you leave the choke alone and instead pump the accelerator pedal a couple of times to inject some fuel from the accelerator pumps.

If your classic has an electric fuel pump you will probably hear it ticking when you switch on the ignition. Starting will be easier if you wait for the rapid ticking to slow down (indicating that the pump has built up some pressure in the fuel system) before using the starter.

Holding the clutch pedal down while starting frees the starter from the onerous task of churning the gearbox internals through cold oil. You are trying to start the engine, not the gearbox, so you might as well give the starter an easier time. But sometimes disengaging the clutch actually puts more load on the starter, particularly if the clutch has an old-fashioned carbon release bearing; so, see what works best on your classic. With the car stationary and the engine running with the gearbox in neutral, press the clutch pedal and listen to the engine note. If the engine speeds up fractionally, disengaging the clutch has reduced the load on the engine so it would be worth declutching while starting.

Usually the choke control can be locked in position by turning it; if not, a slotted wooden stop is useful. A clothes peg works well. Once your engine starts, push the choke in as soon as you can – if the weather is warm you can probably push it in half way almost immediately. If the engine does not start after it has turned over for a few seconds, give the starter motor a rest before trying again – it is not designed for continuous use and may overheat. If the engine still will not fire after a couple of attempts, turn to Chapter 6.

Assuming the engine does start, you need to take some care during the warm-up period. The engine oil will be cold and thick and oil pressure will be abnormally high. Try to avoid high load and high revs until the water temperature is approaching normal, by which time the oil

pressure should have dropped back to its normal value. Gradually push the choke control back in as the engine warms up. Always try to use as little choke as possible to avoid excessive fuel consumption, emissions and engine wear.

It will usually be unnecessary to use the choke when starting a hot engine, but it is often a good idea to open the throttles slightly while turning the engine over to ensure adequate amounts of air/fuel mixture reach the cylinders – but be ready to release your pressure on the accelerator once the engine fires to avoid racing the engine.

OPPOSITE Coaxing your classic's engine to life can take a little more skill than required for a modern car

LEFT Ignition key positions for a typical classic *(iStockphoto)*

BELOW How much you need to use the choke will vary from car to car – get to know what works on your classic

Braking

To drivers brought up on modern cars with modern braking systems, the concept of braking requiring any technique might seem alien. You just push the middle pedal and you stop, right? Well, yes, up to a point. The problem is that drivers of modern cars are spoilt by the efficiency of their braking systems, which make the essential techniques of yesteryear a thing of the past. Servo assistance and disc front brakes are now universal, anti-lock systems are widespread, improvements in cooling and lining materials have all but eradicated brake fade and tyre technology has made cars more forgiving of sloppy, unthinking driving. Classic car drivers are less lucky.

Classic brakes are less efficient than modern ones, and classic cars tend to use much narrower tyres. As a result, a classic is more likely to lock a wheel or to veer off a straight path during heavy braking, particularly on a slippery road, and is more likely to suffer brake fade, so the driver has to apply a bit more thought to how he uses the brakes. Selecting a low gear to use engine braking for a long descent instead of relying solely on the brakes, for instance, and braking in short bursts rather than continuously to give the system time to cool.

In any car, braking around corners is unwise: drivers of modern cars do it all the time and their fat tyres keep them (mostly) out of trouble, but a classic car driver ought to show his machine some respect and take a little more care. A good driver will also use observation and anticipation to avoid unnecessary braking, lifting off early and allowing the car to slow naturally rather than staying on the power to the last moment and then braking hard.

Always aim to brake fairly firmly to begin with, and reduce the braking effort as the car comes closer to the required speed. This gives a greater margin of safety in case conditions suddenly change or there is a failure in the braking system.

Parking brakes

This is one area where standardisation has destroyed some of the interesting variations between marques, between countries of manufacture and between family runabouts and sporting roadsters. Classic handbrakes come in all shapes, sizes and locations, and the details of their operation vary.

Generally, if you press the button and push the brake lever away from you it will disengage the brake. 'Umbrella handle' types often need a twist as you push, as do the dash-mounted pull-handle types used by Mercedes and others. To apply the brake, pull the handle towards you – preferably with the button held down, to avoid that horrid grating noise as the pawl, which holds the brake on, grinds across the quadrant which holds it in place.

Foot-operated parking brakes are easy enough to apply – simply push the small parking brake pedal. A dash-mounted release lever is usually provided to release it, though some American cars automatically released the parking brake when the automatic transmission selector was moved to 'Drive'. Some of these were noted for slipping out of Park into gear, which coupled with an auto-release parking brake allowed them to roll happily away unaided.

More confusing are fly-off handbrakes. Where a normal handbrake locks on if you pull it and let go, a fly-off handbrake does what its name suggests – it flies back to the 'off' position. On a conventional handbrake the button unlocks the lever, but on a fly-off handbrake the button locks the lever. To engage a fly-off handbrake you pull the lever then press the button to lock the lever in place, and to disengage it you pull the lever slightly to disengage the pawl, then push the lever into the 'off' position. Fly-off handbrakes were once popular on sports cars and are often fitted to cars used in rallies or autotests, because they make handbrake turns easier.

Take care with parking brakes which act on discs rather than drums: if the discs are hot when the brake is applied, the brake can slip as the discs cool. Drum brakes pull themselves tighter as they cool. For this reason most parking brakes use drums, even on cars with disc brakes all round for their main braking system.

Left-foot braking

Even experienced drivers can find left-foot braking a challenge when they first attempt it. I suggest practising on a wide, dry road when there is no traffic about: just roll along at 30mph or so and try braking with the left foot instead of the right. Try to brake very, very gently. You will probably be surprised just how fiercely your left foot attacks the brake pedal, a legacy of all that time it has spent booting clutch pedals. It takes time to develop the sensitivity necessary.

Though left-foot braking is not a technique which confers much advantage in everyday driving of manual transmission cars, it does make a big difference with automatic transmission (see below) making progress on a twisty road smoother and safer. It can also be a useful trick in a manual car: I've left-footed the brake pedal in a situation where the engine wasn't running cleanly and needed the throttle kept open to prevent it stalling, but road conditions demanded braking. In the time taken to transfer the right foot to the brakes and then 'heel and toe' the throttle the engine would have stalled; using left-foot braking I could keep the engine running, and keep control of the car.

BELOW Two feet, two pedals: if your classic has an automatic gearbox, left-foot braking will give you maximum control – but it's a skill which takes time to develop

Gear **changes**

Manual gearboxes have not changed enormously over the last few decades, so changing gear in a classic should not pose major problems. The difficulties which do arise are likely to be due to synchromesh – or more accurately the lack of it, either by design or because of wear – or curious control arrangements.

Synchromesh makes gear changes easy in modern gearboxes. Classic car gearboxes may have no synchromesh or, more commonly, synchro on the top three gears but not on first. Synchromesh on second gear works the hardest, and over time it becomes weaker or even non-existent. Double declutching (see below) will help produce crunch-free changes even when synchromesh is absent. Give the system time to operate: rather than jamming the lever into each gear position as fast as it will go, apply gentle pressure in the direction of the next gear and when the synchromesh has equalised the gear speeds, the lever will drop sweetly into place.

With a good gearbox and careful judgement you can do this without using the clutch.

Some gearboxes are recalcitrant when cold, needing slow and careful changes until the gearbox oil has warmed up if nasty noises are to be avoided. Classic Ferraris, famously, refuse to engage second gear until the 'box is warm. Sometimes a gear will refuse to engage, particularly first gear when starting from rest. If this happens pull the lever into the opposite gear position (usually second) and then try first again. Alternatively, leave the lever in neutral, release the clutch, give the throttle a blip, then try to engage the gear again. If you still cannot find a gear, one trick is to allow the car to roll forward or back a few inches, then try again. If none of these techniques works there may be problems with the gearbox, or the clutch could be failing.

Most classics have four gears arranged in the familiar 'H' pattern with first gear to the left and forward. Five-speed gearboxes will either have the first four gears in the 'H' and fifth gear to the right and forward, or will use a 'dog-leg first' arrangement with first gear left and back, and the top four gears in the 'H'. The latter is preferred on high-performance cars (Ferraris again, amongst others) because first gear is not much used once the car is under way, so it makes sense to have the top four gears in the most easily selected positions.

Always pause in neutral before selecting reverse gear, to avoid a nasty graunch (caused by the gearbox internals still moving as you try to select the gear). Reverse gear selection often catches out drivers in unfamiliar cars, because different manufacturers provide different ways to defeat the reverse gear lock-out. The simplest is simply a spring bias away from the reverse gear gate. If a good shove will not get the gear lever into position, try pushing the lever down on its axis, or pulling it up as you move it. Some gear levers are fitted with a collar under the gear knob which must be lifted to allow reverse gear to be selected.

Column-mounted manual gearchanges essentially provide the same gate as a floor-mounted lever, but on its side – so first gear, for instance, will be selected by pulling the lever towards the wheel and up. Gear levers sprouting from the dashboard seem to be a peculiarly French fascination (enjoying a revival in modern MPVs). They are easy enough to get the hang of: whether the lever is moved or twisted or pulled, the gear positions are conventional.

Double declutching

Modern synchromesh gearboxes have made double-declutching a thing of the past, but with many classics it is an essential skill – particularly for those which lack synchromesh, often on first gear. The theory is that a gearchange, usually a downchange, is easier if the gearbox internals are speeded up before the attempt to engage the gear.

The drill goes like this. The driver releases the throttle, declutches and moves the gear lever to the neutral position – so far, so normal. With the gear lever still in neutral the clutch is re-engaged and the throttle blipped, and the faster the car is travelling and the 'shorter' the gear to be engaged the more emphatic the blip should be. The driver

'Double declutching' (or 'double clutching' in the US) can help to make smooth downshifts with non-synchro gears, or gearboxes with worn synchro cones. To make a double-declutched downshift the driver lifts off the throttle

declutches and moves the gearlever to neutral

then re-engages the clutch and blips the throttle

The clutch is then disengaged again and the new gear selected

and finally the clutch engaged and the throttle opened to match the engine revs to the new gear

then declutches a second time, engages the new gear, and releases the clutch pedal.

Because the double-declutching process is most frequently used for downchanges, it is often useful to be braking at the same time. That appears to call for three feet – one per pedal – but the 'heel and toe' technique makes it possible.

Heeling and toeing

Few terms in motoring can be at once so well known and so confusingly inaccurate. 'Heeling and toeing' rarely, if ever, involves the driver's heel and toe.

The idea is to merge the processes of braking and changing down, so that they occur simultaneously. There are several benefits. First,

'Heeling and toeing' is a technique which allows smooth downchanges while braking, improving comfort and safety. The driver lifts off the throttle with the right foot

To correctly match the engine revs to the new gear, the driver blips the throttle without reducing the pressure on the brake pedal by using the side of the foot

Purpose-designed driving shoes like these from Piloti incorporate reinforcement on the outside of the right shoe to make heeling and toeing easier

the whole process can be completed in a shorter time, which means braking can begin later (important in competition driving). Second, braking can be completed in one smooth operation rather than a series of jabs interspersed by gearchanges, making the car more stable and more controllable on its entry to the corner – especially in wet or icy conditions. That makes life easier for the driver, and gives passengers a smoother ride too.

The heel and toe process begins with normal braking, using the ball of the right foot, and when a downchange is required the driver declutches with the left foot as normal. Normally the driver would then have to move his right foot off the brake to the accelerator, to raise the engine speed for the lower gear which is about to be selected. But using the 'heel and toe' technique he keeps on braking with the right foot while either rolling it over sideways to operate the accelerator pedal using the side of his foot, or twisting his ankle to catch the pedal with his heel. The downchange can then be completed as normal.

Double-declutching, if it is necessary, can be combined with heel and toe pedal operation: the driver can brake continuously during the double-declutched downchange, at the same time controlling the throttle using the rolled-over or twisted right foot technique. The benefits in time saved and smoothness gained when double-declutching using the heel and toe technique are even greater because of the longer, more complex double-declutching process.

Depending on the pedal positions in the car, and the anatomy of the driver, the heel and toe process can be simple or tricky, and can involve anything from a gentle roll of the foot to a sharp turn of the ankle. Sometimes the pedal positions can be altered to make heeling and toeing easier: in the 1960s bolt-on pedal extensions which achieved the same ends were all the rage, and some are still available today. The set-up of the brake system also plays a part, because a light brake pedal makes it very difficult to roll your foot across to the accelerator without simultaneously squeezing the brakes a little harder. The effects can be minimised with practice.

The best way to learn is to begin in a stationary car, practising the right foot movement you need to blip the throttle while maintaining pressure on the brake pedal. You can then start using that technique in a moving car, but leave yourself plenty of room for error. When you get it right the result is a smooth, stable entry to a corner or hazard accompanied by smooth and timely downchanges.

Automatic gearboxes

The whole point of an automatic transmission is that the gear selection process is handled for you, so once 'Drive' is selected an automatic gearbox can often be left to its own devices. But there are some circumstances where intervention from the driver is useful.

The automatic transmission responds to the vehicle's speed and the load on the engine – as you go faster it selects higher gears, and if the load on the engine increases, because you are overtaking or climbing a hill, the transmission may 'kick down' into a lower gear. What an auto 'box cannot do is anticipate the road conditions, which is where the driver comes in.

A classic example is a press-on driver accelerating hard along a straight up to a tight bend. The gearbox selects a low gear to aid acceleration, but when the driver lifts off the throttle to brake for the bend, the transmission detects the reduced engine load and selects a higher gear. It has no way of knowing that the driver is about to brake and might prefer to retain the lower gear for extra engine braking up to the corner, and better acceleration out of it. A switched-on driver, therefore, will use the manual over-ride provided to keep the gearbox in a lower gear.

Likewise, a thinking driver can select a lower gear manually before overtaking, rather than begin the manoeuvre with the transmission between gears as it kicks down.

Smoothness and safety can be improved by left-foot braking, which is much simpler in an automatic car because there is no clutch pedal to worry about. Some who regularly switch between autos and manuals suggest left-foot braking in an automatic invites trouble later when driving a three-pedal car, but personally I've never found it a problem.

Pre-selector gearboxes

Walter Wilson's semi-automatic gearbox was used in an impressive array of vehicles, from racing ERAs and Connaughts to Daimler limousines, buses and even tanks. Like the more familiar automatic transmission which began to replace it after the Second World War, the Wilson gearbox is an epicyclic geartrain where ratios are selected by brake bands which can lock each of the annulus gears. Either a centrifugal clutch or a fluid flywheel is provided. The novelty is that each gear is selected manually by the driver before it is needed, then the change made at any time by pressing and releasing a gearchange pedal which takes the place of the clutch pedal. This means that gear selection can be unhurried and can be done whenever is convenient, and then the actual gearchange can be completed swiftly and without the driver removing his hands from the wheel.

The potential benefits for a racing car are obvious. Hill-climb champion Raymond Mays said 'there is no doubt that this type of gearbox is an enormous help', though it was certainly an acquired taste. The great Tazio Nuvolari is reputed to have disliked the Wilson gearbox in the MG K3 with which he won the Ulster Tourist Trophy in 1933, eventually telling his riding mechanic Alec Hounslow to take charge of the lever while he worked the pedal!

The Wilson transmission has a selector quadrant similar to an automatic. The engine should be started in neutral, and then the lever can be moved to either the first or reverse gear position and the gearchange pedal operated. The car will remain stationary, in gear, and will move off when the driver increases the engine revs to a fast tickover. Second gear can be

ABOVE MG K3
Magnette: Nuvolari
disliked the Wilson
pre-selector
transmission, but
that didn't prevent
him from winning
the TT! *(MG Rover)*

immediately pre-selected, then engaged when required by operating the pedal – and so on up to top gear.

It is worth noting that if the gearbox is left in gear and the engine started from cold with the choke out, the car will immediately begin moving – there are lots of tales of unwary mechanics chasing after driverless cars, or being run over by them.

Overdrive

Overdrives are two-speed gearboxes attached to the output shaft of a conventional manual gearbox, offering either a 1:1 ratio (overdrive switched 'out') or an 'overdriven' ratio where the output shaft speed is higher than the input (overdrive 'in'). Usually the overdrive is switched electrically from a stalk on the steering column or dashboard, or a switch in the top of the gearknob. Declutching is not usually necessary, though lifting off the throttle is wise.

Overdrive gives 'longer' gearing which reduces noise, fuel consumption and engine wear at high

speed, and which can fill in gaps between the gears in the main gearbox. So, for instance, a gap between third and fourth might be filled by overdrive third. With practice it's possible to change gear in the main gearbox and switch the overdrive in or out simultaneously, effectively giving you six or seven gear ratios to choose from.

Other transmission systems

There are several other variations on the basic manual gearbox and twin-plate clutch. Some systems have automatic clutches operated by gear lever movement – like the Hydrak clutch used by Mercedes in the 1950s, and Porsche's similar Sportomatic system. The clutch on the NSU Ro80 was operated by a sensor in the gearknob, giving the driver an opportunity to destroy the engine by resting an unthinking hand on the gearknob at motorway speeds. Up to the 1960s, Rover cars often incorporated a freewheel which, in its 'free' setting, allowed clutchless gearchanges.

Steering

Broadly speaking there are three different methods of steering, which have come to be known as 'push-pull', 'rotational' and 'fixed-input'. Sadly, all three terms are misleading.

Push-pull steering should more accurately be called pull-push steering, since it demands that the first steering movement pulls on the wheel. This is the 'shuffle' method of feeding the wheel through the hands, beloved of British driving examiners, police forces and advanced driving organisations. In a left turn, the left hand is moved to the 10 o'clock position then pulled downwards to steer, and when it gets level with the right hand both hands move down together – the left hand turning the wheel while the right hand slides over the rim. When both hands reach the bottom of the wheel, further steering angle can be applied by pushing up with the right hand while the left hand slides up, and if necessary the whole process then repeats. The arms never cross.

Rotational and fixed-input steering use both hands to steer the wheel. In fixed-input steering half a turn of steering lock (or perhaps a little more) in either direction can be applied before the arms cross over so far they touch. Rotational steering begins in the same way, but the left arm (in a left turn) is moved out of the way of the right arm and crossed over above it, gripping the wheel at about 10 o'clock to continue the turn. If you can anticipate a corner requiring more than about half a turn of lock a sensible method is to reposition the hands on the wheel before the corner so most, or all, of the steering movement can be performed in a single, smooth arc.

Most of the time my preference is for the fixed-input/rotational school, for three reasons. First is that you spend more time with both hands holding the wheel. Classics tend to react more violently to bumps in the road, which can throw you off course, and having two hands on the wheel minimises the effects. Second, in an emergency it is very difficult to wind on, or off, as much steering lock as rapidly using the push-pull method – not impossible, but very difficult. Third, there is a point in the push-pull process where both hands are at the bottom of the wheel, and if this coincides with the lock required for the corner, control throughout will be poor.

That said, the size of the steering wheel and the gearing of the steering system are going to make a big difference to the method you use. Rotational steering becomes a lot more difficult with a big wheel, particularly when it is closer to you than you would like – exactly the situation in many a classic. In this situation the push-pull method can be the only way to retain effective control if the wheel has to be turned through a large angle. Rather than being a slave to a single technique, a good driver should understand and practise all the different steering techniques, and will choose the one which is the most effective in any given situation.

Fixed-input steering

Making a left turn using fixed-input steering: from 'ten to two' both hands turn the wheel...

...without changing position through the turn

The driver can complete a half-turn in either direction from the straight ahead position

PULL-PUSH STEERING

Making a left turn using pull-push steering: starting from the 'ten to two' position **1** the left hand is raised and pulls down **2** while the right hand slides down the wheel. When the left hand reaches the bottom **3** the right hand grips the wheel and pushes up to continue the turn **4** while the left hand slides up **5**

ROTATIONAL STEERING

Making a left turn using rotational steering: both hands turn the wheel, as with fixed-input steering **1**, **2**. With the right hand around the 12 o'clock position the left hand is crossed over the top of the right arm **3** to continue the turn **4**, **5**

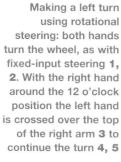

Signalling

Flashing direction indicators have been the norm for decades, but you do not have to go back too far to find semaphore indicator arms in the B pillars and even more weird and wonderful signalling systems (of dubious value). Even flashing indicators of the modern type can be confusing for the novice – by design or through age and wear they may not self-cancel, and the visual and audible warning that the indicator is still flashing may not be as obvious as it usually is in a modern car. Whatever you are driving, it is well worth cultivating the habit of manually cancelling the indicator rather than waiting for the self-cancelling system to operate. That way you will be well able to cope with any system – and your signals should be better-timed, too.

Other visual signals, such as hand signals, have dropped out of use to such a degree that even if you know what they mean and how to give them, they are of little use to other road users. Back in the days when hand signals were more widely used the celebrated motoring writer and former racer S.C.H. 'Sammy' Davis wrote of seeing a driver's forearm and hand appear from a sunshine roof, describe three horizontal circles, and disappear, which he took to mean 'I am about to do something but I do not know quite what.'

It is common practice in some countries for faster vehicles to alert road users ahead that they are about to overtake using a long headlamp flash, but many drivers interpret a headlamp flash to mean 'after you' – a confusion which could have serious implications.

ABOVE Get into the habit of manually cancelling indicators – your signals will be better-timed, and indicators which do not self cancel by design or because of a fault will not faze you

Staying out of trouble

The aim of every driver should be to avoid accidents with alertness and anticipation, but that applies especially to classic car drivers. Road users often use the appearance of a car to make assumptions about its speed and behaviour. Many people will assume that if a car is old it must, therefore, be travelling slowly. That encourages pedestrians to cross in front of you and drivers to pull out of side turnings as you approach, both without actually checking that your rate of approach matches their assumptions. You have to do the thinking for them, and drive 'defensively'. At the same time you need to be aware of the limitations of your classic, and drive in such a way that those limitations never put you or other road users in danger.

Stopping distances are an example. Many older classics will happily reach speeds that would be impressive in a modern car, but in an emergency their inability to brake like a modern car could be a big problem, and you need to drive accordingly.

Sadly, driver education these days seems to be aimed solely at keeping cars to speed limits, which leads many to believe that if they keep to the limit they are driving safely, whatever else they do or do not do behind the wheel. But that is not the case: concentration and observation are also vitally important. You will be a safer driver if you train yourself to constantly assess the road ahead, and anticipate what every other vehicle and road user around you might do next, so that you can plan your own speed and course to ensure that there is always a 'bubble of safety' around your car.

Emergencies

Slides and skids

Steering, braking and acceleration all place demands on a tyre, and there is only so much force a tyre can generate. Beyond that, it slides. It may slide because the driver is asking too much of the tyre, or because the grip offered by the road surface has reduced. In each case the way to deal with the slide is to reduce the force acting through the tyre so that control is regained. The next problem is that the car is no longer travelling along the course you originally intended. Generally speaking the tyres at one end of the car will slide before the other, giving you 'understeer' (known as 'push' in the US) or 'oversteer'.

Understeer is when the front of the car runs wide in a turn, often as a result of going into the bend too fast. The natural reaction is to apply more steering lock, because the car is not turning as much as you would like, but this only adds to the problem – you are asking the front tyres to generate more force, but they are already beyond their limit. The answer is to lift off the throttle and unwind the steering slightly to stop the front sliding, then to reapply steering lock at a slower speed to correct your course.

In an oversteer situation the back of the car 'steps out' and the car aims towards the apex of the bend. Uncorrected, the car will probably spin. In a rear-drive car oversteer is often caused by applying too much throttle on the exit of a bend: the rear tyres use up their grip by accelerating the car, and you run out of cornering force. To regain control you must gently reduce the throttle opening to give the rear tyres a chance to grip, and steer in the opposite direction to the bend to correct your course. Note the emphasis on gently: snapping the throttle shut will unsettle the car and give you even more problems.

It is far better to learn about your classic's limits at a time and place of your choosing, rather than finding out in the middle of an emergency situation. Track days (see Chapter 7) offer a good way to find out how your car handles, in relative safety.

BELOW This Escort is oversteering: the car is trying to spin, and the driver is correcting the slide by steering in the opposite direction to the corner, or 'opposite lock'

Broken windscreen

Laminated glass windscreens are now universal, but classics are more likely to be fitted with toughened glass screens. A laminated screen struck by a stone or similar projectile will chip in one spot, but a toughened glass screen will probably shatter – seriously impairing vision.

To regain enough vision to stop the car, punch through the glass keeping your wrist straight, to make a hole big enough to see through. The glass is designed to crumble into relatively blunt-edged pieces so you are unlikely to do yourself much damage, certainly less than you can expect by trying to drive without being able to see where you are going.

Once you have brought the car to a halt you can push out the remaining glass. If there are air vents in the bonnet, cover them with something like newspaper or a tarpaulin to avoid getting glass in the vents.

Dealing with the weather

Classic cars and their drivers can struggle with different weather conditions, and bad weather is not always the cause of the problem.

Not every classic has sun visors and even when they are provided they may well be inadequate, particularly in an open-topped car. Tiny scratches on the windscreen, common if the screen has been in place for many years, can cause further problems in bright weather by scattering the light and causing fatigue. A cap with a peak can be a useful accessory, provided it is worn in the old fashioned orientation with the peak at the front as the designer intended. Sunglasses can be a boon – shades designed specifically for drivers, like the well known Serengeti range, cut glare while improving recognition of signal colours, and modern wrap-around styles can also help to keep the wind out of your eyes in cars with short screens. Some wrap-around glasses intended either for driving or for skiing and snowboarding have interchangeable lenses, so you can use them with clear lenses to keep the wind out even on dull days.

In bad weather these wrap-around glasses can help to keep cold air and rain out of your eyes. An even better option is to wear proper goggles, though some styles do make you look like a former fighter pilot or retired motorcycle racer – which is fine if, indeed, you are a former pilot or racer, but marks you out as a bit Walter Mitty otherwise. Personally, I like the French Léon Jeantet Aviator goggles, available in the UK from Davida, because they are comfortable, relatively unobtrusive and offer excellent vision in all directions thanks to their curved lenses.

The heater can often be relied upon to keep your feet warm, but the top half of an open cockpit is always going to be cool. In these circumstances driving gloves are an enormous help, even if these days they are resolutely untrendy, because they keep your fingers warm and improve your grip on the wheel. A warm coat is another essential, and there is much to be said for the classic leather flying jacket with its big collar: in an open car much of the air flow curls over the screen and comes at you from behind, and a big collar keeps the wind off the back of your neck.

Classic car demisting systems are nowhere near as effective as those in use today, particularly now that air-conditioning is far more common, and older systems need more careful use to ensure that the glass is kept mist-free. Keep the air temperature control high, if needs be, higher than necessary for comfort, and direct that hot air to the windscreen and side windows. Turn on the fan and open a window or quarter light for ventilation, both to keep the interior comfortably cool and to allow the hot, moisture-laden air a chance to escape.

RIGHT Roadsters can still be driven with the top down if you dress the part. The author demonstrates, with warm coat, leather driving gloves and Leon Jeantet goggles from Davida

Being towed

If your classic ever has to be towed with a rope, remember that the golden rule is to keep the rope taut. That means a lot of gentle braking, together with careful observation of the road conditions ahead so you know when the towing car is about to slow down.

If possible, rather than sit directly behind the towing vehicle pull out slightly so you can see past it. It can be helpful to keep the driver's window open so you can listen to the towing car's engine note and brake gently during gearchanges to avoid the rope going slack.

Bear in mind that power assistance to the brakes and steering, if either is normally available on your classic, will only function if the engine is running. Servo brakes might give you a false sense of security because they will work normally a couple of times even with the engine off, through residual vacuum in the servo – then they suddenly get heavier.

Use a good, strong rope which is clearly visible to you and other road users, and make sure it is fastened on to a strong part of the car. Towing eyes are usually exposed to all the elements, so make sure you check for any corrosion which might have weakened a towing eye before you use it in anger.

ABOVE A highly visible orange rope is easier to see from the driving seat. Keeping the rope taut is essential

LEFT If you need to fix a tow-rope to your classic, choose a strong part of the car. Check for corrosion around towing eyes before using them

When it
goes wrong

Preparing for **trouble**

There is a story (perhaps apocryphal), dating back to the 1920s or 1930s, of a Rolls-Royce owner who took his car on a grand tour of Europe. After many arduous miles the rear axle broke, so at the next town our well-heeled owner cabled Derby for assistance. A technician was duly dispatched with a replacement axle which was fitted to the car, and the tour was completed without further difficulty. Back at base the owner approached Rolls-Royce to settle his account, upon which he was informed that he must have been mistaken, as 'Rolls-Royce axles never fail'.

It illustrates the point that you can't possibly carry everything you might need to fix your classic if something goes wrong. Instead, it makes sense to carry spares you could fit yourself, and the tools you'd need for the job, plus any very rare parts a local garage might find hard to source.

Even then, it's only worth carrying items which would immobilise the car if they failed – anything less important can wait until you get home. If you're planning to take your classic overseas, you also need to check local rules on the equipment you carry.

Spares to carry

The essential items start with the usual fluids. Carry plain water and anti-freeze, either separately (in which case the water can also be used to replenish a windscreen washer, or even for drinking in an emergency) or as a ready-made mixture of the correct proportions. Oil and brake fluid are also worth carrying in case of emergency, but you don't need much unless your car uses a special type which you would not be stocked by the average petrol station.

If your classic uses a lead-replacement additive or an octane booster, carry a good supply in case it proves difficult to find. You can carry extra fuel, too: a couple of gallons in a can might give you some peace of mind if you're in unknown territory and can't easily predict the frequency of petrol stations. But to avoid wasting all that space, it's a much better plan to keep those spare two gallons in the car's fuel tank. In other words, fill up before you really need to. If your fuel gauge is erratic, get to know how many miles you can comfortably achieve on a tank of fuel and fill up at that mileage, whatever the gauge says.

The majority of breakdowns are caused by electrical faults, and these are often fixable by the roadside if you have the right spares to hand. Coils can fail at inopportune moments, and are easy to fit. Condensers, contact breaker points and the rotor arm are worth replacing before a long journey, and take up little space when carried as spares.

A selection of bulbs is always a good idea, and is a legal requirement in some countries. Carry a handful of fuses, covering all the ratings used on your classic (assuming it has any, of course). Many fuse boxes incorporate space for spare fuses – fill up the spaces. If you're happy to tackle electrical repairs, it's worth taking a length of insulated wire, a selection of crimp terminals and a crimping tool, and some insulation tape, for jury-rigging repairs. You can even take an in-line fuse holder to protect any lash-up wiring.

Carry a spare fan belt. Emergency types have a joint which allows them to be fitted without tools, but reduces their life-expectancy. Carry spares for any other essential accessory drives on your particular engine, too.

Split hoses are another common problem. Emergency hose bandages do work, provided the split in the hose is small and the area around the split is clean and dry. Sadly those conditions aren't always easy to arrange, so on long journeys it is worth carrying radiator hoses. To save space you can sometimes carry whichever radiator hose is the longest, and if the shorter one fails you can cut it down to fit. A length of fuel pipe is also useful for making temporary replacements of fuel supply and breather hoses.

Another good idea is to collect a handful of nuts, screws and other fixings of the sizes commonly used on your classic, in case something vibrates loose.

BELOW You cannot carry everything you might need in an emergency, but it is worth carrying a selection of useful spares and the usual fluids

Tools to **carry**

If you end up trying to fix a broken-down classic by the roadside you're unlikely to be able to wash your hands after you complete the job – and inevitably breakdowns happen when you are dressed in your finery, on the way to some grand event. Disposable gloves can be useful (provided you remember to put them on before you start work) or there are now effective 'no water' hand cleaning tissues. Overalls might also be a good idea, if you know you would tackle major roadside repairs yourself.

Jump leads are a commonly-used emergency tool, and you can't always rely on someone else having a set. The same applies to a towrope. Another essential item is the car's jack, but don't just carry it – check that it works properly. It's worth carrying a short plank of wood for the jack to sit on, too, thus avoiding the possibility of it slipping if the ground is wet or uneven.

A fire extinguisher is compulsory in some countries and a good idea everywhere else, as a fire can reduce your prized machine to cinders in minutes. You would hate to stand there with nothing to do but watch it burn. Carry a bigger extinguisher than you think you need – the small ones last only a few seconds in use. In case of accidents a small but comprehensive first aid kit is a good idea, and a disposable camera to photograph the scene may help an insurance claim. A warning triangle is a wise addition to your kit, as it provides early warning to on-coming motorists that there's a static classic in the road ahead. It is compulsory to carry a triangle in some countries, along with a high-visibility vest.

A jam jar is very useful. It takes almost no space because other items can be packed inside it, and it can be used for tasks as diverse as collecting nuts as you remove them, so they don't get lost, and catching fuel from a disconnected fuel line when you spin the engine on the starter to check the flow rate. What else could you use?

Pliers are a must-have tool, essential in all kinds of running repairs. If you're trying to keep the size and weight of your tools to the minimum, carry a multi-tool instead. Choose carefully, testing to see how easy it is to use each item on the tool, and only discard dedicated tools when you are happy that the multi-tool functions equally well.

Spark plugs can be melted by incorrect ignition timing coupled with heavy-duty use, and even if you avoid plug failures you might want to pull the plugs out to help diagnose faults or to clean them. If you're already carrying a socket set, the addition of a spark plug socket won't rob you of much space. Unless your classic is prone to oiling plugs in traffic, say, or the plugs it uses are rare, it's probably not worth carrying a set. But consider carrying one – in case the plugs have to be removed for cleaning, say, and one gets dropped or cracked. A spare HT lead, as long as the longest lead used on your engine, can also be useful.

Rags are vital for cleaning components or hands, and useful in many other ways – folded into anti-vibration pads, knotted to make hose clamps and so on. Worth squashing into a spare gap in the boot.

There's no need to have a full set of screwdrivers or sockets – just take the sizes most commonly used on your classic. If you're also carrying a socket set, consider taking the appropriate socket and a breaker bar rather than carry a dedicated wheelbrace. A full kit of spanners also takes up space, so my preference is to pack one or two of the most widely-used sizes – 1/2in and 5/8in, say – together with a couple of adjustable spanners. Adjustables have had a lot of bad press over the years, but for use in emergencies they are ideal. Always hold an adjustable so the greatest loads are applied to the fixed, not the moving jaw and keep a thumb on the adjusting screw to ensure the jaws don't open up in use.

A torch or work lamp is a vital extra – emergencies are just as likely to happen in darkness, and even in the daytime it can be difficult to see what you are doing in a gloomy engine bay. If space is not a concern, a work lamp powered from the car battery is ideal.

Another must-have item is a water-repelling spray, for chasing water out of the ignition system and for general light lubricating duties. You might also want to carry a water leak additive, but these tend to work only on minor leaks.

Just to remind you, make sure your toolkit contains such invaluable and versatile items as string, electrical wire and crimp terminals, rubber bands and paper clips. Insulation tape is rightly frowned upon for its regular appearance in gruesome 'repairs' but as a short-term get-you-home aid it can be vital. Likewise, stronger tank tape can play a part in everything from replacing broken exhaust rubbers to holding together bits of broken lamps until they can be replaced.

A mobile phone can be your best friend in the event of a breakdown. If you're a member of one of the breakdown services, keep the number close by. It's also worth having the number of your usual garage, and any useful owners' club contacts.

OPPOSITE You cannot carry everything you might need in an emergency, but it is worth carrying a selection of useful spares and the usual fluids

FAR LEFT Adjustable spanners can be useful in an emergency. Keep your thumb on the adjusting screw to ensure the jaws cannot open up in use

LEFT WD40 in use

Engine will not start

If the engine turns over only slowly, or not at all, check that the headlights produce a strong beam: if they don't, the battery is probably flat. See the section later in this chapter on jump starts and bump starts. If the lights suggest that the battery has adequate energy, you need to delve further into the electrical system. A likely culprit will be the battery connections, or the main earth strap between the battery earth terminal and the body or chassis. If all the connections seem sound, connect a test lamp or voltmeter to a good earth and the large terminal on the starter, and try the starter again – if the meter moves or the lamp lights, that indicates power is getting that far, which suggests the problem is the starter itself. Worn brushes are a likely cause. Or the starter could be stuck: see 'Strange Noises'.

If there is no power at the starter, test the power connections to and from the solenoid using your meter or test lamp. If the connections are OK and power is reaching the solenoid but no further, the solenoid is at fault.

On automatic cars there is an inhibitor switch to ensure that the car cannot be started in gear. Try moving the gear selector into gear then back into Park or Neutral, and then try the starter again. If the engine still does not turn over, the switch may be faulty.

If the engine turns over normally but fails to start, and previously it has been working normally, the fault is likely to be in the ignition or fuel systems, and more often than not the problem will be the ignition system. To confirm this, remove one of the plug leads, push the rubber boot back to expose the connector on the end and hold the lead by its cover with insulated pliers close to an earth point on the engine. If you now operate the starter you should get a good strong spark – if not, investigate the ignition system. If the spark is fine, check for fuel at the carburettor – see 'Tracing fuel system faults' below.

If the engine has just been reassembled and has not yet been started, check that the ignition timing is correct. A classic mistake is to refit the distributor 180 degrees out of phase, in which case the spark will never occur at the right time. Turn the engine by hand and check that you get this sequence: the inlet valve should close, then the contact breaker points open, then the exhaust valve opens.

Tracing ignition faults

If there is no spark from a spark plug held against an earth point, remove the distributor cap and hold the end of a screwdriver next to the central contact in the cap – the one which supplies HT current to the rotor arm. Rest the shaft of the screwdriver against an engine earth, and have an assistant turn the engine over on the starter. If you now get a spark,

the fault lies in the distributor cap, rotor arm or plug leads. Look for cracks or burning in the distributor cap or rotor arm. The rotor arm and condenser are cheap and easy to fit, so if there is any doubt about them, replace them. If you get no spark it means there is no power reaching the coil, and this could be caused by faulty wiring or problems with the contact breaker in the base of the distributor. Check that the contact breaker points are fitted correctly and open and close as they should, and check the points gap using feeler gauges.

To investigate further you will need either a multimeter or a test lamp. You can buy a test lamp or make your own – it is simply a bulb in a holder (something like a sidelight or interior bulb is ideal) with two flying leads soldered to the contacts, preferably terminated with small crocodile clips. Whichever tool you use, one of its terminals should be connected to an earth point and the other to the item you are testing. Test that your earth point is sound and that the bulb is good by applying your test lead to the unearthed terminal on the battery – the bulb should light up.

Turn the engine by hand so the contact breaker points are open, and switch on the ignition. Apply your test lead to the moving contact. If the bulb lights (or your meter shows about 12V) the problem is with the contact breakers – check the points are clean, or simply replace the set. Otherwise, follow the low-tension wire back from the distributor to its terminal on the coil and apply your test lead to the terminal. If the bulb lights, the low-tension wire from coil to distributor is damaged, or there is a poor connection to the distributor body or the contact breaker set.

If you still don't get any signs of life, apply your test lead to the other coil terminal, which is the one supplying current from the ignition switch to the coil. If the bulb now lights, the coil is at fault. If there is still nothing, the ignition switch or its wiring must be faulty.

OPPOSITE Use a test lamp or multimeter to check for power at the starter solenoid

FAR LEFT Use a screwdriver blade to check for a spark from the distributor cap's centre contact

LEFT Check for a spark at the plugs by holding one plug near an engine earth using insulated pliers

Tracing fuel system faults

To check that fuel is reaching the carburettor,
remove the fuel supply line from the carb and
place the end in a jam jar, or similar, then turn on
the ignition (for electric pumps) or operate the
starter (for mechanical ones). A strong gush of
fuel from the pipe indicates that all is well at least
as far as the carburettor.

If the ignition system checks out and your
initial test suggests that fuel is reaching the
carburettor, you probably have either too much
or too little fuel in the cylinders. Too little will
probably be cause by blocked carburettor valves
or jets, possibly as a result of running very low
on fuel – debris from the bottom of the tank
sometimes gets drawn into the system. The
carburettor will have to be stripped so the valves
and jets can be removed and cleaned – ideally
they should be blown through with an air line, as
poking bits of wire through can damage them.

Too much fuel could be the result of a sticking
choke, so check all the carburettor linkages for
any signs of damage or seizing through
inadequate lubrication. Another possibility might
be a leaky carburettor float, or debris which is
preventing the float valve from sealing correctly.

Contaminated fuel is another possibility,
particularly if you are trying to start a classic
which has been inactive for some time. It's best
to drain the tank and replenish with fresh fuel.

If no fuel appears to be reaching the
carburettor, first check that there is fuel in the
tank – whatever the fuel gauge may say. Remove
the filler cap and rock the car from side to side,
listening for fuel sloshing around in the tank. If
you have an electric fuel pump you should be
able to hear it ticking as it pumps the fuel – it will
tick rapidly for a few seconds when you first start
the engine, then the ticking will slow down to
once or twice a minute. If you cannot hear the
fuel pump ticking, give it a sharp tap with a piece
of wood or something similar – if that gets it
going, the pump is faulty.

Both mechanical and electric fuel pumps can
incorporate fine mesh filters which may get
blocked by debris from the fuel tank. Try
removing the filter, cleaning it in fresh petrol
and refitting.

Overheating

An overheating engine should be switched off and allowed to cool before you do anything about it. Don't try to remove the radiator cap, because you can easily be scalded by escaping steam. In any case, the radiator cap helps the cooling system to maintain its working pressure, which raises the boiling point of the coolant water – so if you remove the cap from a hot engine, it will boil all the more ferociously. Any attempt to add cold water could easily crack the radiator or header tank, so let everything cool before you investigate the cause of the overheating and before you replenish the coolant.

A broken or loose fan belt will commonly be the cause, not because the fan is being driven too slowly (the fan is of no benefit except when the car is stationary or moving very slowly) but because the water pump is usually driven from the same pulley, so a loose fanbelt means sluggish water circulation around the engine.

Another cause might be a thermostat which is stuck shut, in which case the engine will boil but the radiator will still be cold. As a get-you-home measure you can remove the thermostat completely, but fit a new one as soon as you can – without a thermostat, warm-up will be slower (so engine wear will be greater) and on some engines the water flow-through will be incorrect if there is no thermostat, potentially causing hot spots in the cylinder head.

If the engine is fitted with a temperature-sensitive electric fan, the cause of the overheating might be a failure of the fan itself or, more likely, the thermal switch. Try removing the two wires from the fan switch and bridging them together with short length of wire – if the fan starts up, the switch has died. The fan can be left running to get you home.

ABOVE Keeping a regular watch on the temperature gauge could save you a lot of heartache and expense

Other engine problems

Many different problems can cause the engine to lack power, run roughly or 'miss'. Assuming nothing has been touched on the engine since it last ran without fault, start by looking for air leaks in the intake system, checking that the throttle and choke are operating freely, checking that connections to the coil and distributor are secure and removing the spark plugs to check that they are in good condition and have the correct gaps. Then remove and clean any filters in the fuel system. If this fails to solve the problem, the next step is to look for debris in the carburettor, and to check for water or other contamination in the fuel.

If the engine runs on – continues to run for a moment after the ignition is switched off –

something other than the ignition system is igniting the air/fuel mixture in the cylinders. Incorrect mixture or incorrect ignition timing can cause local overheating, so check both are correct. Very tight valve clearances can allow the exhaust valve to heat up, which is another potential cause, or it may be that the spark plugs are the wrong grade, or one or more of them has a fouled tip.

An engine which is reluctant to start following a short stoppage – after filling-up at a fuel station, for instance – might be suffering from fuel vaporisation. If you wait a few minutes for the fuel to cool down, the car should start and run normally.

Strange noises

Your classic starts making an unfamiliar noise: is it serious? Is something expensive about to happen? Is this a situation where you should pull over as fast as humanly possible, or is it OK to limp home? Or can you ignore it altogether?

Rhythmic knocking noises are a common cause for concern. Check whether the noise is engine-speed or vehicle-speed related: try changing to a different gear, or stopping the car but leaving the engine running. A heavy knocking noise which varies with engine speed might be worn main or big-end bearings – mains tend to rumble as well as knock. A lighter knocking could be a sticking valve, worn small-end bearing or broken piston ring. In any of these cases the engine will not react well to continued use.

Light tapping from the top end of the engine might be caused by excessive valve clearances: you may lose power, but the engine should limp home without drama if you keep the speed and load down. If the noise continues after valve clearance adjustment, the cause will be a worn camshaft or worn valvegear.

A harsh rattle which happens only at idle speed often indicates a worn timing chain or faulty tensioner. When renewing the timing chain, it is wise to change the drive sprockets and tensioner at the same time to minimise future work.

Knocking which varies with vehicle speed indicates a transmission or running-gear problem rather than any problem with the engine. Check for play in propshaft joints, buckled wheels or worn wheel bearings. This sort of fault generally emerges slowly. A speed-related knocking from a front-wheel drive car when driven in a tight curve indicates wear in the constant velocity joints transmitting drive to the wheels.

A screeching noise from under the bonnet may be because of a seized water pump, which will cause rapid overheating. You can get the same effect if the coolant freezes in cold weather. More likely, the screech will be the result of a slack fan-belt, which can be easily tightened. Do not neglect a squealing fan-belt, because the more it squeals the more its inner surfaces become smoothed and glazed, and the less likely it is ever to grip the drive pulleys correctly – and eventually you will lose your dynamo/alternator drive and water pump drive.

A harsh grinding noise after the engine is started indicates that the starter motor pinion is jammed in mesh with the flywheel. To free it, turn the square end of the starter motor shaft clockwise with a spanner. You can also try putting the car in gear and rocking it backwards but beware – it is easy to damage the starter.

LEFT Noises which vary with vehicle speed are usually from the transmission, wheels or suspension. Check for play in suspension joints and wheel bearings

Dial readings and warning lights

The oil pressure warning light should come on when you switch on the ignition and go out when the engine starts. If it comes on at any time while the engine is running (or your oil pressure gauge drops to zero) stop the engine and find the cause. A very low oil level could be the cause, but if the level is correct the problem will lie with the oil light or gauge, or it could be that the oil pump is not delivering enough pressure to the bearings. Find the cause before running the engine again.

If you have an oil pressure gauge, you will probably notice that it reads low when the engine is idling. That's not a problem, provided that the reading rises when the engine is revving. If the oil gets hot, for example when towing or climbing long hills the pressure will begin to drop away again.

On many classics the ignition light will come on while the engine is idling, indicating that the dynamo is not charging the battery. Dynamos produce little current at very low speeds, so this is normal. But the light should extinguish as soon as the revs rise beyond idle speed – if not, there is a charging problem, perhaps a loose or broken fan belt.

Exhaust pipe
smoke and drips

Exhaust gases are usually difficult to see, but in some circumstances you may see white, blue or black vapour. You can also see water dripping from the tailpipe.

The dripping water and white 'smoke' – which is actually water vapour – come from the same source. In cold weather they are normal, caused by the cold exhaust system condensing the water vapour in the exhaust gases. The vapour or drips should disappear as the exhaust system warms up. If you see the white water vapour or dripping water even when the engine has been running for some time, that suggests there is more than the usual amount of water in the exhaust gases – that could be the result of a failing head gasket, or a warped or cracked cylinder head. If you continue to run a car in this condition the problem is only likely to get worse, and there is a danger that you will run out of coolant.

Blue smoke indicates burning oil, which suggests engine wear. Puffs of smoke as you change gear suggest wear in the valve guides or valve stem oil seals. Continuous blue smoke under load indicates worn bores or piston rings.

Black smoke indicates excess fuel. You may see hazy black smoke when the engine is running on choke, but if black smoke is still seen when the engine is warm there is either a problem in the fuel system, such as a sticking choke or holed carburettor float, or there is a blockage in the intake system.

BELOW White smoke from the exhaust suggests a possible failing head gasket *(iStockphoto)*

Alternative means
of starting

Even if the battery is so low in charge that it cannot turn the engine fast enough to start it, there are still ways of getting your motor running. Which of these methods you attempt depends upon the age of your classic and the tools and manpower available. Whichever you choose, make sure you leave the engine running for 10–20 minutes once it has started, to give the charging system a chance to charge up the battery – otherwise you will need assistance again the next time you try to start the engine.

Starting handle

The starting handle all but died out in the 1950s, though they were still used on some long-running cars (often as an option) right into the 1970s. Vintage and veteran machines often had a fixed starting handle protruding from the front of the car, but later a separate handle was provided as part of the toolkit and a discreet aperture provided in the front bumper to allow the handle to mate up with the nose of the crankshaft.

To start a car using a starting handle, ensure the handbrake is on and the gearbox is in neutral, the choke is set for a cold start and if you have an ignition timing lever that it is set to full retard. Turn on the ignition switch to the running position and, if the car has an electric fuel pump, wait for the initial rapid ticking to subside. Grasp the starting handle

and turn the engine over slowly (almost invariably clockwise) until you meet a resistance, which is the sign that one cylinder is reaching the top of its compression stroke. You need to drive the engine 'over the top' against the compression as fast as possible with a good swing of the starting handle. With luck the engine fires at this point but if not you repeat the process until it does – or until you are worn out.

To avoid injury it is important to hold and swing the starting handle correctly. If the engine backfires while starting, it can force the handle backwards against its normal rotation with enormous force. If you grip the handle normally as though you are winding a mangle this could easily dislocate your thumb, so always grip a starting handle with your thumb pushed over onto the same side of the handle as your palm. To avoid arm and shoulder injuries always crank the engine by pulling up on the starting handle, never by pushing down.

Bump-start or tow-start

Both bump-starts and tow-starts use the motion of the car to turn the engine via the transmission. It will work on cars with manual gearboxes, and on some automatics, but not on cars with centrifugal clutches.

Bump-starting is easy if there happens to be a hill down which you can roll the car, though circumstances rarely provide a convenient hill when your car won't start. Without one you will need a

RIGHT Always hold a starting handle with your thumb and fingers on the same side to avoid injury

willing volunteer or two to give your car a push: theoretically you could push yourself then jump in and start the car, but it's a risky procedure that I wouldn't recommend.

Tow-starting is less physically demanding, but requires you to have another vehicle and a tow-rope available. As with any towing, make sure you fix the rope to a substantial part of the car, and agree signals between both drivers before you begin.

Both forms of starting work the same way, except for the manner in which the car is being moved along. Start by making sure that the ignition switch is turned to the running position and the transmission is in neutral. Allow your car to get up a bit of speed – a brisk walking pace will do – then declutch and select second gear. Gently engage the clutch: as you do the car will slow down and the engine will turn over and, hopefully, fire up. As soon as the engine starts, declutch again and select neutral. It can also help if you keep the throttle open slightly so the engine runs at a fast idle.

Note that if the motive power for all this comes from friends pushing your car, you have to be particularly careful about how you engage the clutch. Bang the clutch in fiercely and the car will suddenly slow, causing your friends to run into the back of the car; the engine will then fire and the car will run off down the road, at which point your (soon to be former) friends will probably be left face down in the mud.

Jump-start

If you have access to a set of jump-leads and another vehicle, you can perform a jump-start, using the power of the battery and charging system of the healthy car to boost the flat battery in your classic. Both cars should have electrical systems which run at the same voltage, but there is no reason why a modern negative-earth car should not be used to boost a positive-earth classic provided that care is taken to get the connections correct. Cars with ECUs can be damaged by being jump-started and can even be sensitive to being used as a donor to start another car, so consult the handbook before you begin.

Use good quality jump leads, with fat cables, thick insulation and strong clips. Plastic clips are common nowadays, but in my experience they rarely last long before breaking. The jump leads will be colour-coded red and black, and conventionally the red leads are used to connect the positive side, and the black connects the negative side.

Begin by positioning the donor vehicle so that its battery is within jump-lead distance of the battery in the car you are trying to start, but not too close and

LEFT Jump leads should be connected in the correct order to minimise the danger of igniting gas produced by a charging battery

certainly not touching (which can cause a short circuit), and open the bonnets on both cars. Assuming your donor car is negative earth, use the red jump lead to connect the positive terminals of both batteries together – check for a '+' sign at both battery terminals. Connect the black jump lead to the negative terminal of the classic's battery, ensuring that the other end is kept away from the red lead and from the bodywork of both cars. Now connect the free end of the black lead to an earth point on the engine or body of the donor vehicle – not to the negative terminal of the donor battery. Start the donor car, and if you have an assistant get them to hold the donor car's engine at a fast idle while you start the car with the flat battery. As soon as you have the faulty car running, disconnect the black jump lead from the donor car and keep the free end away from both cars while you remove the other end from the classic's battery. You can then remove the red jump lead, either end first.

There is a good reason for this sequence. When a battery is charged it gives off a small amount of hydrogen, which is potentially explosive. There will be a small spark when you make the last connection between the two cars, and when you remove the first jump lead to break the circuit. It makes sense to keep this spark as far away from the charging battery as possible, which means it should be at the donor vehicle. Making the negative connection on the donor at an earth point rather than directly to the battery post removes the spark from the vicinity of the donor battery.

An alternative to using another car is to use a mains-powered 'starter/charger' or a portable booster battery. Because the leads are already connected to their 'donor' battery the sequence described cannot be used. The safest way to connect them is to use an earth point away from the classic's battery rather than using the battery terminal itself.

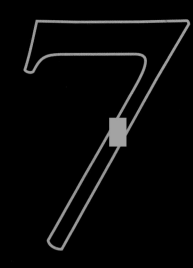

Enjoy your classic

Get the best from **your classic**

We started by saying that there are all sorts of classic cars and all sorts of classic car enthusiasts, with differing interests and varying levels of mechanical knowledge. So it follows that there are plenty of different ways of using your classic, and plenty of opportunities for enjoying it. It might be enough simply to have a wonderful old machine in the garage which comes out at summer weekends and warm evenings, for a gentle jaunt to a local pub or a trundle round the countryside. Lots of classics get used this way, and they bring enormous enjoyment to their owners – and, it should not be forgotten, to the very many other people who are stirred

by the sight of an old car on the road. But the opportunities for using and enjoying your classic go much further.

For instance, you can take part in various different forms of motor sport, from auto tests and trials to hillclimbs, sprints and circuit races. If that sounds a bit too serious but you still like the idea of driving a classic sports car the way it was intended to be driven, you can try a non-competitive track day, where you can explore your cars limits in safety. Or if less strenuous entertainment is the order of the day you can get involved in the many shows and social events which are organised every year, many of them by classic car clubs.

Joining the club

Practically all classics are supported by an owners' club. Membership of a club offers a number of important benefits, not the least of them being the community spirit that prevails: when you're faced with a problem, it is comforting to know that you are not alone, and that there are people who can help.

If you ask classic car owners why they belong to a club, a lot of them will cite insurance deals as the reason – many clubs have special schemes, and the discounts can often be greater than the club's annual membership fee. Sometimes dealers and specialists will give discounts to club members, and they may advertise sales and special deals in club magazines before they become more widely publicised, so members can get to hear about the best deals first.

Many clubs run their own parts supply operations which assist members to find elusive spares. This can range from putting buyers and sellers in contact with each other and recommending sources of supply, to organising the remanufacture or reconditioning of important parts.

Most clubs have knowledgeable technical officers to help with any problems you might have, and publish informative magazines to keep you in touch with other members and with the specialists that can help you look after your car. The magazines are also an excellent source of cars for sale.

Car clubs also organise regular meetings where you can meet other owners, and this social aspect is one of the biggest reasons for joining a club. You can swap advice and information, or simply meet up with like-minded people for a chat. The car clubs are the driving force behind a vast number of shows and motor sport events in the UK and the rest of the world.

Nothing stops you from being a member of more than one club, and often there will be several which are appropriate. To choose between them, start by looking at the benefits the club offers and see how they relate to the way you intend to use the car. If your car is under restoration, a good parts service and knowledgeable technical officers might be what you need. If you are planning to race the car, you might want to join a club which

organises championships for its members – and so on. Try to find out from existing members which club provides the best support for your model.

The appeal of a one-make or one-model club is obvious, but there are other organisations which are worth considering. Local classic car clubs are usually open to drivers of all classics, and are usually strong on the social side with regular local meetings and events. There are also clubs which cater for specific types of car – police cars, commercial vehicles, vintage cars and so on.

All but the very largest clubs are run by unpaid volunteers. Even if a contact telephone number is published, you may not be able to reach anyone during the day. Leave a message if there is an answerphone, or call in the evening (up to about 9pm is generally acceptable). E-mail is a good alternative.

A recent trend is the introduction of internet-based car owners' communities, either offshoots of existing clubs or separate entities. Often these include lively forums full of opinions, which can be a quick and easy way to discuss problems with other owners and find practical solutions born of long experience.

BELOW Club events are generally restricted to one marque or model: it's not often that you will see this many Mercedes SLs in one place *(DaimlerChrysler)*

Car shows

ABOVE Static displays sometimes accompany sporting events. Here a Porsche 911 is on show at the Goodwood Festival of Speed

RIGHT Classics of all types and all ages line up together at shows: a Ford Zephyr heads a line-up of classic saloons

On practically every weekend in the summer you will find local shows at car museums, showgrounds and stately homes in the UK, either dedicated classic car events or more general transport shows which include a section on classic and vintage vehicles. The smaller, local events often struggle to attract enough exhibitors, and will welcome you with open arms if you want to display your classic (or preferably a group of cars, perhaps from the local branch of a club). The big classic car shows have the opposite problem, with more exhibitors than space, and at these shows you will have to pay for your space.

In many countries, annual national or international classic car shows attract hundreds or thousands of cars, and enthusiasts flock in to see them. Often these events will include trade areas (selling car parts, memorabilia and books) and the automotive equivalent of a beauty queen contest – a concours.

Concours d'élégance

The term concours d'élégance is misleading, because these days elegance really has very little to do with it. The experts judging these competitions look for condition and preparation, with prizes awarded for the best cars. Big concours events are major shows in their own right, one of the biggest and best known being the Pebble Beach Concours d'Élégance in the US, which has been staged annually since 1950. Also well known were the Louis Vuitton Classic events held in France, Britain and once in the US, though from 2006 these are being replaced by an award recognising the best of the winners in other major concours events. The Concórso d'Elegànza Villa d'Este in Italy is another high-end event, but not all concours are dripping with

such high levels of investment and social standing: there are concours at most car shows and club events.

Very often concours-winning cars are in astonishing condition and frequently much better presented than they ever were when new. Concours enthusiasts spend vast amounts of time, and often a lot of money, restoring cars to showroom condition, correct in every detail and spotlessly clean. It is one way of enjoying a classic car, and from a spectator's standpoint it can be interesting to see cars in their original condition and to appreciate the effort that has gone into restoring and preparing them. Personally, I'd rather use my classic than trailer it around and polish it, but the choice is yours.

BELOW In Europe one of the biggest concours is the Concórso d'Elegànza at the Villa d'Este *(BMW)*

Motor sport

Many people like the idea of competing in their classic, but are often put off by the costs, the complication and the potential for damage. There are ways to minimise all three, however, and there are so many branches of motor sport that there's something suitable for almost everyone.

Circuit racing is the best-known form of motor sport, of course, and club events take in everything from pre-war sports cars to modified modern machines. On the track the competition is every bit as serious as it is in mainstream motor racing, and in some classes considerable sums are spent on car preparation, but there are numerous club categories where you can take part without needing costly modifications to your car. And the atmosphere is generally one of friendly rivalry.

Circuit racing is not cheap, however, and the more seriously you take it the more expensive it gets. Sprints and speed hill climbs, collectively known as 'speed events', are a cheaper alternative. One car runs at a time against the clock on a short course and the best time in each engine capacity or age class wins. Road-going classes require only a few safety modifications, and it is perfectly feasible to drive your classic to the event, compete, and

drive home. Because cars compete one at a time, organisers are often prepared to accept entries by two drivers sharing one car. The amount of competitive driving is small compared to a circuit race meeting, maybe five runs per driver in a day, each one probably lasting under a minute, but the excitement and adrenaline can reach even higher levels than in racing. In speed events there's no time to play yourself in, as there is in a race – you have to be fully committed from the start.

There is sometimes confusion about the term 'hillclimbing' because some people take that to mean the kind of event where cars battle up grassy slopes or unmade roads, trying to avoid clipping marker posts which define the course. In such events the winner is the driver with the lowest penalty score. These are, in fact, known as trials, and they are often popular with classic car owners. Little car preparation is required and drivers need no personal safety equipment because speeds are low, so you can take part in trials relatively cheaply. Passengers are allowed, too, and play a vital role by 'bouncing' the car through slippery sections. The best known is the Motor Cycle Club's Lands End Trial, held each spring.

Autotests, sometimes called driving tests, are another competition where cars run singly against the clock, this time speeding around a tight course laid out on a flat metalled area. The course

BELOW In sprints and hill climbs cars run singly, against the clock

generally includes slaloms through cones, handbrake turns around cones, reversing into boxes made of (you guessed) cones and precision braking tests. Maximum speeds are low, but autotests are great fun and an excellent test of driving skill. Small, wieldy sports cars such as MG Midgets excel at these events.

Classic sports cars such as Porsche 911s, Big Healeys and Sunbeam Tigers are often seen in another branch of motor sport, historic rallying, which is run along the same lines as mainstream rallying but with classes based on age and engine capacity. In addition to loose-surface 'stage rallying' which generally takes place during the course of one day there are long navigational events on metalled roads, often billed as 'reliability trials'. One of the most famous is LEJOG, the Land's End to John o'Groats Reliability Trial, an extraordinary three-day test of endurance for classic cars and their drivers run by the Historic Endurance Rallying Organisation. Even longer events can encompass many different countries and last for weeks, and rank as some of the most epic motoring events ever staged.

Getting started

In Britain, motor sport is controlled by the Motor Sport Association, and competitors need to apply to the MSA for a competition licence before they can compete. Along with the licence you get the MSA's yearbook – the famous 'Blue Book' – which is the sport's bible. If you are buying a car specifically for competition, the class structure may influence your choice of engine size or age: generally it is better to be at the top end of the engine size range, and the young end of the age range. But the point of the class system is that it levels the playing field to some degree, so it is really only worth considering if you are going all out for class wins, rather than simply enjoying yourself.

The regulations will detail some modifications which are required, and further modifications which are allowable. Usually the former are aimed at improving safety, while the latter will make your car quicker and more competitive should you choose to take advantage of them. At the lower levels, at least, autotests and speed events generally have fairly relaxed safety requirements because you will only be travelling at the kind of speeds you can reach on the road, and each car runs alone. Roll-over bars may be optional (though recommended), race seats may not be required and standard road seat belts may be acceptable. Circuit racing is generally seen as potentially more dangerous because you are racing other cars at higher speeds, so the minimum standards are higher – FIA approved roll bars, safety

electrical cut-off switches, approved race seats with full harnesses and so on.

Should you choose to go further with modifications to your car it makes sense to talk to marque experts to get a better idea of the car's competition weak points and potential. This allows you to get the best value for your preparation budget. If you decide to entrust preparation of your car to a professional, look for one with a track record of building winning cars in the sporting discipline you wish to enter.

Advice about driving techniques could fill several books, and indeed has done, but three oft-quoted adages are a good place for the beginner to start. Keep in mind that 'to finish first you first have to finish', 'brake early to avoid disappointment' and 'always keep one foot on a pedal'.

Driver's equipment

Consult the Blue Book and you will find that the minimum standards for a driver's personal safety equipment vary in the same way as the minimum standards for car preparation. The rules might say you can save money by wearing a race suit which is cheaper but not so effective at protecting you in a fire, and other fireproof gear (socks, balaclava, boots, gloves) may be optional. But how much do you value your safety? It makes more sense to invest in the best fireproof gear you can afford, because better-quality racewear will not only protect you better in an accident – it will also be less irritating to use, and more comfortable to wear.

The same applies to your crash helmet. Cheap helmets will pass the regulations, but a better-quality item will fit better and be more comfortable. Whatever you choose to spend, make sure you try on a helmet before you buy it – and keep it on for some time. It should be as snug as possible without being so small it gives you a headache.

ABOVE Classic racing can be just as spectacular as modern motor sport – often better

Track **days**

If you are keen to drive on a circuit but not so keen on the cut and thrust of competition, consider a track day. Many circuits now offer mid-week sessions for road cars which are relatively cheap, allowing you to drive your sports car at speed without the risks associated with road driving – and without the speed limits imposed on the road. Lap timing is frowned on: the idea is to enjoy handling your car on a circuit, rather than to be looking for the last tenth of a second improvement in lap time.

Track days are another event often organised by car clubs (or by specialist track day companies on behalf of the clubs) giving you another chance to meet up with like-minded owners. Little modification and preparation of your car is required, unlike most forms of racing, but if you regularly use your sports car for track work it makes sense to consider the tyres and brakes carefully. You may want to keep a set of tyres specifically for track use – or at least increase the tyre pressures before you venture out on track. Drivers and passengers are required to wear crash helmets, which organisers often have available for

hire – though it makes sense to buy your own if you plan to do lots of events. A comfortable helmet will make the experience all the more enjoyable.

In some cases you don't even need to find an organised track day. Some circuits, most famously the epic 14-mile Nürburgring Nordschleife, allow drivers to turn up and drive on the circuit after payment of a small fee. You can run your classic at the Nürburgring for just €15 (about £10 or US$18) per lap, and the circuit is open in the afternoon on many days during each month, and for a short session on most evenings. There are also 'Ring taxies' to take you round the circuit to show you the way before you have a go yourself. Some other famous circuits, like Le Mans, Spa-Francorchamps, Dundrod, the Isle of Man TT course and the Monaco Grand Prix circuit use public roads at least in part, and you can drive on these (at more sensible speeds) when racing is not in progress. There are also a number of disused road circuits which you can follow on public roads, such as the Ulster Tourist Trophy course at Newtownards in Northern Ireland and the former French Grand Prix circuit at Reims.

BELOW Track days provide an opportunity to explore the limits of your classic in relative safety *(Jaguar)*

Touring at home and abroad

Every year there are countless tours and runs organised by car clubs and specialist companies, taking convoys of classic cars through interesting scenery and sometimes including runs around famous racing circuits or visits to car shows or to motor museums such as Britain's National Motor Museum at Beaulieu, and the Haynes Museum at Sparkford in Somerset. The pace of these events is usually gentle, the emphasis being on enjoying the drive rather than breaking any speed records. Runs like these vary from short trips lasting no more than a day to 1,000-mile European tours. And every year hundreds of sports cars converge on major motor sport events, in particular the Le Mans 24-hour race – often in organised convoys of similar cars and like-minded enthusiasts.

Doing it yourself rather than relying on someone else's itinerary brings greater flexibility – you can go where you want, when you want, at the speed you prefer.

Preparing for tours

Montagu Napier, of early British motor car fame, apparently hated carrying luggage when touring and would pack nothing more than a toothbrush. Upon arrival at a hotel he would despatch the

staff to buy pyjamas, clean shirts and underwear as appropriate, and his travel-stained garments would be left in the hotel trash.

Few classic car owners will approach a tour in such a minimalist fashion, and in any case many countries have regulations these days about items you must carry. Not pyjamas and clean shirts, but a warning triangle (Cyprus apparently requires you to carry two of them), spare bulbs, a fire extinguisher, or a first aid kit. It's also prudent to carry some·spares and tools, as described in Chapter 6. You'll need to carry your driving licence and, for some countries, an International Driving Permit. You can also be asked to produce your vehicle registration document, insurance certificate and passport – but make sure these are kept with you rather than left in the car, as they make it easier for a car thief to dispose of the vehicle.

How much personal luggage you take will depend on the length of your tour and the carrying capacity of your classic. There is little point skimping so much that you are uncomfortable or irritated by what you don't have, but equally there is no point carrying lots of things you never use.

ABOVE Classic tours attract a huge variety of classic cars from humble saloons to exotic sports cars *(LAT)*

Earning money with your classic

Can a classic car earn its keep? One way is to hire out your car for weddings, assuming you have a classic which looks the part and has space for bride and groom in the back. Reliability is vital, so you need to make sure the car is absolutely spot-on mechanically. You will also need to check that your insurance covers you for hiring out your vehicle – many policies do not.

Another way to earn money from your classic is to join an agency offering old cars as period props for TV and film productions. Again, reliability is important because a static classic could halt shooting, and that could cost the production company huge sums. Make sure your insurance cover is up to scratch, and find out exactly what your car will be used for, who will drive and who will pay for any damage. If possible, be there on the day, but try to keep out of the way. All sorts of classics are needed, so don't imagine only rarities and exotica are of interest – everyday cars are often needed for street scenes, and period panel vans are particularly sought after because they can be parked up to hide immovable modern street furniture like road signs and advertising hoardings.

Using a classic

It is possible to use a classic car as your everyday transport, and lots of people do. In some cases simple modifications can make life a lot easier, particularly during the winter months, and these are covered in Chapter 4.

Particularly worthwhile will be to upgrade the charging system, perhaps fitting an alternator in place of a dynamo, and to think about switching to halogen lights. Depending on the pros and cons of your particular car you might also think about improvements to the brake system, or engine modifications allowing you to run on unleaded fuel.

Leaving a classic unattended in a public car park can be risky, so choose carefully where you park. Try to park in a well-lit area, ideally close to a road or footpath where there is a constant stream of people rather than in a dark area away from passers-by, where a thief can work unnoticed.

Of course there are drawbacks, from the additional maintenance requirements to the joys of draughty convertibles in winter, but for many classic car owners – me included – the sheer enjoyment of driving a classic outweighs the irritations.

OPPOSITE Period films and TV dramas constantly use classic cars – but before you get involved make sure you know how your car will be used *(BBC)*

BELOW It's perfectly possible to use a classic every day, provided you choose the right car and are aware of the limitations

50 classics
to consider

Finding 50 interesting, popular classic cars to feature was not difficult: it was deciding what to leave out that was the problem. There are hundreds of fascinating cars out there and, as we have already said, different cars will appeal to different people. Those I have chosen are cars which have a considerable following both in the UK and the rest of the world, and for the most part I have restricted the list to relatively affordable machinery rather than devote space to exotics we would all like to have but will never own – though a few of the cheapest Astons and Ferraris do make it onto the list.

If your favourite classic, or the car you are thinking of buying, does not feature on the list, you should not take that as an indication that the car is not worthy. Every classic car has its own blend of style, character, comfort, performance and reliability: it is up to you to choose which of those traits is most important to you, and this list is no more than a starting point.

Notes on the entries

Because of space limitations only major model changes are noted. For most cars there will have been numerous minor changes during production.

SPECIFICATIONS Where there are several models or engine sizes, a typical specification, representative of one popular model, has been given. Specifications generally relate to UK and European models; cars for the US market may have lower power outputs and different equipment because of local emissions and safety regulations.

PRICE RANGE Any attempt to provide specific prices in a listing such as this is futile: even if they were correct at the time of going to press they would be out of date by the time the book was on sale. And, in any case, values vary depending on the country in which the car is located, whether the seller is a dealer or a private individual, and many other factors. The guide given here indicates the relative prices of the cars in our list: more **£** means more expensive. Cars with a single **£** are very affordable, those rated **£££££** might carry price tags most of us would expect to see on a house. The rating gives a guide to the value of cars in good, but not concours-standard condition – cars in very good condition, and rare models, will be worth more.

COLLECTORS'S RATING How collectable is this car? The rating will reflect the car's rarity, reputation and desirability. Cars rated ★ are of interest only to a small number of dedicated enthusiasts, while those rated ★★★★★ are much sought-after.

DRIVER'S RATING What is it like to drive? An overall rating of the car's road manners, taking into account many different factors – acceleration, braking, roadholding, ride comfort, cruising ability, refinement, visibility and ease of control. A ★ rating indicates cars which are less satisfying to drive, while a ★★★★★ rating denotes the kind of cars we all want to drive.

MAINTENANCE AND SPARES Cars with a ★ rating may need frequent maintenance, they may be complex and fiddly to work on, and they may require special tools or professional garage equipment for many jobs. Spare parts might be difficult to find – even service consumables like air filters might be a problem. A ★★★★★ rating indicates that the car is easy to service and repair, and finding spares is no problem. The cars in this list tend to be reasonably well-served by specialists or even, in a few cases, the original manufacturer.

ALTERNATIVES For each classic I list alternatives which are either direct rivals or cars which are slightly different, but might appeal to the same sort of buyer.

BELOW One of the more affordable classic sports cars, the MG Midget

ALFA ROMEO 105-SERIES COUPÉ
Two-plus-two coupé and convertible, 1964–77

Confusing variety of names from original Giulia Sprint GT to the final 2000GTV, but the basic recipe remained the same throughout: neat Giugiaro-designed body, running gear from 105-series Giulia saloon and classic twin-cam engine in capacities ranging from 1290cc to 1962cc. Quick, characterful and deliciously well balanced, they demonstrate all that is best about classic Alfas. Sadly, they also share classic Alfa drawbacks: the battle against rust never ends. The lightweight GTA, built for touring car racing, is the ultimate version (lesser cars are often rebuilt as replicas) while the GTC is an elegant four-seat convertible – both are rare and expensive. Alfisti regard the 1750 as the optimum engine – sweeter than the 2000, and with more power than the smaller units.

Specifications (1750GTV)
Construction	Unitary steel body
Engine	1779cc in-line four, twin overhead cam, 132bhp (SAE gross) at 5,500rpm
Transmission	Five-speed manual gearbox, rear-wheel drive
Suspension	Front: Double-wishbones, coil springs, telescopic dampers and anti-roll bar
	Rear: Live axle, coil springs, trailing arms, A-bracket, telescopic dampers and anti-roll bar
Brakes	Discs all round, servo assisted
Wheels/tyres	5.5x14in steel wheels, 165R14 tyres
Performance	0–60mph: 9.5sec. Top speed 115mph
Price range	££
Collector's rating	★★★★
Driver's rating	★★★★
Maintenance & spares	★★★★
Alternatives	Lancia Fulvia coupé, BMW 2002

ALFA ROMEO DUETTO/SPIDER
Two-seat sports, 1966–93

This long-running sports car from the Alfa Giulia family is an attractive package. Launched in 1966 as the 1600 Duetto, with 'boat tail' body by Pininfarina, which was not universally acclaimed but wore well, and the engineering underneath was Alfa's usual top-class standard. Renamed Spider in 1967, and the 1750 engine became standard the same year – later there was a 1300 Spider Junior. Definitive vertical tail body introduced in 1970, and 2000 engine a year later. Beware asthmatic US-market cars with de-smogged engines and impact bumpers. Imports into the UK ceased in 1977, but converted left-hand-drive cars were available from specialists and Alfa relented in the 1980s as roadsters became popular again. Dubious 1980s styling revisions were cleaned up on the Series 4 of 1989. Rust, as always, is the big problem.

Specifications (1600 Duetto)
Construction	Unitary steel body
Engine	1570cc in-line four, twin overhead cam, 109bhp (SAE gross) at 6,000rpm
Transmission	Five-speed manual gearbox, rear-wheel drive
Suspension	Front: Double-wishbones, coil springs, telescopic dampers and anti-roll bar
	Rear: Live axle, coil springs, trailing arms, A-bracket, telescopic dampers and anti-roll bar
Brakes	Discs all round
Wheels/tyres	4.5x15in steel wheels, 155R15 tyres
Performance	0–60mph: 11sec. Top speed: 115mph
Price range	££
Collector's rating	★★★★
Driver's rating	★★★★
Maintenance & spares	★★★★
Alternatives	Fiat 124 Spider, MGB Roadster, Triumph TRs

ASTON MARTIN DB4/5/6
Two-plus-two GTs and convertibles, 1958–70

The definitive post-war Aston Martin, with new 3.7-litre Tadek Marek six-cylinder engine, Harold Beach platform chassis and bodywork based on Touring of Milan's Superleggera system. DB4 of 1958 became Series 2 with larger sump and front-hinged bonnet introduced in 1960, Series 3 (new rear lights) and Series 4 (new grille and rear lights) in 1961. Series 5 had higher roof and longer wheelbase. DB5 with 4-litre engine from 1963 (made famous by its appearance in the James Bond film *Goldfinger*). DB6 of 1965 roomier, but at the expense of frumpier styling. High-performance 'Vantage' engine options available for all types, but don't believe the inflated SAE gross horsepower figures. Convertibles also available, using the Volante name from 1965. DB4GT is shorter, faster and even more expensive.

Specifications (DB5)
Construction	Steel platform chassis, tubular steel body frame with aluminium panels
Engine	3995cc in-line six-cylinder, twin overhead cam, 282bhp at 5,500rpm
Transmission	Four-speed manual with overdrive or five-speed ZF manual, rear-wheel drive
Suspension	Front: Double-wishbone, coil springs, telescopic dampers
	Rear: Live axle, trailing links and Watt link, coil springs, lever-arm dampers
Brakes	Discs all round. Servo assistance
Wheels/tyres	5.5x15in wire wheels, 6.7-15 cross-ply tyres
Performance	0–60mph: 8 seconds. Top speed: 145mph
Price range	£££££
Collector's rating	★★★★★
Driver's rating	★★★★★
Maintenance & spares	★★★
Alternatives	Jaguar E-type, Ferrari 275GTB, AC 428

ASTON MARTIN DBS/V8
Two-plus-two GT and convertible, 1967–89

Stop-gap DBS carried over the DB6's 4-litre straight-six engine into a new William Towns-styled body while the delayed V8 was being developed. Still a 140mph car, and when the V8 arrived in 1969 it proved to be searingly fast. Revised front end from 1973, by which time David Brown had sold Aston Martin and officially the cars were no longer DBs. Six-cylinder cars continued until the end of 1973, simply known as Vantage. Weber carburettors replaced Bosch injection on the V8 that year. High performance Vantage announced in 1977, with drophead Volante following the year after. Weber-Marelli fuel injection was fitted in 1986, and the same year Aston announced a short run of Vantage Zagato two-seaters. V8 models were the mainstay of Aston's production until the Virage came along in 1989.

Specifications (V8)
Construction	Steel platform chassis, box-section body frame with aluminium panels
Engine	5340cc V8, twin overhead cams per bank, approximately 350bhp at 6,000rpm
Transmission	Five-speed ZF manual or three-speed Chrysler Torqueflite automatic, rear-wheel drive
Suspension	Front: Double-wishbone, coil springs, telescopic dampers
	Rear: De Dion axle, coil springs, telescopic dampers
Brakes	Discs all round, inboard at rear. Servo assistance
Wheels/tyres	7x15in alloy wheels, Avon radial tyres
Performance	0–60mph: 7.5 seconds. Top speed: 145mph
Price range	££££
Collector's rating	★★★★★
Driver's rating	★★★★★
Maintenance & spares	★★★★
Alternatives	Jensen Interceptor, Ferrari 400

AUDI QUATTRO
Four-seat coupés, 1980–91

The car which made popular the idea of four-wheel drive for on-road performance cars. Based on the drivetrain of the off-road VW Iltis, the quattro (Audi always insisted on a lowercase 'q') blended unassailable grip with turbo power to produce a formidable rally machine and an all-weather supercar. Single-cam 2144cc engine from launch in 1980, then revisions in 1983: pneumatic diff locking, revised gear ratios and anti-lock brakes. Very rare Sport quattro of 1984 was a shorter and more powerful homologation special, and spawned amazing S1 rally car with huge wings and vast power (over 500bhp). Torsen centre differential adopted in 1988. From 1990 the quattros gained a 20-valve engine and revised transmission, until production ended in 1991. An important car in historical terms, and still an impressive performance machine.

Specifications (20 valve)
Construction	Unitary steel body
Engine	2226cc turbocharged in-line five, twin overhead cam, 220bhp at 5,900rpm
Transmission	Five-speed manual, four-wheel drive with Torsen centre differential and lockable rear differential
Suspension	MacPherson struts all round, anti-roll bars front and rear
Brakes	Discs all round, ventilated at front, anti-lock system
Wheels/tyres	8Jx15 alloy wheels, 215/50R15 tyres
Performance	0–60mph: 5.9 seconds. Top speed: 143mph
Price range	££
Collector's rating	★★★★
Driver's rating	★★★★★
Maintenance & spares	★★★
Alternatives	Lancia Delta Integrale, Ford Sierra/Escort Cosworth, Opel Ascona/Manta 400

AUSTIN-HEALEY 100/3000
Two-seat and two-plus-two sports, 1954–68

Austin mechanicals underpinned the stylish and swift Healey Hundred sports car, which was famously adopted by Austin overnight at the London Motor Show. Original 2660cc 100, high-performance 100M and super-rare 100S (beware of fakes) were followed by smoother but slower 100/6 with 2639cc six-cylinder engine in 1956. Definitive Austin-Healey 3000 arrived in 1959, the 124bhp 2912cc engine of the 'Big Healey' giving it a significant power advantage over the TR3 and MGA competition. Triple-carb MkII, MkIIa with curved screen and wind-up windows and MkIII with 148bhp engine followed. Tens of thousands were built, many of them exported to America, while in Britain the Healeys had a 'tough and capable' image thanks to BMC rally successes. Still very popular, and values reflect that: final MkIII 3000 is well into E-type territory, pricewise.

Specifications (3000 MkIIa)
Construction	Steel ladder chassis with steel body
Engine	2912cc in-line six-cylinder, pushrod overhead valve, 130bhp (SAE net) at 4,650rpm
Transmission	Four-speed manual gearbox with overdrive on 3rd and 4th, rear-wheel drive
Suspension	Front: Lower wishbone, coil spring and lever-arm damper, anti-roll bar
	Rear: Live axle with semi-elliptic leaf springs and Panhard rod
Brakes	Disc front, drum rear
Wheels/tyres	4x15 steel wheels, 5.9-15 Dunlop RS5 cross-ply
Performance	0–60mph: 10.5sec. Top speed: 115mph
Price range	££££
Collector's rating	★★★★★
Driver's rating	★★★★
Maintenance & spares	★★★★
Alternatives	Triumph TR4/5/6, MGB/C, Sunbeam Alpine

AUSTIN-HEALEY SPRITE/MG MIDGET
Two-seat sports, 1958–80

Geoffrey Healey designed the Sprite as a baby brother to the successful Austin-Healey 100, but it's better known today as the latterday MG Midget. The 'Spridget', as the Healey and MG versions are collectively known, is one of the most enjoyable and affordable classic sports cars of all. Although its straight-line performance figures are nothing to get very excited about today, its fun-per-mile and cost-to-smile ratios are almost unbeatable. No wonder it is still so popular.

Only the first Sprites have the Frogeye/Bugeye shape largely penned by Healey body designer Gerry Coker. It's cute, and some racers prefer it because it's said to generate less air resistance than the later 'square body' shapes. Otherwise Sprite and Midget are identical but for badges and trim, only the latter surviving beyond 1970. Sprites were badged as Austins rather than Austin-Healeys from 1969–70 as the Healey contract had been terminated. Running gear is essentially Austin A35, with compact wishbone front suspension and a live axle plus BMC A-series engines of 948cc, 1098cc and ultimately 1275cc. The Midget was given a Triumph Spitfire engine in 1974 as a money-saving measure – it allowed Leyland to get both the Midget and the Spitfire through US emissions regulations without having to work on two different engines. Ugly black 'rubber' bumpers were another part of the 1974 makeover and are widely disliked, so the optimum Spridget for most people is an early-1970s 1275 of which the 'round arch' model is the best liked. Production ended in 1980.

Specifications (1275cc)

Construction	Unitary steel body
Engine	1275cc in-line four-cylinder, pushrod ohv, 70bhp at 5,800rpm
Transmission	Four-speed manual, rear-wheel drive.
Suspension	Front: Double wishbone, coil springs, lever-arm dampers. Rear: Live axle, leaf springs
Brakes	Front: Disc. Rear: Drum. Servo assistance
Wheels/tyres	5x14in steel disc wheels, 145R14 tyres
Performance	0–60mph: 12 seconds. Top speed: 100mph
Price range	£
Collector's rating	★★★
Driver's rating	★★★
Maintenance & spares	★★★★★
Alternatives	Triumph Spitfire, Mazda MX-5 Miata/Eunos Roadster, Fiat 850 Spider, Honda S800

BMW 1602/2002/TOURING
Four-seat saloons, hatchbacks and convertibles, 1966–77

'Neue Klasse' compact saloons saved BMW in the 1960s and sired two-door '02-series sports saloons, which were hugely successful in the showroom and on the race track. Progressively swifter, from initial 1600-2 to definitive 2-litre 2002, twin-carb 2002TI and rapid fuel-injected 2002tii. Successful in saloon car racing, eventually in turbocharged 2002TIK form – technology which later resurfaced as the rare 2002 Turbo road car of 1973/4. Left-hand-drive-only Turbo was quick, but tricky to handle, thanks to monstrous turbo lag, and short-lived because of 1973 oil crisis. Four-seat convertibles, by Baur, are also rare. Another option is the three-door hatchback Touring, a practical semi-estate. Replaced by the E21 3-series in the mid-1970s, though many enthusiasts continued to prefer the sharper, sportier feel of the 2002.

Specifications (2002tii)

Construction	Unitary steel body
Engine	1990cc in-line four, single overhead cam, 130bhp (SAE net) at 5,800rpm
Transmission	Four-speed manual gearbox, rear-wheel drive
Suspension	Front: MacPherson struts and anti-roll bar Rear: Semi-trailing arms, coil springs, telescopic dampers and anti-roll bar
Brakes	Disc front, drum rear. Servo assisted
Wheels/tyres	5x13in steel wheels, 165HR13 tyres
Performance	0–60mph: 8.5sec. Top speed: 117mph
Price range	££
Collector's rating	★★★
Driver's rating	★★★★
Maintenance & spares	★★★★
Alternatives	Ford Escort Twin-Cam/RS, Triumph Dolomite Sprint, Vauxhall Firenza/Magnum

BMW CS, CSi AND CSL
Four-seat coupés, 1968–77

The definitive BMW coupé, descended from the oddly-styled 2000CS of the mid-1960s. Supremely elegant styling and luxurious accommodation, and a choice of lusty 'big six' engines. Carburettors were fitted when 2500CS and 2800CS were launched in 1968, but in 1971 Bosch injection appeared on the 3.0CSi (though a carb'd 3.0CS was still available). The automatic 3.0CSA was a favourite of Beatle George Harrison, who ran his for five years in the 1970s. A lightweight CSL was built in 1972 for touring car racing, and some cars had 'Batmobile' aerodynamic devices – genuine road-going examples with all the aero kit are rare and expensive. The CSL's on-track battles with Ford's RS Capris are now the stuff of legend. Wholesale revision of the BMW range included replacement of the CS coupés by the 6-series in 1977.

Specifications (3.0CS)

Construction	Unitary steel body
Engine	2985cc in-line six-cylinder, single overhead cam, 180bhp (SAE net) at 6,000rpm
Transmission	Four-speed manual transmission, rear-wheel drive
Suspension	Front: MacPherson struts and anti-roll bar Rear: Semi-trailing arms, coil springs, telescopic dampers and anti-roll bar
Brakes	Discs all round, ventilated at front. Servo assisted
Wheels/tyres	6x14in alloy wheels, 195/70R14 tyres
Performance	0–60mph: 8.0sec. Top speed: 130mph
Price range	£££
Collector's rating	★★★★
Driver's rating	★★★★★
Maintenance & spares	★★★★
Alternatives	Mercedes-Benz SL/SLC, Jaguar XJC/XJ-S, Opel Commodore coupé, Lancia Flavia coupé

CHEVROLET CORVETTE
Two-seat sports/coupé, 1953–present

America's sports car was a bit lukewarm to begin with, but was refined through successive generations into an effective road and competition tool. Early styling had hints of Jaguar XK120, then Mercedes-Benz 300SL, but found its feet in the 1960s with the classic Bill Mitchell Sting Ray and Mako Shark shapes. All the Corvettes have glassfibre bodies on steel chassis with cruciform bracing. Six-cylinder engines to start with, but V8s from 1955 were available in a multitude of options over the years, up to full-house 7-litre V8s which delivered blistering performance in a straight line. Handling was sorted by independent rear suspension from 1963, and disc brakes were available from 1965. Corvettes still form part of GM's line-up in the US and increasingly in Europe, with the new-generation C6 model.

Specifications (1963 347ci Sting Ray)

Engine	5346cc V8, pushrod overhead valve, 360bhp (SAE gross) at 6,000rpm
Transmission	Four-speed manual gearbox, optional three-speed automatic. Rear-wheel drive
Suspension	Front: Wishbones, coil springs and anti-roll bar, telescopic dampers Rear: Lower wishbones, transverse leaf spring, telescopic dampers
Brakes	Drums all round, servo assisted
Wheels/tyres	15in centre-lock alloy wheels, 7.10x15 or 7.60x15 tyres
Performance	0–60mph: 6.2sec. Top speed: 147mph
Price range	££££
Collector's rating	★★★★
Driver's rating	★★★★
Maintenance & spares	★★★★
Alternatives	Jaguar E-type, Ford Mustang

CITROËN DS/ID
Four-seat saloons, 1955–75

Extraordinary rocket ship of a saloon car that makes jaws drop today, so imagine the impact it had back in 1955 when it replaced the long-running Traction Avant (itself innovative in its day). Aerodynamic shape makes for refined and economical cruising on the Routes Nationales, while sophisticated hydro-pneumatic suspension provides the ultimate magic-carpet ride. The hydraulic system also powers the brakes (operated by a pressure-sensitive button on the floor), assists the steering and operates the clutch, and can even jack the car up for wheel-changing. Only the ancient, unrefined engines let the side down. Hydraulics widely feared, then as now, which led to the introduction of the cheaper and slightly simpler ID, but actually the system is very reliable. Complexity means expert care is needed for some jobs.

Specifications (DS23 Pallas)

Construction	Unitary steel structure with unstressed outer panels
Engine	2347cc in-line four, pushrod overhead valve, 130bhp (DIN) at 5,250rpm
Transmission	Five-speed manual gearbox with column change, front-wheel drive
Suspension	Front: Double wishbones with hydro-pneumatic struts and anti-roll bar. Rear: Trailing arms with hydro-pneumatic struts and anti-roll bar. Hydraulic systems interconnected front to rear
Brakes	Disc front, drum rear. Hydraulic power assistance
Wheels/tyres	5.5x380 steel wheels, Michelin XAS 185HR380 tyres
Performance	0–60mph: 10.5sec. Top speed: 120mph
Price range	££
Collector's rating	★★★★
Driver's rating	★★★★
Maintenance & spares	★★★★
Alternatives	Citroën CX, Mercedes-Benz W115/W123

FERRARI 308GT4

Two-plus-two coupé, 1973–80

Unusual for a Ferrari in that it seats four (just) and that the styling was by Bertone rather than Pininfarina. Wedge-shaped, cab-forward styling by Marcello Gandini is distinctive and has aged well, though at the time many preferred the Pininfarina curves of its predecessor, the Dino 246. Dino name continued on 308 GT4 at first, but the car gained Ferrari badges in 1976. The 3-litre V8 provides sparkling performance and all the right noises, though handling can be tricky on the limit. Cheap, for a Ferrari, which can mean that it attracts owners without the commitment and depth of pockets necessary to cope when the big bills come along, as inevitably they will. But the 308 GT4 is a characterful and under-rated machine.

Specifications (308GT4)

Construction	Tubular steel chassis, steel body with aluminium bonnet and engine cover
Engine	2927cc V8, twin overhead camshafts per bank, 250bhp at 7,700rpm
Transmission	Five-speed manual, rear-wheel-drive
Suspension	Front: Double wishbones, coil springs and telescopic dampers and anti-roll bar. Rear: Double wishbones, coil springs, telescopic dampers and anti-roll bar
Brakes	Ventilated discs all round, with servo assistance
Wheels/tyres	7.5x14in alloys, 205/70VR14 tyres
Performance	0–60mph: 6.4sec. Top speed: 152mph
Price range	££££
Collector's rating	★★★★
Driver's rating	★★★★★
Maintenance & spares	★★★
Alternatives	Ferrari Mondial, Maserati Merak, Lamborghini Urracco

FERRARI 308/328 GTB/S

Two-seat sports/coupé, 1975-81

Archetypal 1970s Ferrari, the GTB is the true successor to the two-seat Dino 246GT. Arrived two years after the 308GT4, which donated its four-cam V8 engine (308 indicating 3.0-litres and 8 cylinders) and basic chassis design, though GTB had a shortened wheelbase. Faultless styling is by Pininfarina. Tubular steel chassis originally carried a mixture of steel and glassfibre panels, but in 1977 the GTB went all-steel, and the following year a targa-top 308GTS was added. Also an Italy-only 208 tax special. Final carb engines were down on power because of more stringent emission-controls, and fuel-injection motors for 1980 were cleaner but even less powerful, though four-valve heads on the Quattrovalvole (or 'QV') models in 1983 restored some of the output. Revised 3.2-litre 328 from 1985, replaced by 348 in 1989. Characterful, capable and surprisingly practical.

Specifications (308GTBi Quattrovalvole)

Construction	Tubular steel chassis, steel body
Engine	2927cc V8, twin overhead camshafts per bank, 240bhp (DIN) at 7,000rpm
Transmission	Five-speed manual, rear wheel drive
Suspension	Front: Double wishbones, coil springs and telescopic dampers and anti-roll bar. Rear: Double wishbones, coil springs, telescopic dampers and anti-roll bar
Brakes	Ventilated discs all round, with servo assistance
Wheels/tyres	165TR390 alloys, 220/55VR390 Michelin TRX tyres
Performance	0–60mph: 6.4sec. Top speed: 155mph
Price range	£££££
Collector's rating	★★★★★
Driver's rating	★★★★★
Maintenance & spares	★★★★
Alternatives	Porsche 911, Lotus Esprit, BMW M1

FIAT X1/9

Two-seat sports, 1972–88

Bertone's 'baby Ferrari' offers mid-engined handling precision in a small and cheap package. Surprisingly comfortable and practical (with luggage space in the nose and tail) but noise level can be wearing. Early cars, rare now in the UK, were powered by the 1290cc Fiat 128 engine, but from 1978 the X1/9 received the 1498cc engine used in the Ritmo/Strada, and a five-speed gearbox. Even then, there was only 85bhp to play with, and in the US emissions regs resulted in as little as 67bhp. Bertone always built the bodyshells, and from 1983 they took over complete assembly as Fiat divested itself of some low-volume production burdens: Pininfarina took over the 124 Spider the same year. The X1/9 survived until 1988, when production ended with a 'Gran Finale' special edition.

Specifications (1500)

Construction	Unitary steel body
Engine	1498cc in-line four, single overhead cam, 85bhp (DIN) at 6,000rpm
Transmission	Five-speed manual gearbox, rear-wheel drive
Suspension	Front: MacPherson struts Rear: MacPherson struts
Brakes	Discs all round
Wheels/tyres	5x13in alloy wheels, 165/70SR13 tyres
Performance	0–60mph: 10sec Top speed: 110mph
Price range	£
Collector's rating	★★★
Driver's rating	★★★★
Maintenance & spares	★★★
Alternatives	Triumph TR7, Mazda MX-5, Toyota MR2

FIAT/PININFARINA SPIDER
Two-seat sports, 1966–85

Pretty Pininfarina-styled sports car based on a shortened Fiat 124 Berlina platform. Early AS-series cars have 1438cc twin-cam engines and 90bhp. BS from 1969 similar, but from 1970 there was the option of a 1608cc, 110bhp motor (BS1) with bonnet humps to clear twin-Webers. Single-carb 1592cc (CS) or 1756cc (CS1) engines from 1972–74, when production for Europe ended. North America received emissions-strangled CS2 in 1978 – 1995cc but just 87bhp, though fuel injection from 1979 boosted output to 102bhp. Fiat approved a US-market turbo kit which took power up to 122bhp. Pininfarina took over production in 1982, producing the DS-series Spider Azzura for the US and Spidereuropa for Europe, with injected 1995cc engines. Look out for Spider rarities: 1972 Spider Abarth Rally, with 128bhp engine and alloy panels (1,000 built) and supercharged 135bhp Spidereuropa VX of 1985 (500 built).

Specifications (1800)

Construction	Unitary steel body
Engine	1756cc in-line four, twin overhead cam, 116bhp at 6,000rpm
Transmission	Four-speed manual gearbox, rear-wheel drive
Suspension	Front: Double wishbones, coil springs and telescopic dampers
	Rear: Live axle with coil springs, trailing arms and Panhard rod
Brakes	Discs all round, servo-assisted
Wheels/tyres	5x13in steel or alloy, 165R13 tyres
Performance	0–60mph: 9sec. Top speed: 115mph
Price range	££
Collector's rating	★★★★
Driver's rating	★★★★
Maintenance & spares	★★★
Alternatives	Alfa Duetto/Spider, MGB, Lancia Beta Spyder

FORD ESCORT TWIN CAM AND RS Mk1/2
Four-seat sports saloons, 1968–80

Ford's mass-market saloons spawned high-performance derivatives for racing and rallying, first the Lotus-engined Escort Twin Cam and then the successful RS range beginning with the RS1600 in 1970 which went on to be highly successful in rallying. RS2000 uses bigger but less highly-strung 2-litre Pinto engine from the Mk3 Cortina, while the cheaper Mexico has a lightly-tuned 1.6-litre motor. Mk2 cars follow a similar pattern, but the rally weapon became the RS1800 (rare now in road-going trim) and the RS2000 now had a glassfibre 'shovel nose' front end. Not particularly clever in engineering terms, with carburettored engines and a cart-sprung live-axle at the back, but the hot Escorts are well sorted and great fun. There are plenty of tuning options even today.

Specifications (RS2000 Mk1)

Construction	Unitary steel body
Engine	1993cc in-line four, single overhead cam, 100bhp at 5,700rpm
Transmission	Four-speed manual gearbox, rear-wheel drive
Suspension	Front: MacPherson struts, anti-roll bar
	Rear: Live axle, radius arms, semi-elliptic leaf springs, telescopic dampers
Brakes	Disc front/drum rear, servo-assisted
Wheels/tyres	5x13in steel or alloy, 165R13 tyres
Performance	0–60mph: 9sec
	Top speed: 110mph
Price range	££
Collector's rating	★★★★
Driver's rating	★★★★
Maintenance & spares	★★★
Alternatives	BMW 2002, Alfa Giulia Sprint, Triumph Dolomite Sprint

FORD CAPRI Mk1/2/3 & CORTINA Mk1/2
Four-seat coupés, saloons and estates, 1962–82

Cortina brought Ford into the modern era and proved an enormous sales success. Enthusiasts drooled over Cortina GT and then the awesome twin-cam-engined Lotus-Cortina, but today beware of fakes. Square-styled Mk2 Cortina from 1966 spawned cult 1600E 'executive' saloon. Cortina running gear underpinned Capri coupé of 1969, famously advertised as 'the car you always promised yourself' though surely few people promised themselves the 1300. Thousands of Pinto-powered 1.6-litre and 2-litre cars sold, but Capris with 3-litre Essex and 2.8-litre Cologne V6s were Ford's performance highlights until the 1980s: rare RS2600 and RS3100 were built for racing, and later Ford's Special Vehicle Engineering team built the Capri 2.8 Injection road car. Look out for rare (less than 100) Tickford Turbo Capri.

Specifications (Capri Mk1 3000GT)

Construction	Unitary steel body
Engine	2994cc V6, pushrod overhead valve, 128bhp at 5,200rpm
Transmission	Four-speed manual gearbox, rear-wheel drive
Suspension	Front: MacPherson struts, anti-roll bar
	Rear: Live axle, radius arms, semi-elliptic leaf springs, telescopic dampers
Brakes	Disc front/drum rear, servo-assisted
Wheels/tyres	5.5x13 steel, 185HR13 tyres
Performance	0–60mph: 9.6sec. Top speed: 113mph
Price range	£–££
Collector's rating	★★★
Driver's rating	★★★
Maintenance & spares	★★★★
Alternatives	Capri: Opel Manta, Fiat 124 Spider, Vauxhall Firenza. Cortina: Hillman Avenger/Hunter, Vauxhall Viva/Magnum

FORD MUSTANG

Four-seat saloons, coupés and convertibles, 1964–1973

Lee Iacocca's sporty compact car took America by storm, offering looks, performance, a low basic price and a roster of options to entice buyers. Slow straight-sixes or punchy V8s on offer, with Shelby-developed GT-350 at the top of the range. Revised styling and big-block V8s for 1967, topped by 428ci Shelby GT-500. Bigger and heavier for 1969, with yet more power: Super Cobra Jet 428 was rated at 335bhp, but actually over 400bhp. Though not as quick off the mark as the Cobra Jets, the Boss Mustangs were better handling as they were the street versions of Ford's racing machines, with 429ci engine for NASCAR and 302ci for Trans-Am racing. As America's 'power' era ended, Mustang outputs dropped – by 1973 the top engine was a 156bhp V8, and the Mustang II of 1974 was a lukewarm replacement.

Specifications (Shelby GT-350)

Construction	Unitary steel body
Engine	4736cc (289ci) V8, pushrod overhead valve. 306bhp (SAE gross) at 6,000rpm
Transmission	Four-speed manual gearbox Rear-wheel drive
Suspension	Front: Wishbones, coil springs and anti-roll bar
	Rear: Live axle with semi-elliptic leaf springs
Brakes	Disc front, drum rear
Wheels/tyres	Several options, e.g. 6x15in alloy wheel/steel rim, 7.75x15 Goodyear tyres
Performance	0–60mph: 6.5sec. Top speed: 127mph
Price range	££–£££££
Collector's rating	★★★★
Driver's rating	★★★
Maintenance & spares	★★★★
Alternatives	Chevrolet Corvette, Chevrolet Camaro, Pontiac Firebird, Plymouth Barracuda

JAGUAR Mk1/Mk2/S-type/420 AND DAIMLER V8-250/SOVEREIGN

Four-seat saloons, 1955–68

Favourite for saloon car racing (and getaway driving) when they were new, the compact Jaguars of the 1950s and 1960s have since become classic icons. The Jaguar 2.4 of 1955 began the line, its thick window frames betraying Jaguar's first attempt at monocoque construction. Swifter 3.4 introduced in 1957. Mk2 of 1959 was restyled and offered a 3.8-litre engine option – favourite with underworld 'wheelmen' who always stole cars wearing club badges, because they were the best maintained. S-type was a half-way house between Mk2 and the big MkX – E-type/MkX independent rear suspension gave it a more comfortable ride and better grip, but the longer tail unbalanced the styling and it was heavier, so slower, than a Mk2. The 420 (not to be confused with the much larger, MkX-derived, 420G of the same period) was a further development of the S-type theme with a 4.2-litre engine and four-headlamp front end.

Daimler came under Jaguar control in 1960, and produced its own versions of the compact Jaguars from 1962. The first was the 2½-litre V8, a Mk2 fitted with the lovely Edward Turner-designed V8 engine from the SP250 and a fluted grille. The Sovereign of 1966 was a Daimler-badged 420.

From 1967 the Mk2s were revised to make them cheaper to build, with slimline bumpers and vinyl trim as standard. The 2.4 and 3.4 were renamed 240 and 340, and the smaller Daimler became the V8-250. All were replaced by Jaguar and Daimler versions of the XJ6 in 1968/69.

Specifications (3.8 Mk2)

Construction	Unitary steel body
Engine	3781cc in-line six-cylinder, twin overhead cams, 220bhp (SAE gross) at 5,500rpm
Transmission	Four-speed manual, optional overdrive or three-speed automatic, rear-wheel drive
Suspension	Front: Double wishbone, coil springs, telescopic dampers
	Rear: Live axle, trailing links and radius arms, leaf springs, telescopic dampers
Brakes	Discs all round. Servo-assistance
Wheels/tyres	5x15in wire wheels, Dunlop cross-ply tyres
Performance	0–60mph: 9 seconds Top speed: 125mph
Price range	££–£££££
Collector's rating	★★★★
Driver's rating	★★★★
Maintenance & spares	★★★★
Alternatives	Mercedes-Benz 220SE, Rover P6 3500

JAGUAR XJ6/XJ12 S1/S2 AND XJ-S
Four-seat saloons, two-plus-two coupés, 1968–96

Masterly XJ6 replaced the whole range of old-school Jaguars at a stroke in 1968. Road manners are amazing, with a supple and near-silent ride, yet precise, roll-free cornering. XJ6 had 2.8-litre or 4.2-litre XK engine, and 1972 XJ12 added ultra-refined V12 from the E-type. XJ6L and XJ12L were long-wheelbase versions. Two-door XJC coupés looked great but never sold sufficiently well, and unreliable racing versions didn't help. Series 2 models with revised styling and 3.4-litre base engine from 1973. XJ-S had a shaky start in 1975 with adverse comments about its styling, but a

renaissance in the 1980s came via 'High Efficiency' heads on the V12, new cabriolet and convertible bodies, a 3.6-litre engine option and TWR's successful racing programme. TWR later built road-going XJR-S. XJ6 replaced by XJ40 in 1986, but XJ12 continued until 1992 and XJ-S until 1996.

Specifications (XJ6 Series 2 4.2)

Construction	Unitary steel body
Engine	4235cc in-line six-cylinder, twin overhead cams, 167bhp at 4,500rpm
Transmission	Four-speed manual or three-speed automatic, rear-wheel drive.
Suspension	Front: Double wishbone, coil springs, telescopic dampers, anti-roll bar. Rear: Lower wishbones, trailing links and fixed-length driveshafts, twin coil spring/telescopic damper units
Brakes	Discs all round, inboard at rear. Servo-assistance
Wheels/tyres	6x5in steel wheels, 205/70VR15 Dunlop SP Sports tyres
Performance	0–60mph: 9 seconds. Top speed: 116mph
Price range	££
Collector's rating	★★★
Driver's rating	★★★★
Maintenance & spares	★★★★
Alternatives	XJ6/12: Mercedes-Benz S-class, BMW 7-series XJ-S: Porsche 928, Mercedes-Benz SL

JAGUAR E-TYPE
Two-seat sports, two-seat and two-plus-two coupés, 1961–75

Perhaps the most recognisable classic car of them all. Stunned press and public on its launch in 1961 for its wild shape – a refinement of the low-drag D-type racing car – and supposed 150mph top speed, plus its bargain £2,000 price tag. Early 'flat floor' 3.8s are sought after, despite improvements which made later cars better. From 1964 a 4.2-litre engine was adopted, along with a Jaguar gearbox instead of the vague and notchy Moss 'box of the 3.8. A two-plus-two coupé was added to the range in 1966, with a longer wheelbase and taller roofline which made it look gawky from some angles. Uncowled, sealed-beam headlights were adopted on the 'Series 1½' of 1967 while the Series 2 introduced late in 1968 had a larger air intake to cope with air-conditioning, now offered as an option to placate US customers.

Jaguar's new V12 engine was slotted into the Series 3 E-type of 1971. Despite the jump in capacity to 5.3-litres the E-type's top speed still hovered around the 150mph mark, though the V12 car had swifter acceleration. In this form the E-type soldiered on until 1975, when it was effectively replaced by the XJ-S.

A dozen racing 'lightweight E-types' were built in the 1960s, though many road cars have been modified as replicas since. There is a strong market for restored, rebuilt and re-engineered cars with tuned engines and many modern conveniences – at a price.

Specifications (3.8 Series 1)

Construction	Unitary steel body tub with tubular front subframe
Engine	3781cc in-line six-cylinder, twin overhead cam, 265bhp at 5,500rpm
Transmission	Four-speed manual, rear-wheel drive
Suspension	Front: Double wishbone, coil springs, telescopic dampers, anti-roll bar Rear: Lower wishbones, trailing links and fixed-length driveshafts, twin-coil spring/telescopic damper units
Brakes	Discs all round. Servo-assistance
Wheels/tyres	Wire wheels, 7.50-14 or 6.40-15 tyres
Performance	0–60mph: 7 seconds. Top speed: 150mph
Price range	££££
Collector's rating	★★★★★
Driver's rating	★★★★★
Maintenance & spares	★★★★
Alternatives	Aston Martin DB4

LANCIA DELTA HF TURBO/INTEGRALE

Four-seat hatchback, 1983–93

Giugiaro-styled Lancia hatchback was given a 130bhp 1.6-litre turbo engine in 1983 to form the HF Turbo. A 165bhp four-wheel-drive version followed in 1986, and the 185bhp Integrale followed in 1987. Integrale 16v with 200bhp was launched in 1989 and Integrale Evolution with 210bhp was launched 1991. The final mainstream version was the 1993 Evolution II with 215bhp and catalytic converters, but throughout the Integrale production run there were many special editions – be careful of fakes and 'replicas'. Delta HF Turbo and Integrale became ultra-successful rally machines in the post-Group B era, winning six consecutive World Rally Championship titles from 1987 onwards until Lancia retired from the sport. They are inspirational road cars with solidity, power and poise, but can be awful if neglected or badly rebuilt.

Specifications (Integrale 8v)

Construction	Unitary steel body
Engine	1995cc turbocharged transverse in-line four-cylinder, twin overhead cams, 185bhp at 5,000rpm
Transmission	Five-speed manual, four-wheel drive with centre epicyclic differential controlled by viscous coupling and rear Torsen-type differential
Suspension	Front: MacPherson struts, anti-roll bar. Rear: MacPherson struts, anti-roll bar
Brakes	Discs all round. Servo-assistance
Wheels/tyres	6x15in alloy wheels, 195/55R15 tyres
Performance	0–62mph: 6.4 seconds. Top speed: 133mph
Price range	£–££££
Collector's rating	★★★
Driver's rating	★★★★
Maintenance & spares	★★★
Alternatives	Audi quattro, Toyota Celica GT-Four

LAND ROVER SI/II/III

Four-wheel drive vehicle, 1948–85

World-beating four-wheel-drive vehicle developed by Rover immediately after the Second World War. Became progressively less agricultural and more comfortable over the years, relatively speaking. Choice of four-, six- and eight-cylinder engines – fours are cheapest to run, the V8 performs better. Very early Series 1 models (up to 1954) have 80in wheelbase. V8s only available from 1979 in the long 109in wheelbase, but many of the usual 88in short-wheelbase vehicles have been converted. Land Rovers are designed to be easy to work on but not quite as simple as they appear: there are traps for the unwary. Big change came with the introduction of the Ninety and One Ten from 1983, with Range Rover-style coil springs – though some diehards argue that leaf-spring Land Rovers (on sale into 1986) are still the most effective in really tough terrain.

Specifications (Series 2 petrol)

Construction	Steel ladder chassis, aluminium body panels
Engine	2286cc in-line four, pushrod overhead valve, 77bhp
Transmission	Four-speed manual gearbox, two-speed transfer gearbox and four-wheel drive
Suspension	Front: Live axle with leaf springs. Rear: Live axle with leaf springs
Brakes	Drums all round. Transmission handbrake
Wheels/tyres	5x16 steel wheels, 6.00x16 tyres
Performance	0–60mph: 25sec. Top speed: 70mph
Price range	£
Collector's rating	★★★★
Driver's rating	★★
Maintenance & spares	★★★★★
Alternatives	Jeep CJ-5/CJ-7, Toyota Landcruiser

LOTUS SEVEN, CATERHAM SEVEN

Two-seat sports, 1957–present

Remarkable road/racing machine at first using BMC, Ford or Coventry Climax engines in a simple spaceframe chassis with aluminium body panels. Replaced by Series 4 Seven of 1970 using an Elan-like backbone chassis and a GRP body. Distributor Caterham Cars took over production in 1973, quickly reverting to the more popular Series 3 cars. Caterham continues to refine the basic design (notably introducing a longer cockpit and de Dion rear suspension) and to fit ever more modern engines – currently Rover K-series units with up to 230bhp. Very rapid acceleration with almost any engine, and unrivalled road manners, but stark and uncompromising – so not for everyone. Good access to engine and suspension, hence fairly easy to work on, but watch for rusting spaceframe chassis on older cars.

Specifications (S3 1600GT)

Construction	Steel spaceframe chassis with aluminium body panels
Engine	1598cc Ford in-line four, pushrod ohv, 84bhp at 6,500rpm
Transmission	Four-speed manual gearbox, rear-wheel drive
Suspension	Front: Double wishbone, coil springs, telescopic dampers and anti-roll bar. Rear: Live axle with coil springs, radius arms, A-bracket and telescopic dampers
Brakes	Disc front, drum rear
Wheels/tyres	5.5x13 alloy wheels, 165R13 tyres
Performance	0–60mph: 7.7sec. Top speed: 100mph
Price range	£££–£££££
Collector's rating	★★★★
Driver's rating	★★★★
Maintenance & spares	★★★★
Alternatives	Westfield, Clan Crusader, Ginetta G15, Lotus Elise

LOTUS ELAN/+2

Two-seat sports, two-seat and two-plus-two coupé, 1962–74

Successor to the glassfibre monocoque Elite, the Elan earned Lotus's bread and butter in the 1960s. Originally intended to be another GRP monocoque, but sheet steel backbone chassis jury-rigged for development worked so well it was retained, with a GRP body on top and Ford-based Lotus twin-cam engine, shared with Lotus Cortina, to provide the motive power. Coupés and convertibles available, unlike hardtop-only Elite. Extraordinary roadholding despite tiny tyres, with terrific balance and adjustability and a supple ride for a sports car. Interiors are attractive, too, as Colin Chapman was aiming further upmarket, so you get a well-stocked wooden dashboard and many have electric windows. Theoretically 'big valve' SE versions are the quickest, but many cars have been rebuilt to non-standard spec. Elan Plus 2 was built as a coupé only: longer and wider, with two small rear seats.

Specifications (S4 SE)

Construction	Steel backbone chassis, glassfibre body
Engine	1558cc in-line four, twin overhead cam, 115bhp at 6,250rpm
Transmission	Four-speed manual gearbox, rear-wheel drive
Suspension	Front: Double wishbones, coil springs and anti-roll bar. Rear: Chapman struts
Brakes	Discs all round
Wheels/tyres	4.5x13 centre-lock steel wheels, 155R13 Dunlop tyres
Performance	0–60mph: 7.5sec Top speed: 120mph
Price range	££–£££
Collector's rating	★★★★
Driver's rating	★★★★★
Maintenance & spares	★★★★
Alternatives	TVR Vixen, Ginetta G15, Lotus Elite, Mazda MX-5

LOTUS ESPRIT/TURBO/V8

Two-seat coupé, 1976–2004

Long-running mid-engined Lotus began as a 2-litre, 16-valve sports coupé with brisk but not Ferrari-baiting performance. Early profile raised by an eye-catching underwater performance opposite Roger Moore in the 1977 James Bond film *The Spy Who Loved Me*. Chassis changes and a 2.2-litre engine in normally-aspirated and turbocharged versions renewed the Esprit's appeal in 1980. Sharp-edged Giugiaro styling lasted until 1988, when an in-house restyle by Peter Stevens softened the edges. In 1996 a 349bhp, 3.5-litre V8 turned the Esprit into a true supercar, but the raucous four was still available until 1999. Progressively faster and better handling over the years, but build quality and irritating design flaws were regular bugbears compared to foreign opposition (which, to be fair, was generally more pricey).

Specifications (Turbo Esprit)

Construction	Steel backbone chassis, glassfibre body
Engine	2179cc turbocharged in-line four, 210bhp at 6,000rpm
Transmission	Five-speed manual gearbox, rear-wheel drive
Suspension	Front: Wishbone, transverse links and anti-roll bar, coil springs and telescopic dampers Rear: Transverse links, radius arms, coil springs and telescopic dampers
Brakes	Discs all round, inboard at rear. Servo-assisted
Wheels/tyres	15in alloy wheels, Goodyear NCT 195/60VR15 tyres
Performance	0–60mph: 5.6sec Top speed: 152mph
Price range	£££–£££££
Collector's rating	★★★
Driver's rating	★★★★★
Maintenance & spares	★★★
Alternatives	Porsche 911, Maserati Merak, Ferrari 308GTB

MAZDA MX-5 MIATA ROADSTER S1/S2

Two-seat sports, 1989–2005

Mazda's Elan for a new era, the MX-5 Miata made small rear-drive sports cars cool again. Early cars were powered by a smooth twin-cam four (which looked remarkably like a Lotus Twin-Cam) developing 116bhp from 1.6-litres, with a 1.8-litre being added to the range in 1994. Series 2 models from 1998 were recognisable by exposed headlamps (rather than pop-up lamps of earlier car). Further styling revisions in 2001 were accompanied by uprated engines, the 1.8 now featuring variable valve timing and delivering 156bhp. None of the MX-5s were particularly fast, but the car's fine handling made up for its performance deficiencies with great balance and grip. Replaced by a new MX-5, based on the platform of the rotary-engined RX-8 coupé, late in 2005.

Specifications (1.8)

Construction	Unitary steel body
Engine	1839cc in-line four, twin overhead cam, 140bhp at 6,500rpm
Transmission	Five-speed manual gearbox, rear-wheel drive
Suspension	Front: Double wishbones, coil springs, telescopic dampers and anti-roll bar. Rear: Double wishbones, coil springs, telescopic dampers and anti-roll bar
Brakes	Discs all round. Servo-assisted
Wheels/tyres	5.5x14 alloy wheels, 185/60R14 tyres
Performance	0–60mph: 8.0sec Top Speed: 128mph
Price range	££
Collector's rating	★★
Driver's rating	★★★★
Maintenance & spares	★★★★
Alternatives	Triumph Spitfire, MG Midget, MGB

MERCEDES-BENZ 200-280 W123
Four-seat saloons, coupés and estates, 1976–85

Rugged mid-size Merc saloons have a deserved reputation for enormous strength and reliability, though they are not quite as comfortable or refined as you might imagine. Range of engines, from 2-litre four to swift 2.8-litre twin-cam six, and even a choice of diesels – a 3-litre five-cylinder with or without turbo, or a normally-aspirated 60bhp 2-litre which makes the W123 glacially slow. Best compromise for most people is the 2.3-litre 230E petrol engine with much of the 2.8's performance but without its appetite for specialist maintenance. Rust is the major enemy, parts availability is not a major worry, though prices can be high and W123s are unlikely ever to be valuable. Still a target for thieves who dismantle for parts to sell into third world countries, where legions of W123s are still in use.

Specifications (230E)	
Construction	Unitary steel body
Engine	2299cc in-line four, single overhead cam, 132bhp at 5,100rpm
Transmission	Four-speed manual, five-speed manual or four-speed automatic gearbox. Rear-wheel drive
Suspension	Front: Double wishbone, coil springs and telescopic dampers
	Rear: Semi-trailing arms, coil springs, telescopic dampers and anti-roll bar
Brakes	Discs all round. Servo-assistance. ABS optional.
Wheels/tyres	5.5x14 steel or alloy wheels, 175HR14 tyres
Performance	0–60mph: 12sec. Top speed: 112mph
Price range	£
Collector's rating	★★
Driver's rating	★★★
Maintenance & spares	★★★★
Alternatives	Peugeot 505/604, BMW 5-series, Ford Granada

MERCEDES-BENZ SL/SLC
Two-plus-two sports, 1971–89

Long-running Mercedes roadster (SL) and coupé (SLC) have always been effortlessly cool. First cars were powered by V8s of 3.5-litres (350SL) or 4.5-litres (450SL), always with automatic transmissions, but after the 1973 oil crisis Mercedes added a 280SL with a 2.8-litre twin-cam six and a choice of manual or automatic gearboxes. A 5-litre V8 was introduced in 1977 in what was originally called (confusingly) the 450SLC 5.0, and was later available in the SL body. The smaller V8 grew to 3.8-litres and then to 4.2-litres, while the twin-cam six was replaced by a new 3-litre single-cam six in the 1985 300SL. A US-only 560SL was also made in the final years until an all-new SL was introduced in 1989. Tank-like build quality earned it the nickname of 'panzerwagen'.

Specifications (Euro 450SL)	
Construction	Unitary steel body
Engine	4520cc V8, single overhead cam per bank, 225bhp at 5,000rpm
Transmission	Three-speed automatic, rear-wheel drive
Suspension	Front: Double wishbones, coil springs, telescopic dampers and anti-roll bar
	Rear: Semi-trailing arms, coil springs, telescopic dampers and anti-roll bar
Brakes	Discs all round. Servo-assisted. ABS optional from 1980
Wheels/tyres	6.4x14 steel or alloy wheels, 205/70VR14 tyres.
Performance	0–62mph: 8.8sec. Top speed: 134mph
Price range	££–£££
Collector's rating	★★★★
Driver's rating	★★★★
Maintenance & spares	★★★★
Alternatives	Mercedes-Benz SL W113, Porsche 928, Jaguar XJ-S

MG MGA/TWIN-CAM
Two-seat sports/coupé, 1955–62

Cracker of a sports car, which proved what MG could do when BMC let them do it instead of insisting they stick with the increasingly old-fashioned T-series line. Still with a separate chassis, but now clothed in full-width low-drag bodywork derived from the 1951 Le Mans MG TD, UMG 400. Production MGA was available in roadster or (from 1956) coupé form. BMC B-series engine of 1489cc and 72bhp powered the early cars, but from 1958 there was a high-performance alternative: a 1588cc twin-cam unit with 108bhp, which proved to be rather temperamental. Twin-Cam also had discs all round and centre-lock Dunlop wheels. Base MGAs gained the 1588cc capacity – but not the twin-ohc head – in 1959 and 1622cc in 1961 MGA Mk2, the latter recognisable by its recessed grille bars.

Specifications (1600 Mk2)	
Construction	Steel chassis, steel body
Engine	1622cc in-line four, pushrod overhead valve, 93bhp at 5,500rpm
Transmission	Four-speed manual gearbox, rear-wheel drive
Suspension	Front: Wishbones, coil springs and lever-arm dampers
	Rear: Live axle with semi-elliptic leaf springs and lever-arm dampers
Brakes	Disc front, drum rear
Wheels/tyres	Steel disc wheels; centre-lock wires optional
Performance	0–60mph: 13sec. Top speed: 101mph
Price range	££–£££
Collector's rating	★★★★
Driver's rating	★★★
Maintenance & spares	★★★★
Alternatives	Austin-Healey 100, Triumph TR2/3, Morgan Plus 4

MG MGB/C

Two-plus-two sports/coupé, 1962–81

The MGB was *the* affordable sports car in the 1960s and 1970s, and it's now *the* affordable classic sports car. While its monocoque body was all-new in 1962, much of the engineering underneath was carried over from the successful MGA – which meant a BMC B-series engine (now 1798cc), disc front brakes and coil-spring independent front suspension. Five-bearing engine from 1965, the same year that the MGB GT was introduced – a pretty and useful fastback with a rear load door. MGC of 1967 was an attempt to build a Big Healey successor, not least because BMC's George Harriman wanted to end Donald Healey's contract. Heavy iron engine and woolly torsion bar front suspension robbed it of any sporting pretensions in road-going form – though highly developed MGC GTS racers showed promise. V8 MGBs proved to be a more enduring performance idea, first the conversions by Ken Costello and later Leyland's own MGB V8 in GT form only – there were no factory V8 roadsters. Like the four-cylinder 'B (and the Midget) the V8 was given 'rubber' bumpers and a hike in ride height in response to new US 'safety' rules which were actually aimed at reducing the costs of insurance claims. Apart from that there was little real development during the 1970s. Final MGB Limited Edition models were built in 1981.

A healthy market for MGB parts led British Motor Heritage to track down all the tooling and restart the manufacture of bodyshells. That kick-started 'Project Adder', a tuned and updated MGB which became Rover's MG RV8 in 1992.

Specifications (MGB Mk1)

Construction	Unitary steel body
Engine	1798cc in-line four, pushrod overhead valve, 95bhp (SAE net) at 5,400rpm
Transmission	Four-speed manual gearbox, rear-wheel drive
Suspension	Front: Wishbones, coil springs and lever-arm damper
	Rear: Live axle with semi-elliptic leaf-springs, lever-arm dampers
Brakes	Disc front, drum rear
Wheels/tyres	14in steel, 5.60-14 tyres (optional wire wheels with 5.90-14 Dunlop Road Speed tyres)
Performance	0–60mph: 12sec. Top speed 110mph
Price range	££
Collector's rating	★★★
Driver's rating	★★★
Maintenance & spares	★★★★★
Alternatives	Triumph TRs, Austin-Healey 100/3000

MINI COOPER/COOPER S/1275GT

Four-seat small saloon, 1961–71

Alec Issigonis's masterpiece was intended as a small family car, but its superior grip and manoeuvrability were highlighted when John Cooper dropped a Formula Junior engine in one to produce a pocket-sized performance saloon. Twin-carb 997cc engine (55bhp) until 1963, then 998cc engine with more torque. Cooper S 1071cc from 1963, then 1275cc from 1964, and there was also a homologation special 970cc Cooper S in 1964/65. 'Wet' Hydrolastic suspension replaced 'dry' rubber cones in 1964: good in theory, but not so good in practice and many have been converted to 'dry' spec. The 1275GT of 1969 was never as fast or quite as sharp, with a single-carb engine, bluff-front Clubman body style and none of the competition-derived equipment of the Coopers (front discs not withstanding). All hot Minis are terrific fun.

Specifications (998)

Construction	Unitary steel body
Engine	998cc in-line four, pushrod overhead valve, 55bhp (SAE net) at 5,800rpm
Transmission	Four-speed manual gearbox, front-wheel drive
Suspension	Front: Wishbones and Hydrolastic spring/damper units
	Rear: Trailing arms and Hydrolastic spring/damper units. Hydrolastic units connected front to rear
Brakes	Disc front, drum rear
Wheels/tyres	10in steel wheels, 145R10 Dunlop tyres
Performance	0–60mph: 15sec. Top speed: 90mph
Price range	££
Collector's rating	★★★★
Driver's rating	★★★★
Maintenance & spares	★★★★
Alternatives	Sunbeam Stiletto/Imp Sport, Abarth-Fiat 500/600/850, NSU TT/TTS, Simca 1000 Rallye

MORRIS MINOR/1000 & RILEY 1.5
Four-seat saloons, convertibles and estates 1948–71

Minor was the first British car to sell a million, celebrated by a mauve-coloured Minor Million special edition in 1960. Early MM-series 'low light' models are truest to designer Alec Issigonis's intentions, but none came with the flat-four engine originally envisaged – instead it was a wheezy 918cc Morris sidevalve, then the 803cc Austin A-series in the 1952 Series II and finally the 948cc A-series in the Minor 1000 of 1956. Tourer convertible was available from the start, Traveller estate from 1953 – there were also vans and pickups.

Wolseley and Riley launched in 1957 with plusher, roomier bodies and bigger engines but the same running gear: they were popular mid-range quality saloons, the cheaper Wolseley outselling the Riley two-to-one. Also made in Australia, as the Austin Lancer and Morris Major.

Specifications (Minor 1000)
Construction	Unitary steel body
Engine	948cc in-line four-cylinder engine, overhead valve, 48bhp (SAE net) at 5,100rpm
Transmission	Four-speed manual, rear-wheel drive
Suspension	Front: Transverse links, radius arms, torsion bars and lever-arm dampers. Rear: Live axle with semi-elliptic leaf springs and lever-arm dampers
Brakes	Drums all round
Wheels/tyres	14in steel, 5.20-14 Dunlop tyres
Performance	0–60mph: 24sec
	Top speed: 74mph
Price range	£
Collector's rating	★★
Driver's rating	★★
Maintenance & spares	★★★★
Alternatives	Austin A35, Renault 4CV, Austin 1100, Ford Anglia

PORSCHE 911/912
Two-plus-two coupé and convertible, 1964–90

Iconic air-cooled sports coupé, designed to offer more space and more refinement than Porsche's outgoing 356. Original coupé of 1964 with 130bhp, 2-litre flat-six engine was joined by the Targa, with a lift-out roof panel, in 1965. A 911S with bigger valves and higher compression appeared in 1967, and in 1970 the engine was bored out to 2.2-litres. In 1971 the flat-six grew again, an increase in stroke taking it to 2341cc and up to 190bhp. In 1973 came the Carrera RS, with a big-bore 2687cc engine, generating 210bhp, and a lightweight body. The first turbo 911 arrived in 1975, and the definitive 300bhp 3.3-litre Turbo came in 1978.

Regular revisions kept the range fresh, with body changes (including fully galvanised shells from 1976) and ever larger engines – 2.7-litres, 3-litres and finally a 231bhp 3.2-litre normally-aspirated unit. The Targa was also supplemented by a full cabriolet. The 911 sired a rare twin-turbocharged four-wheel drive derivative, the 959, which proved to be one of the fastest supercars ever, with a top speed approaching 200mph.

A new Type 964 car arrived in 1989, with broadly the same shape but a host of detail differences. At first it was only available in four-wheel drive Carrera 4 form, but later two-wheel drive and Turbo versions were added to the range. The Type 964 was revised to become the Type 993 in 1994, and replaced by the Type 996 in 1998.

Specifications (1968 911S 2.0)
Construction	Unitary steel body
Engine	1991cc flat-six, single overhead camshaft per bank, 170bhp (SAE net) at 6,800rpm
Transmission	Five-speed manual gearbox, rear-wheel drive
Suspension	Front: Wishbones, telescopic damper struts, torsion bars and anti-roll bar. Rear: Trailing arms, torsion bars and anti-roll bar
Brakes	Discs all round
Wheels/tyres	6x15 alloy, 185/70VR15 Dunlop SP tyres
Performance	0–60mph: 7.5sec
	Top speed: 137mph
Price range	££–£££
Collector's rating	★★★★
Driver's rating	★★★★
Maintenance & spares	★★★★
Alternatives	Porsche 356, Lotus Elan/Esprit/Excel

PORSCHE 924/944/968
Two-plus-two coupés and convertibles, 1975–95

Porsche designed this sports coupé for Volkswagen, but when the project was shelved Porsche took it on themselves. Built at the Audi Neckarsulm works, using lots of VW/Audi bits to keep the price down – including a rather insipid four-cylinder engine, mounted at the front and water-cooled (a first for Porsche). More power from 924 Turbo in 1979, then Porsche fitted its own 2.5-litre four (effectively one bank of the 928's V8) to produce the 944. The 944 Turbo followed in 1985, seriously challenging the 911 as the ultimate driver's Porsche. Hefty revisions produced the 968 of 1991, with 3-litre turbo and normally aspirated engines giving up to 305bhp. The 968 continued until 1995, its place in the Porsche range being taken by the Boxster.

Specifications (944)
Construction	Unitary steel body
Engine	2479cc in-line four, single overhead cam, 163bhp at 5,800rpm
Transmission	Five-speed manual gearbox, rear-wheel drive
Suspension	Front: MacPherson strut and anti-roll bar
	Rear: Semi-trailing arms, torsion bars, telescopic dampers
Brakes	Ventilated discs all round
Wheels/tyres	7x16 alloy wheels, 225/55VR16 tyres
Performance	0–62mph: 8.3sec.
	Top speed: 138mph
Price range	££–£££
Collector's rating	★★★
Driver's rating	★★★★
Maintenance & spares	★★★★
Alternatives	Lotus Eclat/Excel, Alfa GTV, Toyota Supra

RELIANT SCIMITAR GT/GTE/GTC
Two-plus-two coupé and estate, 1964–86

Scimitar GT was a convincing package: fast, sure-footed, and good-looking. Steel chassis and GRP body styled by Ogle. Original GT (known internally as SE4) was fitted with Ford Zephyr/Zodiac straight-six, but later gained the new Essex V6 in the SE4a/4b, along with revised chassis. Rare SE4c has 2.5-litre engine. Coupé is now almost forgotten thanks to the success of the 'sporting estate' GTE (SE5) variant introduced in 1968. Revised interior and more powerful V6 in 1971 SE5a. SE6 of 1975 was longer and wider, revised to become SE6a the following year. In 1980 Reliant adopted the Ford Cologne V6 (SE6b) and introduced the Stag-like convertible GTC (SE8b). Financial troubles halted production in 1986 and the GTE was sold to Middlebridge Motors, which made only a handful of cars before it, too, succumbed.

Specifications (GTE SE5a)
Construction	Box-section steel chassis, glassfibre body
Engine	2994cc V6, pushrod overhead valve, 138bhp at 5,000rpm
Transmission	Four-speed manual gearbox. Rear-wheel drive
Suspension	Front: Double wishbones, coil springs, anti-roll bar and telescopic dampers. Rear: Live axle, radius arms, Watt linkage, coil springs
Brakes	Disc front/drum rear, servo-assisted
Wheels/tyres	5.5x14 steel or aluminium alloy/steel wheels, 185R14 tyres
Performance	0–60mph: 10.5sec. Top speed: 110mph
Price range	£–££
Collector's rating	★★★
Driver's rating	★★★★
Maintenance & spares	★★★★
Alternatives	Ford Capri 3000, BMW 2002 Touring, Volvo 1800ES, Lancia Beta HPE, Gilbern Invader/Estate

ROVER P6
Four-seat saloon, 1963–77

Though aimed at a conservative market, the P6 was an advanced car with an unusual endo-skeletal structure and unstressed outer panels, and overhead-cam engines – plus the 3.5-litre ex-Buick V8 later on. All models are refined and capable saloons with welcoming interiors and fine handling, thanks to de Dion rear end (though planned air suspension never made it into production). The V8 adds storming performance despite P6's weight, particularly in manual-gearbox 3500S form, though fuel economy is not a strong point. Series 1 cars distinguished by their bright aluminium grille, swapped for a plastic egg-box affair on the 1971 Series 2, while V8s all have an auxiliary air intake under the bumper. External panels easy to remove, and can be quickly restored to hide terminal rot underneath – so check structure is sound when buying.

Specifications (3500S)
Construction	Unitary steel structure with unstressed outer panels in steel and aluminium
Engine	3528cc V8, pushrod overhead valve, 152bhp (SAE net) at 5,000rpm
Transmission	Four-speed manual gearbox, rear-wheel drive
Suspension	Front: transverse lower links, longitudinal upper links, horizontal coil springs, anti-roll bar and telescopic dampers. Rear: De Dion with Watt linkages, coil springs and telescopic dampers
Brakes	Discs all round, inboard at rear, servo-assisted
Wheels/tyres	5.5x14in steel wheels, 185R14 tyres
Performance	0–60mph: 9.5sec. Top speed: 120mph
Price range	£–££
Collector's rating	★★★
Driver's rating	★★★
Maintenance & spares	★★★
Alternatives	Ford Consul/Granada Mk1, Triumph 2000/2500, Humber Sceptre

ROVER SD1
Four-seat hatchback, 1976–86

The much-maligned SD1 was a great car hampered by the worst of mid-1970s Leyland build 'quality', which led to the early onset of rust and a raft of electrical problems. Basic design, a team effort by engineers from Rover and Triumph, was sound though not as innovative as the P6 it replaced. Engines eventually included Austin-Morris O-series 2-litre, Triumph-designed 2.3-litre and 2.6-litre sixes and a 2.4-litre turbo-diesel, but the jewel in the crown is the 190bhp 'twin plenum' V8 which powered the final Vitesse models. An alternative is the V8-engined Vanden Plas, which was the luxury model in the range. SD1 was widely used by British police forces and had an interesting motor sport career both as an outsized rally car and a successful racing machine.

Specifications (Vitesse)

Construction	Unitary steel body
Engine	3528cc V8, pushrod overhead valve, 187bhp at 5,280rpm
Transmission	Five-speed manual gearbox, rear-wheel drive
Suspension	Front: MacPherson strut and anti-roll bar
	Rear: Live axle with Watt linkage, coil springs and telescopic dampers
Brakes	Discs front/drum rear, servo-assisted
Wheels/tyres	6.5x15 alloy wheels, 205/50VR15 tyres
Performance	0–60mph: 7.1sec
	Top speed: 130mph
Price range	£
Collector's rating	★★
Driver's rating	★★★
Maintenance & spares	★★★★
Alternatives	Jaguar XJ6, BMW 7-series, Ford Granada

ROLLS-ROYCE SILVER SHADOW, BENTLEY T-SERIES
Four-seat saloon/coupé/convertible, 1965–80

The first modern-era Rolls-Royce (and almost identical Bentley) with a monocoque body and 6230cc pushrod V8 engine. Masterly in-house styling looked spot-on from the start, and the Shadow was very successful. Two-door coupés available from 1965, convertibles from 1967, but from 1971 these were called Corniche rather than Silver Shadow. Long-wheelbase cars available from 1969, and bigger 6750cc engine from 1970. Revisions in 1977 produced the Shadow II (and Bentley T2), the most noticeable difference being an air dam under the front bumper and more precise rack-and-pinion steering. Long-wheelbase cars were called Silver Wraiths (recalling a 1946–59 model name) from 1977. Replaced by Silver Spirit and long-wheelbase Silver Spur in 1980. Not all that rare, so values are surprisingly low. White ones are invariably ex-wedding cars.

Specifications (Shadow 1)

Construction	Unitary steel body
Engine	6223cc V8, pushrod overhead valve, power not quoted but approximately 180bhp
Transmission	Four-speed automatic gearbox, rear-wheel drive
Suspension	Front: Wishbones, coil springs, automatic self-levelling system, telescopic dampers and anti-roll bar. Rear: Semi-trailing arms, coil springs, automatic self-levelling system, telescopic dampers and anti-roll bar
Brakes	Discs all round, power-assisted
Wheels/tyres	6x15in steel wheels, 8.15-15 Avon tyres
Performance	0–60mph: 10.8sec
	Top speed: 115mph
Price range	£££
Collector's rating	★★★
Driver's rating	★★★★
Maintenance & spares	★★★
Alternatives	Mercedes-Benz S-class, Jaguar XJ6/XJ12

SUNBEAM ALPINE AND TIGER
Two-plus-two sports cars, 1959–68

Rootes' competitor for MG, Triumph and Austin-Healey. Cruciform chassis shared with Hillman Husky and four-cylinder Rapier engine sound prosaic, but the combination worked pretty well with neat handling and reasonable ride comfort, though competitors generally offered more outright performance. Pretty styling, with trendy finned rear wings until 1964 Alpine IV, by which time engine had grown to 1592cc. Final Alpine V of 1965–68 boasted 1725cc and 100mph performance. Tiger used Ford V8 power (260ci at first, 289ci in the 1967 Tiger II) though performance was not quite in the Cobra league. Killed off because of the conflict between the Ford motor and Rootes' takeover by Chrysler in 1967. Look out for rare fastback Alpines converted by Harrington, often featuring tuned engines.

Specifications (Alpine V)

Construction	Cruciform steel chassis, steel body
Engine	1725cc in-line four, pushrod overhead valve, 92bhp (SAE net) at 5,500rpm
Transmission	Four-speed manual gearbox with overdrive on third and top, rear-wheel drive
Suspension	Front: Wishbones, coil springs, anti-roll bar and telescopic dampers
	Rear: Live axle with semi-elliptic leaf springs and telescopic dampers
Brakes	Disc front, drum rear, servo-assisted
Wheels/tyres	4.5x13 steel wheels, 5.90-13 Dunlop tyres
Performance	0–60mph: 13sec
	Top speed: 100mph
Price range	££–££££
Collector's rating	★★★
Driver's rating	★★★
Maintenance & spares	★★★★
Alternatives	MGB, Triumph TR4/TR4A

TRIUMPH TR2/3/3a

Two-seat sports, 1953–62

'TR1' never saw production. Short-tailed prototype 20TS seen at London Motor Show in 1952, but reactions were mixed. Much-revised TR2 of 1953 was a big improvement, and gave Triumph a viable Austin-Healey 100 competitor. Tough four-pot engine came from Standard Vanguard, chassis and body were all-new. TR3 of 1955 had flush grille and from 1956 disc brakes were available. TR3a of 1957 had a full-width grille and latterly the

option of a 2138cc engine. Theoretically the TR3a was replaced by the Michelotti-styled TR4 in 1961, but the conservative US market liked the side-screen TRs so an updated TR3a remained available for a while – later dubbed TR3b. Production ended in 1962. More capable and more fun than their rather 'vintage' appearance might suggest.

Specifications (TR3)

Construction	Steel ladder chassis with steel body
Engine	1991cc in-line four-cylinder, pushrod OHV, 90bhp at 4,800rpm
Transmission	Four-speed manual, optional overdrive, rear-wheel drive
Suspension	Front: Double wishbones and coil springs, telescopic dampers. Rear: Live axle with semi-elliptic leaf springs, lever-arm dampers
Brakes	Drums all round; later disc front/drum rear
Wheels/tyres	15in steel wheels, 5.50x15 tyres. Wire wheels optional
Performance	0–60mph: 12 seconds. Top Speed: 107mph
Price range	£££
Collector's rating	★★★★
Driver's rating	★★★★
Maintenance & spares	★★★★★
Alternatives	Austin-Healey 100, MGA

TRIUMPH TR4/4a/5/6

Two-seat sports, 1961–76

Classic open sports car: simple separate chassis, tough and torquey engines. Mechanicals and bodywork developed in alternate stages, beginning with TR4 which was essentially a longer, Michelotti-restyled TR3a with mild improvements to the running gear. Interesting 'Surrey top' was an option. TR4a used the same body but replaced old-fashioned live rear axle with an independent coil spring and semi-trailing arm rear end. Short-lived TR5 of 1967–68 kept the same body style once again but added a long-stroke, 2.5-litre version of the Standard Vanguard/Triumph 2000 straight-six engine with new-fangled petrol injection (a first for a British car) giving it 150bhp and sparkling performance. Sadly the injected engine could not meet US emissions laws, so a lukewarm carburettored TR250 was sold in America. Karmann cleverly restyled the front and rear, while leaving the centre body section unchanged, for the 1969 TR6, but the chassis and engine were much the same. Home-market production continued until 1975, while milder US-market cars continued into 1976, but eventually the very different TR7 took over. Handling was better than reputation suggests, particularly on cars with IRS. Just about the last old-school sports car.

Specifications (TR5)

Construction	Steel ladder chassis with steel body
Engine	In-line six-cylinder, pushrod OHV, 2498cc, 152bhp at 5,500rpm, 159lb ft at 3,000rpm
Transmission	Four-speed manual with optional overdrive, rear-wheel drive
Suspension	Front: Double wishbone, coil springs, telescopic dampers. Rear: Semi-trailing arms, coil springs, lever-arm dampers
Brakes	Disc front, drum rear. Servo-assistance
Wheels/tyres	5x15in steel or wire wheels. 165HR15 tyres
Performance	0–60mph: 9 seconds. Top speed: 120mph
Price range	£££
Collector's rating	★★★★
Driver's rating	★★★★
Maintenance & spares	★★★★★
Alternatives	MGB/C, Austin-Healey 3000, Datsun 240Z

TRIUMPH TR7/8
Two-seat sports, 1976–81

Big change for TR range: out goes the fuel-injected six-cylinder engine, the traditional separate chassis and the classic open roadster body, and in comes a modern monocoque with wedge-shaped styling and a fixed hard top, with a Dolomite-derived overhead-cam four-cylinder engine. Diehard TR enthusiasts were horrified. Emissions and safety legislation were the culprits, as ever, though a proposed ban on convertible cars never materialised. The TR7 was slower and softer than the TR6, and the lack of a convertible for the first few years of production hampered sales, as did strikes among the Leyland workforce and relocation of the production line – TR7s were made at first at Speke, then Canley and finally at Solihull.

The TR7 matured during its production run, with the long-awaited convertible version arriving in 1980 and improving specifications including a five-speed gearbox. But – questionable styling aside – TR buyers' biggest problem with the TR7 was its lack of pace. A TR7 Sprint with the 16-valve Dolomite Sprint engine was planned but only a few prototypes were ever built. Instead, works rally TR7s used the Rover V8 engine and a production TR8 road car appeared in 1980. Sadly less than 3000 were made, the bulk of them for export to the US. Since then dozens of TR7s have been converted with V8 power (and often uprated brakes, dealing with another of the TR7's weak spots). Conversions are often good, but the rarity of the 'real' TR8 will always give it a price premium.

Like the Rover SD1, the TR7/TR8 suffered from the mismanagement of the whole Leyland operation – but somewhere in there a good car is trying to get out.

Specifications (TR7)

Construction	Unitary steel body
Engine	1998cc in-line four, single overhead camshaft 105bhp (DIN) at 5,500rpm
Transmission	Four-speed manual gearbox (later five-speed manual), rear-wheel drive
Suspension	Front: MacPherson struts and anti-roll bar. Rear: Live axle, trailing arms, coil springs and anti-roll bar
Brakes	Disc front, drum rear, servo-assisted
Wheels/tyres	5.5x13 steel or alloy wheels, 175/70SR13 tyres
Performance	0–60mph: 9.6sec, Top speed: 112mph
Price range	££
Collector's rating	★★★
Driver's rating	★★★
Maintenance & spares	★★★★
Alternatives	MGB/GT/V8, Mazda RX-7, Matra Bagheera

TRIUMPH HERALD, VITESSE, SPITFIRE & GT6
Four-seat saloons, two-seat sports/coupé, 1959–80

This replacement for the monocoque Standard Eight and Ten reverted to separate chassis construction because Standard-Triumph's body suppliers were bought up by competitors. Herald had four-cylinder 'SC' engine (948cc, 1147cc or 1296cc) and was available as a two-door saloon, coupé, convertible or estate. Four-headlamp Vitesse was powered by a related in-line six (1596cc until 1966, when it was enlarged to 1998cc) and was a saloon or convertible (plus a handful of unofficial wagons). All were famed for their extraordinary 25-foot turning circle. The Spitfire sports car used a modified version of the Herald's chassis and engine, and was a deadly rival for the Midget and Sprite throughout the 1960s and 1970s (generally outselling its Abingdon rival). The GT6 was a fixed-roof fastback version of the Spitfire with six-cylinder power and three different designs of rear suspension during its life.

Specifications (Spitfire)

Construction	Steel backbone chassis with steel body
Engine	1147cc in-line four, pushrod overhead valve, 63bhp (SAE net) at 5,750rpm
Transmission	Four-speed manual gearbox, rear-wheel drive
Suspension	Front: Wishbones, coil springs, anti-roll bar and telescopic dampers. Rear: Swing axle with transverse leaf spring, radius arms and telescopic dampers
Brakes	Disc front, drum rear
Wheels/tyres	3.5x13 steel wheels (4.5x13 wires optional), 5.20-13 Dunlop tyres
Performance	0–60mph: 16sec. Top speed: 92mph
Price range	£–££
Collector's rating	★★★
Driver's rating	★★★
Maintenance & spares	★★★★
Alternatives	Austin-Healey Sprite/MG Midget, Honda S800

TRIUMPH 2000/2500/STAG

Four-seat saloons, two-plus-two sports, 1963–77

Big Triumph saloons were comfortable and well-equipped rivals for Rover P6, with good road manners and smooth engines. All powered by six-cylinder engines, from a carburettored 2000 to the fuel-injected 2.5PI with detuned TR5 motor, which was a family man's hot-rod. Sadly, the Lucas injection system was unreliable in service, though today the problems are all fixable. The Stag could have been a cut-price Mercedes SL, but instead it was dogged by problems with its in-house 3-litre V8 engine.

Mk2 versions of the saloons echoed Stag styling and had much-improved interiors with comfortable seats and wooden dashboards with comprehensive instrumentation. Fuel-injection was eventually dropped in favour of a twin-carb 2500S. Continued until 1977, effectively being replaced by its BL family rival, Rover's SD1.

Specifications (Stag)

Construction	Unitary steel body
Engine	2997cc V8, single overhead cam per bank, 145bhp (DIN) at 5,500rpm
Transmission	Four-speed manual with overdrive on third and top or three-speed automatic gearbox, rear-wheel drive
Suspension	Front: Wishbones, coil springs, telescopic dampers and anti-roll bar. Rear: Semi-trailing arms, coil springs and telescopic dampers
Brakes	Disc front/drum rear, servo-assisted
Wheels/tyres	5x14 steel or alloy wheels, 185HR14 tyres
Performance	0–60mph: 9.5sec. Top speed: 125mph
Price range	£–££
Collector's rating	★★★
Driver's rating	★★★
Maintenance & spares	★★★★
Alternatives	Saloons: Rover P6, Ford Zephyr/Zodiac, Ford Consul/Granada. Stag: Reliant Scimitar GTC,

TVR 1600M/2500M/3000M/TAIMAR

Two-seat sports/coupé, 1972–80

Sports coupés which established TVR as a serious player in the specialist sports car market. 'M' designation denotes the takeover of the Blackpool firm by Martin Lilley. All models have GRP bodies on steel-tube chassis, with all-independent suspension. In the UK the cars were powered by the 1.6-litre Ford Crossflow four (1600M) or 138bhp, 3-litre Essex V6 (3000M). For the US the 2500M had the 'federal' carburettored version of Triumph's 2.5-litre in-line six, as used in the TR250 and US-spec TR6, so only 105bhp on tap.

Joined by Taimar, a hatchback version of the 3000M, in 1976, but 3000M continued in production. Rare Broadspeed-developed Turbo versions of the V6 cars available from 1975. V6 convertible introduced in 1978. All replaced by wedge-shaped Tasmin in 1980.

Specifications (3000M)

Construction	Steel tubular chassis with glassfibre body
Engine	2994cc V6, pushrod overhead valve, 138bhp at 5,000rpm
Transmission	Four-speed manual gearbox, rear-wheel drive
Suspension	Front: Double wishbones, coil springs, anti-roll bar and telescopic dampers. Rear: Double wishbones, coil springs and telescopic dampers
Brakes	Disc front/drum rear
Wheels/tyres	6x14in alloy wheels, 185HR14 tyres
Performance	0–60mph: 7.6sec Top speed: 124mph
Price range	££
Collector's rating	★★★★
Driver's rating	★★★★
Maintenance & spares	★★★
Alternatives	Lotus Elan, Morgan Plus 8, Marcos 3-litre, Alpine-Renault A310

TVR 'WEDGE' MODELS

Two-seat and two-plus-two sports/coupé, 1980–1991

Striking sharp-edged styling was a seismic shift for TVR. Began in 1980 with the Tasmin using Ford running gear and Cologne V6 engine from the Capri 2.8 Injection. Budget Tasmin 200 used four-cylinder Pinto power. Tasmin became 280i in 1983, and a 3.5-litre Rover V8 engine was made available in the 350i. Enlarged and tuned V8s powered the 390SE, 400SE, 420SE and 450SE, the latter boasting 320bhp and 150mph performance. The ultimate 'wedge' was 420/450SEAC with wings and lightweight Kevlar body – though, in fact, many had GRP bodies. The wedge style was right for its time but aged quickly, and would be outlived by a reborn version of the 1970s cars, the S series, and replaced by the notably curvaceous Griffith. But the 'wedge' cars defined the TVR of today, and will surely rise in value over time.

Specifications (350i)

Construction	Steel tubular chassis with glassfibre body
Engine	3528cc V8, pushrod overhead valve, 190bhp (DIN) at 5,280rpm
Transmission	Five-speed manual gearbox, rear-wheel drive
Suspension	Front: Double wishbones, coil springs, anti-roll bar, telescopic dampers. Rear: Lateral links, trailing arms, fixed-length driveshafts, coil springs and telescopic dampers
Brakes	Discs all round, servo-assisted
Wheels/tyres	7x15in alloy wheels, 205/60VR15 Goodyear NCT tyres
Performance	0–60mph: 6.0sec. Top speed: 135mph
Price range	££–£££
Collector's rating	★★★
Driver's rating	★★★★
Maintenance & spares	★★★
Alternatives	Triumph TR7/8, Porsche 924/944, Lotus Excel

VOLVO P1800/E/ES
Two-seat sports/estate, 1960–73

Sporting Volvos initially had a convoluted build process, with bodies built at Pressed Steel in Scotland, trimmed and painted by Jensen in West Bromwich and mechanicals fitted in Sweden. Poor quality pressings and common transit damage persuaded Volvo to take on the whole job themselves from 1963. Always remembered for its appearance in the TV series *The Saint* – many restored cars are white with Minilite wheels, like the TV car. Apparently, Roger Moore liked it so much he bought one for himself. Early models have more ornate detailing, and curved 'cowhorn' bumpers at the front; later cars are cleaner but arguably less characterful. A fuel-injected engine appeared on the 1969 1800E, while the ES is a Scimitar-like sporting estate with a lift-up glass rear window for access to the load space.

Specifications (1800E)	
Construction	Unitary steel body
Engine	1985cc in-line four, pushrod overhead valve, 120bhp (SAE net) at 6,000rpm
Transmission	Four-speed manual gearbox with overdrive operating on top gear only, rear-wheel drive
Suspension	Front: Wishbones, coil springs, anti-roll bar and telescopic dampers
	Rear: Live axle with trailing arms, Panhard rod, coil springs and telescopic dampers
Brakes	Disc front/drum rear, servo-assisted
Wheels/tyres	5x15in aluminium alloy wheels with steel rims, 165HR15 tyres
Performance	0–60mph: 9.6sec. Top speed: 110mph
Price range	££
Collector's rating	★★★★
Driver's rating	★★★★
Maintenance & spares	★★★★
Alternatives	Reliant Scimitar GTE, Alfa Romeo GTV

VW GOLF GTI Mk1
Four-seat hatchback, 1975–83

The car that started the 'hot hatch' revolution of the 1980s. Light, handy-sized hatchback with a 1.6-litre four-cylinder engine boosted by Bosch K-Jetronic fuel injection. Originally built as a spare-time project by VW engineers, then adopted by the management as a short-run production car with a view to homologation for motor sport – but it proved enormously popular and became a fixture in the Golf range. Left-hand drive only until 1979, and three-door bodyshell only in the UK – though some markets had a choice of three doors or five. Adopted a 1.8-litre engine in 1983. Every Golf generation since has had a GTI of its own, but each one bigger and heavier than before – straying ever further from the original, successful recipe.

Specifications (1.6)	
Construction	Unitary steel body
Engine	1588cc in-line four, single overhead camshaft, 110bhp (DIN) at 6,100rpm
Transmission	Five-speed manual transmission, front-wheel drive
Suspension	Front: McPherson struts, anti-roll bar
	Rear: Twist beam, coil springs, anti-roll bar, telescopic dampers
Brakes	Disc front/drum rear, servo-assisted
Wheels/tyres	5.5x13 steel or alloy wheels, 175/70HR13 tyres
Performance	0–60mph: 8.2sec Top speed: 112mph
Price range	£
Collector's rating	★★★
Driver's rating	★★★★★
Maintenance & spares	★★★★★
Alternatives	Peugeot 205 GTI, Fiat Strada Abarth, Vauxhall Chevette 2300HS, Alfasud Ti

VW 'BEETLE'
Two-door saloons, and cabriolets, German production: 1945–79

Designed for Adolf Hitler as a 'people's car' in the 1930s, but serious production did not begin until 1945, with Wolfsburg under British control. 'Beetle' went on to become the best selling car ever, eclipsing the Model T Ford. Early cars have split rear window (until 1953) and 1131cc engine (to 1954). Bigger rear window on big-selling 1200 model of 1954–64, then square rear window from 1965 on with a variety of engines. The 'Super Beetle' of 1970 introduced MacPherson strut front suspension, curved windscreen and a bulbous nose for greater luggage space. Too many Beetles around for them to fetch 'collectors' prices, but cabrios (available from 1949 right through to the end of German production in 1979) always command a premium. Production continued in Brazil and Mexico.

Specifications (1300)	
Construction	Steel platform chassis and steel body
Engine	1285cc horizontally-opposed air-cooled four, pushrod overhead valve, 50bhp (SAE net) at 4,000rpm
Transmission	Four-speed manual transmission, rear-wheel drive
Suspension	Front: Trailing arms, torsion bars, anti-roll bar and telescopic dampers. Rear: Swing axles, trailing links, torsion bars and telescopic dampers
Brakes	Drums all round
Wheels/tyres	4x15 steel wheels, 5.60x15 tyres
Performance	0–60mph: 25sec. Top speed: 77mph
Price range	£
Collector's rating	★
Driver's rating	★★
Maintenance & spares	★★★★★
Alternatives	Morris Minor, Mini, Renault 4CV

Useful contacts

In the space available it is impossible to provide a comprehensive list of contacts – there are, for instance, more than 500 car clubs in the UK alone – but details are given for the organisations mentioned in the book and a selection of other useful contacts (including archives, museums, clubs and specialists) which will provide some starting points.

Alfa Romeo Museum
Arese, Milan, Italy
Web: www.museoalfaomeo.com
Alfa Romeo's factory museum has six floors packed with dozens of historic Alfas, from the early Grand Prix cars like the Jano-designed Tipo B/P3 to the 1970s 33 racers. Prototypes and significant production machines are also represented. Entry is free.

Aston Martin Heritage Operations
Telephone: +44 (0)1908 305551
Fax: +44 (0)1908 305554
Web: www.astonmartin.com/parts/heritage
Formed in 2002, catering for all models from the 1958 DB4 to the final V8 Vantage built in 2000. The Milton Keynes-based operation is primarily concerned with re-sourcing obsolete parts, supplied to a network of 11 Aston Martin Heritage Specialists – seven in the UK, one each in Switzerland, Belgium, France and the US.

Aston Martin Heritage Trust
PO Box 207, Wallingford, Oxfordshire OX10 TU
Telephone: +44 (0)1491 837736
Fax: +44 (0)1491 825454
E-mail: amht@email.com
Web: www.amheritrust.org
Founded in 1998 by the Aston Martin Owners Club as an independent charitable trust which would look after the club's extraordinary collection of Aston Martin documentation and memorabilia. The collection includes engineering drawings, artwork, photographs, trophies (some of them from Sir David Brown's widow, Paula) and even whole cars, all stored at the Trust's HQ in Drayton St Leonard, near Oxford.

Aston Martin Works Service
Tickford Street, Newport Pagnell,
Buckinghamshire MK16 9AN
Telephone: +44 (0)1908 610620
Fax: +44 (0)1908 613708
Web: www.astonmartin.com/worksservice
Aston Martin also has its own service department, Works Service at the Newport Pagnell factory, which maintains Astons and Lagondas of all ages and carries out restoration and modification work.

BMW Mobile Tradition
Schleißheimer Straße 416, Corner of BMW Allee, 80 935 Munich, Germany
Fax: +49 (0) 89 38 22 70 22
E-mail: st.empfang@partner.bmw.de
Web: www.bmw.com/mobiletradition
The arm of BMW which looks after the company's heritage operations, including archives, parts supply and a collection of more than 400 historic cars, motorcycles and engines displayed at its Munich museum (currently undergoing major refurbishment). A small collection of classic BMWs, from an Isetta to a Z1, are available for self-drive hire from the Munich workshop.

British Commercial Vehicle Museum
King Street, Leyland, Preston,
Lancashire PR5 1LE
Telephone: +44 (0)1772 451011
Fax: +44 (0)1772 623404
The most important collection of historic commercial vehicles in the UK, with more than 50 exhibits on display.

British Motor Industry Heritage Trust
Heritage Motor Centre, Banbury Road, Gaydon, Warwickshire CV35 0BJ
Telephone: +44 (0)1926 641188
Fax: +44 (0)1926 641555
Web: www.heritage-motor-centre.co.uk
Based at the Heritage Motor Centre at Gaydon, the Trust looks after the largest collection of British cars in the world – not just production road cars, but also race and rally machines, one-offs and prototypes. Originally formed from British Leyland's historic vehicle collection, the cars in BMIHT's care now include other marques, including nearby Aston Martin. There's also an extensive archive of photographs, records and technical documents. BMIHT offers 'Heritage Certificates' showing a car's original build data, to owners of classics built by the former British Leyland marques – MG, Rover, Austin and so on – and Aston Martin.

Brooklands Museum
Brooklands Museum Trust Limited, Brooklands Road, Weybridge, Surrey KT13 0QN
Telephone: +44 (0)1932 857381
Fax: +44 (0)1932 855465
E-mail: info@brooklandsmuseum.com
Web: www.brooklandsmuseum.com
Collection of cars, bikes and aircraft relating to Brooklands, the world's first purpose-built racing circuit. The Museum hosts many events throughout the year, and visitors can see the old Test Hill and the remaining section of the Members' banking. Brooklands was also an important site in the history of British aviation as the home of Vickers, and was involved in such projects as the VC10 and Concorde. Exhibits include the Napier Railton, holder of the Brooklands Outer Circuit lap record.

The Bugatti Trust

Prescott Hill, Gotherington, Cheltenham,
Gloucestershire GL52 9RD
Telephone: +44 (0)1242 677201
Fax: +44 (0)1242 674191
Web: www.bugatti.co.uk/trust
The Trust was founded in 1987 by the late
Hugh Conway, a renowned Bugatti expert.
Based at the famous Prescott hill climb, which
has long-standing Bugatti connections, the
Trust encourages research in all aspects of
Ettore Bugatti's work.

Cars of the Stars Museum

Standish Street, Keswick, Cumbria CA12 5LS
Telephone: +44 (0)17687 73757
Fax: +44 (0)17687 72090
E-mail: cotsmm@aol.com
Web: members.aol.com/cotsmm
A remarkable collection of vehicles used in
films and television shows, including several
cars from the James Bond films.

Walter P. Chrysler Museum

One Chrysler Drive, Auburn Hills, Michigan
48326-2778 USA
Telephone: 248-944-0001
Web: www.chryslerheritage.com
This three-storey museum to the north of
Detroit is the only collection operated by a
US car maker. It includes 65 vehicles from
throughout Chrysler's history, together with
numerous other exhibits.

Cobra Supaform Limited

Units D1 and D2, Halesfield 23,
Telford TF7 4NY
Telephone: +44 (0) 1952 684020
Fax: +44 (0) 1952 581772
Web: www.cobraseats.com
Manufacturer of road and race seats,
including the Classic and Cub seats
ideal for classic cars.

Corbeau Seats Ltd

Wainright Close, Churchfields Industrial Estate,
St Leonards-on-Sea, East Sussex TN38 9PP
Telephone: +44 (0)1424 854499
Fax: +44 (0)1424 854488
Email: sales@corbeau-seats.co.uk
Web: www.corbeau-seats.co.uk
Manufacturers of road and race seats,
including the Classic and Alpine models
ideal for classic cars.

Coventry Transport Museum

Millennium Place, Hales Street,
Coventry CV1 1PN
Telephone: +44 (0)24 7623 4270
Fax: +44 (0)24 7623 4284
E-mail: museum@transport-museum.com
Web: www.transport-museum.com
Excellent museum celebrating Coventry's
history as Britain's 'motor city', telling the story
of the motor car with well-planned exhibits and
information. The car collection is interesting,
too, combining good examples of everyday
cars (including some from the 1970s, which
are becoming rarer) and unique items such
as the original Aston Martin DB7 show car,
a Jaguar XK8 glassfibre styling mock-up and
the Thrust SSC Land Speed Record car.
Entry is free.

Davida UK Limited

Millhouse, Holt Avenue, Moreton,
Wirral CH46 0SS
Telephone: +44 (0)151 678 4656
Fax: +44 (0)151 677 5398
E-mail: sales@davida.co.uk
Web: www.davida.co.uk
Manufacturer of period-style crash helmets –
intended for motorcycle use, but may also
be of interest for some car applications.
Distributors of Léon Jeantet goggles in the
UK and several other countries, and suppliers
of a number of other styles of goggles.

Donington Grand Prix Collection

Donington Park, Castle Donington, Derby
DE74 2RP
Telephone: 01332 811027
Fax: 01332 812829
E-mail: enquiries@doningtoncollection.co.uk
Web: www.doningtoncollection.com
Donington circuit owner Tom Wheatcroft's own
collection of racing cars has become the
Donington Collection, the world's largest
collection of single-seater racing cars.

Federation of British Historic Vehicle Clubs (FBHVC)

Jim Whyman, Federation Secretary,
Kernshill, Shute Street, Stogumber,
Taunton, Somerset, TA4 3TU
Telephone: +44 (0)1984 656995
Fax: +44 (0)1984 656762
E-mail: admin@fbhvc.co.uk
Web: www.fbhvc.co.uk
A group of 370 classic car clubs and more

than 1,500 traders and individual members
which aims to 'uphold the freedom to use old
vehicles on the roads without any undue
restriction and to support its member
organisations in whatever way it can'.

Fédération Internationale de Véhicules Anciens (FIVA)

Richard Sanders, General Secretary, Duckets
House, Steeple Aston, Oxfordshire OX25 4SQ
Telephone: + 44 (0) 1869 340077
Fax: +44 (0) 1869 347524
Email: fivasecgen@aol.com
Web: www.fiva.org
The international federation of historic vehicle
clubs, formed in 1966. Since its merger in
2004 with another international federation, the
IHVO, FIVA spans 50 countries and represents
more than three quarters of a million members.

Haynes International Motor Museum

Castle Cary Road (A359), Sparkford,
Somerset BA22 7LH
Telephone: +44 (0)1963 440804
Fax: +44 (0)1963 441004
Email: mike@haynesmotormuseum.co.uk
Web: www.haynesmotormuseum.co.uk
More than 340 cars and bikes, from the
classics of the 1950s to more modern
machines like the Jaguar XJ220. The famous
'Red Room' is an amazing display of classics,
from MGs to Lamborghinis, every one of which
is red. There are another ten display halls, plus
activities for children and regular events at the
museum and its dedicated test track.

Heritage Motor Centre

See British Motor Industry Heritage Trust.

Historic Endurance Rallying Organisation (HERO)

Ynysymaerdy Farm Cottage, Ynysymaerdy
Road, Briton Ferry, Neath SA11 2TS
Telephone: +44 (0)1639 820864
Fax: +44 (0)1639 812863
Email: info@hero.org.uk
Web: www.hero.org.uk
Organisers of long-distance rallies for
classics, including the well-known LEJOG
from Land's End to John o'Groats.

Jaguar Daimler Heritage Trust

Jaguar Cars Ltd, Browns Lane, Allesley,
Coventry CV5 9DR
Telephone: +44 (0)2476 203322
Fax: +44 (0)2476 202835
Jaguar's museum at the Browns Lane factory,
and the company's historic archives and photo
collection, are maintained by the JDHT.

Lakeland Motor Museum

Holker Hall and Gardens, Cark-in-Cartmel,
Grange-over-Sands, South Lakeland, Cumbria
LA11 7PL
Telephone/fax: +44 (0)1539 558509
Most notable for the Campbell Bluebird
Exhibition, paying tribute to the World Land
Speed and Water Speed record holders Sir
Malcolm Campbell and his son Donald.

Land Rover Museum

Dunsfold Land Rovers Limited, Alfold Road,
Dunsfold, Nr Godalming, Surrey GU8 4NP
Telephone: +44 (0)1483 200567
Fax: +44 (0)1483 200738

Mercedes-Benz Classic Center

Stuttgarter Straße 90, 70736
Fellbach, Germany
Telephone: +49(0) 711 17 8 40 40
Fax: +49(0) 711 17 8 34 56
M-B's own classic workshop, 'the largest and
most extensive vintage car service department
worldwide', offering repair, restoration and parts
for classic Mercedes-Benz models.

Motor Sports Association

Motor Sports House, Riverside Park,
Colnbrook SL3 0HG
Telephone: +44 (0) 1753 765000
Fax: +44 (0) 1753 682938
Web: www.msauk.org
Governing body for motor sport in the UK.

Museo Lamborghini

Automobili Lamborghini SpA, via Modena 12,
40019 Sant'Agata Bolognese, Italy
Lamborghini's official museum. Entry is free,
but visits are by appointment.

Museum Mobile

Ingolstadt, Germany
Web: www.museummobile.de
Audi's historic vehicle museum alongside
its Ingolstadt car production facility.

National Motor Museum

Beaulieu, Brockenhurst, Hampshire SO42 7ZN
Telephone: +44 (0)1590 612345
Fax: +44 (0)1590 612624
Web: www.beaulieu.co.uk
Britain's best-known motor museum, in the
grounds of Beaulieu House, seat of Lord
Montagu. Interesting collection of vehicles,
including a Lotus 49, a Jaguar Le Mans car,
and a variety of other competition and road
machines from the 19th, 20th and 21st
centuries. Also includes a fascinating
reconstruction of a vintage-era motor vehicle
workshop, and regular special displays.

Pace Products (Anglia) Ltd

Homefield Road, Haverhill, Suffolk CB9 8QP
Telephone: +44 (0)1440 760960
Fax: +44 (0)1440 708787
Web: www.paceproducts.co.uk
Manufacturers of alloy radiators, oil coolers,
intercoolers, oil pumps, oil tanks and
accessories.

Piloti Inc

790 Hampshire Road, Suite D, Westlake
Village, CA 91361
Telephone: +1 805 494 0756
Fax: +1 805 856 0319
Web: www.piloti.com
Makers of specially designed driving shoes,
and other clothing.

Ridgard Seats

Parsons Farm, Tilbury Road, Ridgewell, Essex
CO9 4RL
Telephone: +44 (0)1440 788141
Fax: +44 (0)1440 788208
Email: bob@ridgardseats.co.uk
Web: www.ridgardseats.co.uk
Manufacturers of classic race and rally seats.

Saab Bilmuseum

Trollhåtten, Sweden
Telephone: +46 (0)520 84344
Fax: +46 (0)520 320 51
E-mail: saab.carmuseum@saab.com
Web: www.saab.com
More than 60 Saabs on show at the Trollhåtten
production plant, including the original 92.001
prototype built in 1946. Bookings can also be
made for guided tours of the car plant.

Science Museum

Exhibition Road, South Kensington,
London SW7 2DD
Telephone: +44 (0)20 7942 4000
Fax: +44 (0)20 7942 4572
Web: www.sciencemuseum.org
The Science Museum's remit extends far
beyond motoring, but the Museum does have
a fair collection of motor vehicles and engines,
and hosts motoring exhibitions.

Superpro Europe Ltd

Home Farm, Middlezoy, Somerset TA7 0PD
Telephone: +44 (0)1823 690281
Fax: +44 (0)1823 698109
Web: www.superpro.eu.com
European distributors for Australian SuperPro
polyurethane suspension bushes.

Think Automotive

292, Worton Road, Isleworth,
Middlesex, TW7 6EL
Telephone: +44 (0)208 568 1172
Fax: +44 (0)208 847 5338
Email: info@thinkauto.co.uk
Web: www.thinkauto.com
Suppliers of oil coolers, hoses and fittings,
including the well-known Mocal range.

Vauxhall Heritage Centre

Griffin House, Osborne Road, Luton,
Bedfordshire LU1 3YT
Telephone: +44 (0)1582 426527
Fax: +44 (0)1582 426926

Vauxhall Heritage Services

Freepost MID30328, Tipton,
West Midlands DY4 9BR
Telephone: +44(0)121 522 5566
Fax: +44(0)121 522 5521
E-mail: enquiries@vauxhallheritage.com
Web: www.vauxhallheritage.com
Parts and merchandise for older Vauxhalls.
The lively website includes an owners' forum.

Glossary of terms
& abbreviations

Accelerator pump
Carburettor component which delivers a squirt of extra fuel when the throttle is opened suddenly, giving better response.

AF (American Fine)
Screw thread standard, also known as Unified Fine (UNF). Spanner size is measured between the flats of a nut; AF is often taken to mean 'across flats'. The most common sizes used on classics are 7/16in, 1/2in, 9/16in and 5/8in.

Alfin drum
A high-performance brake drum made from a finned (for cooling) alloy casting with a bonded-in iron wearing surface.

Alternator
Later type of electrical generator, producing alternating current which is turned into direct current using a rectifier. On many classics, particularly cars in everyday use, it replaces the original dynamo.

Anti-roll bar
Solid bar or tube connected between the suspension arms on either side of a car, so that it twists when the car rolls in cornering. The torsional stiffness of the bar reduces roll. Known as 'sway bars' in the US.

A-pillar
The windscreen pillar.

Aquaplaning
On a wet road, when a tyre rides on top of the water, losing grip on the road. The steering feels very light, and directional control is lost.

Armature
The rotating coils in a dynamo or magneto.

Aspect ratio
Ratio of width to height, used to describe tyre profiles.

Autovac
Vacuum-operated fuel feed system which sucks fuel from the main tank using intake depression, then delivers it under gravity feed to the carburettor. Made obsolete by mechanical and electric fuel pumps.

BA (British Association)
Screw thread standard. Small fasteners, often used for electrical components. The largest size is 0BA, the smallest in common use is 6BA.

Backfire
Unburnt fuel exploding in the exhaust system, often on the over-run when the throttle is closed.

Backlash
See *Play*.

Baulk ring
Used in some synchromesh gearboxes to prevent engagement until gears are synchronised.

Bias-belted tyre
American tyre design with angled casing plies like a cross-ply, and semi-rigid breakers under the tread like a radial.

Big end
The bearing at the bottom end of the connecting rod, where it connects to the crankshaft.

Bleed
Drain part of the hydraulic fluid in, for instance, a brake system to expel the air it contains.

Blow-by
Combustion gases which have found their way past the piston rings and into the crankcase.

Bore
The internal diameter of the cylinders in an engine (or of any cylinder or pipe).

Bottom dead centre (BDC)
The point in the engine's rotation where a piston is at the lowest position.

Boxer
A horizontally-opposed or 'flat' engine. Strictly speaking a specific type of flat engine with a crankpin for every conrod: where each crankpin carries two conrods (as in the Porsche 917) the engine is really a 180-degree 'V'.

Box spanner
Tube formed into a hexagon at one end, and provided with a 'tommy bar' for extra leverage. Less likely to slip than an open-jawed spanner.

B-pillar
The pillar behind a car's front doors.

BSF (British Standard Fine)
Screw thread standard. Shallow, fine-pitched thread.

BSP (British Standard Pipe)
Screw thread standard. Used in pipework, such as oil pipes and coolers.

BSW (British Standard Whitworth)
Screw thread standard. Coarser than BSF, making it good for soft metals.

Bump
Suspension movement which compresses the springs.

Bump steer
(1) Steering geometry fault which causes the steering angle to change as the suspension moves up and down. (2) Change in the car's direction over bumps, which can be caused by poor rear axle location or a stiff front anti-roll bar.

Bush
A simple bearing allowing axial or limited rotational movement. Where continuous rotational movement occurs, the term 'plain bearing' is used.

Camber angle
Angle to the vertical of a wheel and tyre, as viewed from in front or behind. 'Positive' camber means the tyre is leaning outwards at the top, 'negative' camber means the wheel leans in. As a general rule, a tyre generates more grip running at negative camber.

Camshaft
Rotating shaft driven from the crankshaft at half engine speed by a gear train, a chain or a toothed belt. The camshaft lobes operate the valves in the correct sequence and with the correct timing.

Capacity
Or 'swept volume'. The difference between the volume in the cylinder at BDC and TDC. Measured in cubic centimetres (cc) or litres in the UK and Europe, and in cubic inches in the US.

Carburettor
Device which creates a combustable air/fuel mixture and regulates its flow into the engine.

Caster angle
Angle to the vertical of the steering axis, when viewed from the side. Castor improves straight-line stability and self-centring.

Chassis
(1) The structural frame of the car. In unitary construction, the chassis members are formed as part of the bodyshell. (2) 'Chassis' is also used to denote the suspension and brake systems, as opposed to the powertrain (engine and transmission).

Choke
(1) Device which reduces air flow into the carburettor to enrich the air/fuel mixture during starting and warm up – strictly speaking a 'choke flap'. (2) A carburettor venturi – a 'twin choke' carburettor has two venturis.

Circlip
Flat, circular clip, which looks like a split washer. Commonly used to retain the gudgeon pin connecting con rod to piston.

Combination spanner
Spanner with a ring at one end and an open jaw at the other.

Commutator
Ring of copper conductors, separated by insulation, which transfers current from the rotating coils in a dynamo to the stationary brushes.

Compression ratio
The ratio of the volume in the cylinder at BDC to the volume at TDC.

Condenser
Capacitor fitted in a distributor to prevent 'arcing' across the contact breaker points, which would cause the points to wear rapidly.

Constant velocity joint
A universal joint in which the angular velocity of both shafts remains constant even when the shafts are angled. Used in front-wheel drive cars.

Cotal gearbox
An epicyclic automatic gearbox in which gears are selected by electromagnetic clutches.

C-pillar
The third pillar from the front of the body. Usually adjacent to the rear screen, but on a 'six light' body the C-pillar is between the rear door and the rearmost side window.

Crank pin
The bearing surface on the crankshaft to which a connecting rod is attached.

Crankshaft
The main rotating shaft in the engine, which converts the vertical motion of the pistons into a rotary motion to drive the wheels.

Cross-ply tyre
Older type of tyre where the threads of the casing materials run across the crown of the tyre at an angle.

Crown wheel
Reduction gear in the rear axle, driven by the pinion, which is connected to the propshaft.

Damper
Suspension component which damps out spring movement. Often inaccurately called a 'shock absorber'. Early versions were mechanical friction devices (the Andre Hartford type), while modern dampers are hydraulic.

Decoke
A maintenance job where carbon deposits are removed from the combustion chamber. Just about extinct, thanks to cleaning additives in modern fuels.

Detonation
Explosion of the air/fuel mixture when too high a compression ratio causes the mixture to reach high pressure and temperature. Another form, called pinking or (in the US) pinging, occurs after the spark while the flame front is burning through the mixture – the temperature and pressure of the mixture rises until it explodes.

Differential
Gear system within the driving axle which allows the driving wheels to turn at different speeds in a corner.

Disc brake
A flat disc attached to the wheel hub which is slowed by pads pressed into the disc faces.

Dive
Suspension movement caused by braking, where the front suspension compresses and the rear extends.

D-pillar
The rear screen pillars on a 'six light' body.

Driveshaft
In the UK, the shaft from differential to wheel hub, sometimes called a halfshaft. In the US, the shaft from gearbox to final drive, sometimes called a propellor shaft.

Drum brake
A wide, shallow drum, the rotation of which is slowed by curved brake shoes which are applied to the inside of the drum.

Dry sump
System of engine lubrication commonly used on racing cars, less frequently on road cars, with a remote oil reservoir, oil pressure pump and oil scavenge pump.

Dwell
The angle of rotation of the distributor in each engine cycle where the contact breaker points are closed. Often expressed as a percentage of the total distributor rotation per cylinder cycle: dwell angles are different depending on the number of cylinders in the engine, but dwell percentages are always around 50 per cent.

Duralumin
An aluminium alloy containing copper, magnesium and manganese.

Dynamo
Early electric generator, producing direct current. Less efficient at low engine speeds than an alternator.

Epicyclic gear
Otherwise known as a 'planetary' gear train. A central 'sun' wheel meshes with two or three 'planet' gears, which are connected by a U-shaped planet carrier. The planets mesh with the annulus, a ring-shaped gear with teeth on the inside. Conventional automatic transmissions use combinations of epicyclic gear trains.

Feeler gauge
Tool for measuring small gaps, used to set contact breaker points, spark plug gaps and valve clearances. Consists of several blades, each of a specified thickness.

F-head
Another name for an Inlet over Exhaust (IOE) valve layout (q.v.).

Final drive
The reduction gear within the rear axle consisting of a crown wheel and pinion, or more generally the whole rear axle assembly, including the differential.

Fixed-jet carburettor
Carburettor with a fixed choke or venturi size, such as the common designs from Weber and Dellorto. Compare variable-jet carburettor.

Fluid coupling or 'fluid flywheel'
A hydraulic coupling which takes the place of the clutch. As one half turns, the fluid it displaces impinges on the other half of the coupling and tries to rotate it. *See* torque converter.

Flywheel
Heavy steel or iron disc which rotates with the crankshaft, smoothing out torque variations. The flywheel normally carries the clutch and has a ring gear around its periphery which the starter motor uses to turn the engine.

Grease nipple
A lubrication point through which grease can be injected into a bearing, using a grease gun.

Gudgeon pin
A short shaft which connects the piston to the connecting rod. Also known as a piston pin or wrist pin.

Halfshaft
The driveshaft taking power from the final drive to the wheel hub.

Heron head
Bowl-in-piston combustion chamber with a flat cylinder head, a design developed by aircraft-engine specialist Sam Heron.

Hot spot
Area on the intake manifold which is heated by the exhaust manifold underneath, improving fuel atomisation during warm-up.

HP Horse Power
Usually equivalent to brake horsepower (bhp) but may refer to the RAC horsepower rating once used for vehicle taxation. RAC hp is the product of d^2 multiplied by n divided by 25, where 'd' is bore in inches and 'n' is the number of cylinders. A designation such as '12/50' indicates a 12hp RAC rating and 50bhp true power output.

HT High Tension
The high-voltage electrical system which causes the spark at the spark plugs.

Hydraulic tappets
Valve lifters which are 'pumped up' by engine oil pressure. They do not need periodic checking like 'solid' tappets, but can sometimes be unreliable at very high engine speeds.

Hypoid bevel
Bevel gear with a special curved tooth form, which allows the pinion to be mounted lower relative to the crownwheel. This lowers the propshaft line.

Ignition advance
The spark at the spark plug is usually timed to occur just before (in advance of) top dead centre. In a mechanical distributor, a centrifugal advance system increases ignition advance at higher engine speeds.

Inlet over exhaust (IOE)
Engine with the exhaust valves situated in the block, next to the cylinders, with overhead inlet valves operated by pushrods and rockers.

Injection
Fuel system which replaces carburettors with a metering system which delivers precisely controlled amounts of fuel to the inlet manifold or directly into the cylinders.

Journal
The part of a shaft, for instance the crankshaft, which runs in a bearing.

Kick down
On an automatic transmission, a mechanical or electrical system which selects a lower gear (improving acceleration) if the throttle pedal is pressed to the floor.

King pin
Substantially vertical member in the front suspension which provides the axis about which each front wheel steers. More modern designs replace the king pin with a cast steering swivel and ball joints.

Knocking
Uncontrolled combustion which causes a 'knocking' sound. A general name for detonation, pinking (or pinging) and pre-ignition.

Lash
See *Play*.

Leading shoe
In a drum brake with a single piston and a single pivot, the leading shoe is the one where the rotation of the drum drags the shoe towards the pivot. It does twice the braking of the trailing shoe, so wears much faster.

Leaf spring
Suspension spring usually made from several strips of steel held together by clips, which is mounted to the body or chassis at either end and carries the axle in the centre. More modern versions are made from a single leaf of composite material.

Lean mixture
Air/fuel mixture with excess air, i.e. an air to fuel ratio greater than 14.7:1.

Lever-arm damper
Hydraulic damper with an arm which is connected to the suspension, and a separate body containing the valves which provide damping.

Little end
See *Small end*.

Live axle
Conventional beam axle driving the rear wheels of a car through a differential and halfshafts. The classic arrangement of a live rear axle suspended by leaf springs is also known as the 'Hotchkiss drive'.

LT Low Tension
The low-voltage side of the ignition system which provides current to the coil.

Magneto
A type of dynamo which generates HT current.

Main bearings
The plain bearings in which the crankshaft rotates.

MacPherson strut
A front suspension system, designed by Earl S. MacPherson for Ford in the 1940s, consisting of a lower wishbone and a telescopic damper strut with a concentric suspension spring.

Monocoque
A 'unitary' body/chassis.

Negative earth
Electrical system where the negative terminal of the battery is connected to the chassis or bodyshell.

Nip up
Tighten a fixing just enough to steady the component it is holding, but not fully tight. Sometimes 'nipping up' is used to mean tightening a hand-tight fastener up to its full tightness.

Octane rating
Petrol's resistance to detonation or 'knocking' is denoted by its octane rating. There is no advantage in using a higher octane rating than necessary. There are two octane ratings, the Research Octane Number (RON) and Motor Octane Number (MON). European 'Premium' fuel is 97RON, 85MON.

OHC Overhead cam
The camshaft is mounted above the valves, and driven from the crankshaft by a gear system, chain or toothed belt.

OHV Overhead valve
Generally meaning an engine with its camshaft low down in the block, and valves operated by vertical pushrods and rockers.

Opposite lock
Steering in the 'wrong' direction to deal with oversteer. Also known as counter-steering.

Overdrive
(1) A supplementary gearbox, usually with two speeds, which can be used to provide extra ratios higher than those of the main gearbox alone. (2) Any gearbox ratio greater than 1:1, i.e. where the output speed is greater than the input speed.

Overrun
When the momentum of the vehicle is powering the engine, for example when descending a hill in gear with the throttle closed.

Oversquare
Engine dimensions where the bore exceeds the stroke.

Oversteer
In a curve, when the slip angle of the rear tyres is greater than that of the front tyres. The car tends to turn into the bend more sharply than the driver intends.

P&J
'Pride and joy': your classic car.

Panhard rod
Transverse suspension arm fitted to a live axle which allows vertical movement but limits sideways movement.

Phosphor bronze
Alloy of copper, tin and phosphorous, often with traces of zinc, lead or iron. Good wearing properties, so used for bearings. Not the same as bronze, which is an alloy of copper, zinc and tin.

Pinion
Small gear connected to the propshaft, which drives the crown wheel in the rear axle.

Pinking/Pinging
See *Detonation*.

Piston slap
A metallic slapping noise in the cylinders, caused by the pistons rocking in their bores. Can be because of wear, or a result of large clearances in a cold engine.

Pitch
Fore and aft movement of a vehicle on its suspension. See *Dive and squat*.

Plain bearing
Simple cylindrical bearing, which may be split into two halves or 'shells' so that the bearing surfaces can be replaced.

Play
Free movement between moving parts. For example, the amount the steering wheel must be moved before the front wheels turn. Also known as backlash, or just 'lash'.

Plenum chamber
In an intake system, the main volume from which air is distributed to individual cylinders.

PO
Previous owner.

Porous
Said of a faulty cylinder head or bore which allows combustion gases to escape.

Port
Passageway allowing gas into or out of the combustion chamber.

Positive earth
Electrical system in which the positive terminal of the battery is connected to the chassis or bodyshell.

Pre-ignition
Form of engine knock caused by a hot spot in the combustion chamber igniting the mixture before the spark. Compare detonation.

Pre-selector
Type of gearbox in which the next gear required is selected by the driver before it is needed, and then the change is made by pressing a gearchange pedal.

Propellor shaft (propshaft)
The shaft transferring power (usually) from the gearbox to the final drive. Sometimes called a cardan shaft, and known as a driveshaft in the US. Older technical manuals sometimes use the term 'arbor shaft'.

Pushrod
Rod transferring motion from the camshaft and tappets to the valves or rockers.

Quarter-elliptic spring
Effectively half a semi-elliptic spring. Usually mounted to the chassis at the 'thick' end with the axle cantilevered from the 'thin' end.

Radial tyre
Modern type of tyre used from the 1950s where the threads of the casing material run at right angles to the direction of rotation. The sidewalls are flexible, allowing the tread to remain on the road even when the tyre is distorted in hard cornering.

Radius rod
Suspension link which provides additional fore/aft location for a live axle.

Rebound
Suspension movement which extends the springs.

Rectifier
Group of diodes which convert the AC current produced by an alternator into DC current which can charge the battery.

Regulator
Electrical control box which regulates the dynamo voltage and current to prevent damage to the battery.

Relay
A switch activated by a small electric current, used to control a large current.

Rich mixture
Air/fuel mixture with excess fuel, i.e. a ratio of air to fuel less than 14.7:1.

Ring spanner
Spanner with 12-sided holes at each end instead of conventional jaws. Preferable to open-jawed spanners because they are far less likely to slip, and useful in confined spaces.

Rocker
(1) Valve gear component which transfers motion from the camshaft (often via pushrods) to the valve. (2) The sill panel.

Rheostat
Variable resistor. Often the dashboard lights will be provided with a rheostat so the driver can vary their brightness.

Roll bar
(1) A roll-over bar – a safety structure fitted to a car to protect occupants if the car rolls over. (2) An anti-roll bar, also known as a stabiliser or sway bar.

Roll centre
Instantaneous point about which one end of the car rolls in a corner. The line joining the front and rear roll centres is known as the roll axis.

Running on
The engine continues to run for a few seconds after the ignition has been switched off.

Screamer
A highly-tuned engine, particularly one with a very high rev limit.

Sealed beam
Type of headlamp in which the bulb, reflector and glass are a single, sealed unit.

Servo
Vacuum unit which provides assistance to the brake pedal.

Semi-elliptic spring
Leaf spring in the shape of a half ellipse.

Shackle
Pivoting bracket used to mount one end of a leaf spring.

Shim
Thin spacer used, for instance, to set valve clearances in some types of valve gear.

Shimmy
Vibration of a beam front axle, caused by gyroscopic effects.

Shock absorber
See *Damper*.

Side valve
Engine with valves situated in the block, alongside the cylinders.

Silentbloc bush
Type of rubber bush with a metal central sleeve, used in steering and suspension systems.

Slip angle
The difference between the direction a tyre is pointing and its direction of travel.

Small end
The bearing at the top of the connecting rod, where the rod is connected to the gudgeon pin.

Solenoid
An electrically operated plunger.

Spin-on filter
Disposable 'canister' oil filter, as distinct from the replaceable element type.

Splash lubrication
Simple lubrication system where the crankshaft dips into the oil in the sump and splashes it over the bearings.

Splines
Grooves machined onto a shaft to mate two components, for instance the steering wheel hub and the top of the column.

Sprung weight
The mass of the car carried by the suspension. Compare to unsprung weight.

Squat
Suspension movement caused by acceleration, where the rear springs compress and the front springs extend.

Steering arm
Lever acted on by the steering system which steers a front wheel about its kingpin or ball joints.

Straight cut
A gearbox in which the gear teeth are parallel to the shafts, rather than at an angle. Straight cut gears are stronger, but noisier, and are used on competition gearboxes.

Stroke
In engine specifications, the distance moved by the piston from TDC to BDC. More generally, the range of movement of a moving part.

Stub axle
Short axle which carries a non-driven wheel in an independent suspension system.

Supercharger
An air pump which forces intake mixture into the engine. Superchargers are driven from the crankshaft by a belt or gear system.

Sway bar
US term for anti-roll bar.

SWG (Standard Wire Gauge)
System for measuring the thickness of sheet metal.

Synchromesh
A cone clutch system which synchronises the rotation of gears before they are engaged.

Tappet
Also known as a valve lifter or cam follower. Bears on the cam lobe, transferring the motion from the camshaft to the pushrod or valve. 'Setting the tappets' is slang for adjusting valve clearances.

Throw
The distance between the centre line of the crankshaft and any of the crank pins, equal to half the stroke.

Thrust bearing
A bearing designed to resist end thrust.

Tie rod
Rod joining the steering arms so that they operate in unison.

Toe
Angle from straight ahead, commonly used to describe static positions of the wheels. 'Toe in' means a wheel is turned towards the car, 'toe out' means it is turned outwards.

Top dead centre (TDC)
The point in the engine's rotation where a piston is at the highest position.

Torque
Turning effort, known in physics as a moment or couple. A force acting at some distance from a pivot produces a torque equal to the force multiplied by the distance. Hence torque is expressed in units combining force and distance, often pound (lb) feet or Newton metres.

Torque convertor
Usually taken to mean a fluid flywheel with an extra internal element which multiplies torque. Used in place of a clutch with (usually) an automatic gearbox.

Torsion bar
A spring made from a rod which is fixed at one end and free to rotate at the other.

Track
The distance between the centrelines of the wheels from one side of the car to the other.

Track rod
An arm or linkage system which steers the front wheels.

Trailing shoe
In a drum brake with a single piston and a single pivot, the trailing shoe is the one where the rotation of the drum drags the shoe towards the piston. The trailing shoe is less effective, and wears more slowly, than the leading shoe.

Trunnion
Joint which allows one component to swivel relative to another. Used to connect a steering swivel to the king pin.

Twin-leading shoe
A drum brake where both shoes are provided with a piston at one end and a pivot at the other. Both shoes now operate as leading shoes.

Turbocharger
A pump forcing intake air into the engine. Unlike a supercharger (q.v.) a turbocharger is not driven directly from the engine – instead it is powered by a turbine driven by exhaust gas.

Undersquare
Engine dimensions where the stroke exceeds the bore.

Understeer
In a curve, when the slip angles of the front tyres are greater than those of the rear. The car drifts out to the outside of the bend.

UNC (Unified coarse)
Screw thread standard. Spanner sizes are measured 'across flats'. See *AF*.

UNF
See *AF*.

Unitary construction
'Chassisless' or 'monocoque' construction where the separate chassis is replaced by structural members which are part of the bodyshell itself.

Universal joint
A coupling which allows one shaft to drive another that is at an angle.

Unsprung weight
The mass of the wheels, tyre, suspension and brake components.

Valve clearance
The running clearance in the valve gear. Often measured between the end of the rocker and the top of the valve stem.

Valve guide
Short tube in the cylinder head into which the valve stem fits.

Valve seat
Precision-cut surface against which the valve seals.

Valve seat recession
Wear of the valve seat, causing the valve to recess into the head and the valve clearances to close up. Often the result of using unleaded fuel in an engine not designed for it.

Variable-jet carburettor
Carburettor containing a piston which drops to reduce the size of the venturi at small throttle openings, maintaining an almost constant vacuum in the venturi – hence also known as a 'constant vacuum' carburettor. SU and Stromberg are the best known.

Venturi
The main air passage in a carburettor, consisting of a tube with a constriction. The pressure of the air drops in the narrow part of the tube, causing fuel to be sucked from the carburettor jet.

Wankel engine
Rotary engine developed by Dr Felix Wankel. Favoured by NSU and Mazda, and also used in Norton motorcycles from the 1980s.

Webs
The parts of a crankshaft between the machined bearing surfaces.

Whitworth
See *BSW*.

Wilson gearbox
See *Pre-selector*.

Index